THE LITTLE BOOKROOM
GUIDE TO

New York City
with
Children

PLAY • EAT • SHOP

ANGELA HEDERMAN
MICHAEL BERMAN

PHOTOGRAPHS BY
MICHAEL BERMAN

THE LITTLE BOOKROOM

NEW YORK

Library of Congress Cataloging-in-Publication Data
Hederman, Angela.
The Little Bookroom guide to New York City with children / Angela Hederman and
Michael Berman ; photographer: Michael Berman.
pages cm
Includes bibliographical references and index.
ISBN 978-1-936941-09-4 (alk. paper)
1. Children--Travel--New York (State)--New York--Guidebooks. 2. Family recreation-
-New York (State)--New York--Guidebooks. 3. New York (N.Y.)--Guidebooks. I. Berman,
Michael, 1967- II. Title.
F128.18.H3895 2014
917.47'10444--dc23
2014001053

Printed in the United States of America

Published by The Little Bookroom
435 Hudson Street, Suite 300
New York NY 10014
editorial @littlebookroom.com
www.littlebookroom.com

2 4 6 8 0 9 7 5 3 1

Contents

Quick! Which of the activities below are for children, and which are for parents?

1. Spending the night in a world-famous museum, in a Gothic cathedral, or on an aircraft carrier;

2. Eating a delectable meal in a tiny no-frills Chinatown restaurant where, from your seat, you can watch the mesmerizing process of the chef making hand-pulled noodles;

3. Raising and lowering the sails of a historic schooner as you navigate New York Harbor;

4. Relaxing pre–Happy Hour at an outdoor bar that floats in the Hudson River, taking in views that include the Statue of Liberty, the George Washington Bridge, and two storybook (literally) landmarks;

5. Stargazing for free from the top of a historic observatory, moving from telescope to telescope, with astronomers as your guides.

If you're having trouble deciding which activities are for kids and which are for adults, it may be because all of them are fun for both children and their parents. The single most important thing to know about visiting New York is its impressive ability to delight both adults and children simultaneously. The premise of our guide is that in New York, you don't have to choose between what kids and grownups like to do.

As New Yorkers who have raised—and are still raising—children here, we know that the city is filled with "only in

New York" places to play, eat, and shop where everyone can have fun together. With *The Little Bookroom Guide to New York City with Children* in hand, parents won't have the feeling that they're missing out on anything just because the kids are along.

HOW THE GUIDE IS ORGANIZED

We've organized our recommendations by neighborhood, and within each of them, by Play, Eat, and Shop. Listings are alphabetical with one exception: each Play section starts with our choice of the best local park, so you'll always know where your kids can work off some energy. Visiting a playground in each neighborhood is not only fun for kids, but a great way for parents to get the vibe of different parts of the city.

PLAY

Using this guide, parents who want to take their kids to the city's great cultural institutions can do it with ease. We suggest ways to navigate museums so that you can see the "greatest hits" in the most efficient way, which isn't always obvious—the Met is enormous, the American Museum of Natural History is a labyrinth, and there are times when every museum can be absolutely packed. Nonetheless, with our well-thought-out plan, a visit will be doable and memorable.

In fact, having a child along often offers parents opportunities they otherwise wouldn't enjoy: the chance to stroll through galleries before they're open to the public, or go backstage while a child dances with ballerinas or makes music with world-class performers. NYC's great cultural institutions offer scores of special events for

kids that give adults privileged behind-the-scenes looks, including the wildly popular museum overnights.

Beyond museums, we've compiled scores of activities that appeal to kids, whether they're interested in sports, crafts, animation, ballet, magic, history, movies, books, computers, music, dolls, chess, theater, and more.

Tired of indoor activities? Take to the great outdoors. NYC has spectacular wide-open spaces. Michael, who lives in Brooklyn, takes you on a walk over the Brooklyn Bridge, and, once you're there, to his favorite places, including a restored carousel, historic pizza joints (his specialty), the Coney Island boardwalk and amusement parks, and many more insider places in his—the hippest—borough.

Stay on the island of Manhattan and follow our itinerary through Central Park; or spend a day in glorious Battery Park City, where sites such as the Irish Hunger Memorial and Tom Otterness's whimsical sculptures are unexpected surprises that will delight the whole family.

We hope you'll occasionally follow us a bit off the beaten track to some small or old-fashioned places that we deeply love: a classic sandwich shop, a matzo factory, a ribbon store, a bakery that makes the iconic black-and-white cookies. We couldn't resist sharing some of these quieter corners of the city that, along with its exciting and glamorous attractions, make New York New York. There's beauty and energy everywhere you look.

EAT

There's no need to resort to chicken fingers when you're in New York. With so much great food, kids' menus are almost beside the point. World-class pizza, dumplings, and bagels are only some of the many mouthwatering bargains—and finger food—in the city. There are restaurants that have raised mac 'n' cheese, meatballs, donuts, French fries, and even pudding to culinary glory. Adults and kids alike will have fun at the charming café in Greenwich Village that specializes in cupcake and wine pairings, brunch at a big and busy dim sum place in Chinatown, and a no-attitude pub where kids dance along to traditional Irish music on Sunday evenings.

From infancy, New York children eat in restaurants, and not just at casual, no-frills spots. We've includes places that span a range of styles and prices, from ultra-casual to trendy, where the food is fabulous and where families with kids will feel totally comfortable—even though there may be a super model or a famous chef dining at the next table.

Local chain restaurants in NYC are expected to be a notch above (or miles beyond) national fast food chains, so you won't be settling if you have a meal at the serene Pain Quotidien, the popular Shake Shack, the much-loved Sarabeth's, Luke's Lobster, or others.

Many of our choices are, frankly, cheap (4-for-$1 dumplings; a pizza slice; food truck food). Others are pricier, but always fair value. There are even bargains to be had at some of the most upscale venues, including a hip and trendy restaurant on the Lower East Side. They may not appear on the printed menus, but we share them in the pages of this guide.

SHOP

Fashion-forward New York is a world-class shopping destination where you can find something fabulous for as much or as little as you want to spend. Splurge on something special—there's no shortage of luxury stores here, and we've pointed out the best, from classic to cutting edge. We're partial to stylish boutiques featuring talented local designers. Also, museum shops are treasure troves for fun New York souvenirs like a wooden bagel yoyo or a purse in the shape of a hot dog. We've named the best.

PRACTICALITIES

Walking and taking the subway are quintessential New York experiences, and you'll do a lot of both, but because you'll be climbing stairs and covering many blocks, remember to travel light.

Last, and hopefully unnecessarily, make a plan in the event you are separated from your child (see page 26).

A REMINDER

Things change all the time in the city. We've picked places with staying power, but call ahead to avoid inconvenience and disappointment. Restaurants may be closed for a private event, shops for renovation; chefs and proprietors take vacations.

One last piece of advice: ask anyone on the street if you need directions, information, or the answer to a question. Chances are they'll like nothing more than to help you. We take pride in the welcoming attitude shown by New Yorkers, who want visitors to love the city, and who remember with gratitude their support after 9/11.

Angela Hederman and Michael Berman
New York, January 2014

For Rea: "The flight was a bold and perilous one;
but here [we are], in the great city of New York, safe and sound."
(Frederick Douglass)
And for Taylor, Patrick, Jenie, Gaye Taylor, and Rea Jr.,
with whom we discovered the great city.—AH

Thank you, Kristin and Julia. Your spirit of adventure and love of good restaurants are embedded into the pages of this book.—MB

Call 311 for general citywide information.

The official New York City website is www.nyc.gov. Visitors will find all sorts of assistance by clicking on "NYC Resources," then "Culture & Recreation." Information is for both residents of New York as well as visitors, so you may have to weed through some things that don't apply, but this is a superbly complete and up-to-date site that covers everything from Citi Bike information and sign-up, calendar of events, free things to do, which parks have free Wi-Fi, to virtual tours of attractions in all five boroughs.

Here are a few direct links from within the site:

Getting Around: www1.nyc.gov/nyc-resources/categories/transportation/getting-around/index.page

Parks & Nature: www1.nyc.gov/nyc-resources/categories/culture-recreation/parks-nature/index.page

Sightseeing: www1.nyc.gov/nyc-resources/categories/culture-recreation/sightseeing/index.page

Sports & Recreation: www1.nyc.gov/nyc-resources/categories/culture-recreation/sports-recreation/index.page

Wi-Fi in Parks: www.nycgovparks.org/facilities/wifi

New York City's official marketing and tourism organization is NYC & Company; its website is www.nycgo.com. As would be expected, the site is filled with ads from the organization's partners (restaurants, hotels, etc.), but it's a useful compilation of information beyond the obvious, including current TV show tapings, the location of official information centers, suggested amounts to tip, and lists of deals, discounts, and promotions that can be browsed by date.

Time Out New York
www.timeout.com/new-york-kids

New York magazine
nymag.com/family/kids

The New York Times's daily rundown of events and news occurring in New York City, including listing of free summer concerts: twitter.com/NYTMetro

Family-friendly activities, events, and attractions: mommypoppins.com/ny-kids

MenuPages (website and app containing a thorough collection of menus, reviews, and mapping for Manhattan and Brooklyn restaurants): www.menupages.com

Metropolitan Transit Authority:

NYC MTA homepage: new.mta.info

NYC MTA maps: www.mta.info/maps

NYC MTA App Gallery (an array of transit-related apps, sortable by device type): web.mta.info/apps

Arts for Transit website and apps (a tour of artwork publicly displayed throughout the subway & rail systems): www.mta.info/mta/aft

Hop Stop (transit and walking directions): www.hopstop.com

A Walk in New York by Salvatore Rubbino (Candlewick)

All-of-a-Kind Family (and the All-of-a-Kind Family series) by Sydney Taylor (Yearling)

Eloise by Kay Thompson (Simon & Schuster Books for Young Readers)

Emma's Journey by Claire Frossard and Etienne Frossard (Enchanted Lion Books)

Fireboat: The Heroic Adventures of the John J. Harvey by Maira Kalman (Puffin)

From the Mixed-Up Files of Mrs. Basil E. Frankweiler by E.L. Konigsburg (Atheneum Books for Young Readers)

Good Night New York City by Adam Gamble, illustrated by Joe Veno (Our World of Books)

Harriet the Spy by Louise Fitzhugh (Yearling)

Hello, New York City! by David Walker (Sterling)

Knuffle Bunny: A Cautionary Tale (and the Knuffle Bunny series) by Mo Willems (Hyperion)

Jenny and the Cat Club (and the Jenny Linsky series) by Esther Averill (New York Review Children's Classics)

Larry Gets Lost in New York City by Michael Mullin and John Skewes (Sasquatch Books)

Lyle, Lyle, Crocodile and *The House on East 88th Street* (and the Lyle the Crocodile series) by Bernard Waber (HMH Books for Young Readers)

Milly and the Macy's Parade by Shana Corey and Brett Helquist (Scholastic)

My New York by Kathy Jakobsen (Little, Brown Books for Young Readers)

New York, New York: The Big Apple from A to Z by Laura Krauss Melmed and Frané Lessac (HarperCollins)

Next Stop Grand Central by Maira Kalman (Puffin)

Phoebe the Spy by Judith Berry Griffin and Margot Tomes (Puffin)

Roller Skates by Ruth Sawyer (Viking Penguin)

Storied City: A Children's Book Walking-Tour Guide to New York City by Leonard M. Marcus (Dutton Juvenile)

Stuart Little by E.B. White and Garth Williams (HarperCollins)

The Adventures of Taxi Dog (Maxi the Taxi Dog) by Debra Barracca, Sal Barracca, Mark Buehner (Dial)

The Cricket in Times Square by George Selden and Garth Williams (Square Fish)

The Little Red Lighthouse and the Great Gray Bridge by Hildegarde H. Swift and Lynd Ward (HMH Books for Young Readers)

The Magic Tunnel by Caroline D. Emerson (Scholastic Book Services)

The Man Who Walked Between the Towers by Mordicai Gerstein (Square Fish)

The Philharmonic Gets Dressed by Karla Kuskin and Marc Simont (HarperCollins)

The Pushcart War by Jean Merrill (Yearling)

The Saturdays by Elizabeth Enright (Square Fish)

This Is New York by Miroslav Sasek (Universe)

What Zeesie Saw on Delancey Street by Elsa Okon Rael and Marjorie Priceman (Simon & Schuster Children's Publishing)

When Zaydeh Danced on Eldridge Street by Elsa Okon Rael and Marjorie Priceman (Simon & Schuster Children's Publishing)

A PLAYLIST FOR CHILDREN AND PARENTS

There's nothing like a playlist of classic New York City tunes to get your family in the mood.

"42nd Street" (Ruby Keeler or cast recording from *42nd Street*)

"59th Street Bridge Song (Feelin' Groovy)" (Simon and Garfunkel)

"American City Suite" (Cashman and West)

"Anything Can Happen in New York" (Mickey Rooney, Richard Quine, and Ray McDonald from *Babes on Broadway*)

"Arthur's Theme (The Best That You Can Do)" (Christopher Cross)

"Empire State of Mind" (Jay-Z featuring Alicia Keys)

"Give My Regards to Broadway" (James Cagney)

"I Guess the Lord Must Be in New York City" (Nilsson)

"I Happen to Like New York" (Judy Garland)

"I've Gotta Get Back to New York" (various artists)

"Jenny from the Block" (Jennifer Lopez)

"Lullaby of Broadway" (Doris Day)

"Manhattan" (Blossom Dearie, Bobby Short, Ella Fitzgerald, and various artists)

"Mona Lisas and Mad Hatters" (Elton John)

"Native New Yorker" (Odyssey)

"New York City Rhythm" (Barry Manilow)

"New York Groove" (Ace Frehley)

"New York, New York" (Frank Sinatra)

"New York, New York" (original cast of *On the Town*)

"New York, New York" (Ryan Adams)

"New York Serenade" (from the musical *Rosalie* by George and Ira Gershwin)

"New York State of Mind" (Billy Joel)

"NYC" (from *Annie*)

"On Broadway" (The Drifters or George Benson)

"Spanish Harlem" (Ben E. King)

"Sunday in New York" (Mel Tormé)

"Take Me Back to Manhattan" (Rosemary Clooney)

"Take the 'A' Train" (Duke Ellington)

"The Boy from New York City" (The Ad Libs)

"The Brooklyn Bridge" (Mel Tormé)

"The Only Living Boy in New York" (Simon and Garfunkel)

"The Rising" (Bruce Springsteen)

"The Sidewalks of New York (East Side, West Side)" (various artists)

"There's a Boat Dat's Leaving Soon for New York" (Louis Armstrong)

EATING EASILY AND WELL

Chain Restaurants

These restaurants are parts of chains, most small, some large, that have more than one location throughout the city and can be depended upon for a much-better-than-reliable meal in a kid-friendly setting. Check individual websites for locations; we've referred you to the page on which one of the locations is described.

Bareburger (page 223)
Dig Inn (page 173)
Luke's Lobster (page 428)
The Meatball Shop (page 284)
Melt Shop (page 318)
Oaxaca Taqueria (page 429)
Pain Quotidien (page 429)
Petit Abeille (page 92)
Pio Pio (page 319)
Sarabeth's (page 93)
Shake Shack (page 260)
Whole Foods (page 159)

Department Store Restaurants

Midtown's department store restaurants are true democracies. Used to accommodating lots of people—all kinds of people—and centrally located, they can be lifesavers if you need to sit down and eat without worrying about reservations, how welcome children will be, the menu's appeal, affordability, or other practicalities. From Herald Square (Macy's) to the Grand Central Terminal/Bryant Park area

(Lord & Taylor), and the Upper East Side (Bloomingdale's), these venues are casual and easy. Each of the stores has several options, so the possibilities are even broader than this selection; below are the best choices in each store. As for the food: in contrast to the dreary tearooms of days gone by, Macy's offers a splendid bit of Italy in Manhattan, Sarabeth's is a New York classic, and Bloomingdale's offers healthy choices and legendary frozen yogurt.

Note: The prices at Café SFA at Saks Fifth Avenue are more appropriate for ladies-who-lunch than families with children ($19 for a cup of soup and half-sandwich; a $21 cheeseburger). The restaurants at Bergdorf Goodman and Barneys New York have a less casual atmosphere than the places we suggest.

Stella 34 Trattoria at Macy's Herald Square
See page 320 for full description.

Sarabeth's at Lord & Taylor
See page 320 for a full description

Forty Carrots at Bloomingdales
See page 372 for a full description

PUBLIC RESTROOMS

Lots of restrooms are open to the public. Department stores, branches of the New York Public Library, fast-food places, and chain stores are all possibilities; or duck into a restaurant or a bar—most won't turn away a parent with a child who needs to use the facilities. An essential resource is nyrestroom.com.

On the subway recently, a worrisome announcement was made: "If the teenager who became separated from his family is on this train, please walk up the platform and see the conductor." Although the chances of becoming separated from your child on the street or in the subway are remote, it's a good idea to have a plan. First, make sure your child has your name, your cell phone number, and the name of your hotel pinned in his or her pocket.

Make a simple plan in the event you are separated on the street ("look around for a mom with kids and ask her to help you," "go into a store or a restaurant and tell one of the staff you're lost," etc.). Keep your kids near you on the subway when boarding and getting off; when the cars are crowded, it can take longer than you'd think to get to the door. Have a clear contingency plan: if your child is left on the train, tell him/her to get off at the next stop and stay there—you'll come get them via the next train, which arrives every few minutes. If your child is left at a station, tell them to stay there, too; you'll get off at the next stop and take the next train back. If there's a station attendant in the booth, your child should tell them the plan is to stay put until the parents arrive. If there's no attendant, your child should stay on the platform next to the wall, away from the tracks, and wait for you.

It's easy to lose sight of your child in a crowded museum, too. One general strategy is to make a rule that no one leaves a gallery unless everyone is together. If children do get separated, they can ask a museum guard to call a parent's cell phone number.

NYC BY BICYCLE

Riding a bicycle in New York City requires competence, confidence, and extreme care. If you're interested in riding in the city with your family, the path along the West Side that runs alongside the Hudson River from the Battery all the way up to Fort Tryon Park near Manhattan's northernmost point offers remarkable views. Although it is virtually car-free, cycle with caution. There are lots of pedestrians and other bike riders, many cycling at lightning speed. Other appealing options are Central Park and Governors Island. If you wish to rent a bike, there are two good options.

The city's new Citi Bike program provides bikes for pick-up and drop-off at hundreds of locations in the city, including dozens within a block of the West Side Highway. The bikes are the same size; the saddles are adjustable. Riders must be at least 16 years old. ($9.95/24-hour pass; $25/one-week pass; 30-minute time limit per use; see citibikenyc.com for regulations).

Bike and Roll has ten locations in NYC, including two along the West Side Highway (one at Battery Park, across the street from 17 State Street; the other at Pier 84, at Twelfth Avenue and West 43rd Street); one in Central Park near Tavern on the Green (enter at 67th Street and Central Park West); and one on Governors Island. Bike and Roll's adult bikes accommodate riders from 4'10" to 6'5"; the children's bikes accommodate kids 4'4" to 4'10". Specialty equipment, including toddler seats and tandem bikes for young people, called tagalongs, are available. Adult rates are about $14 per hour.

Bike and Roll also offers several guided tours, including Central Park, Brooklyn Bridge, and New York at Night. Tours range from 6–14 miles in length, last about three hours each, and are held during warm weather only; prices are $25–$50 for kids and $40–$64 for adults. Only one Bike and Roll location is open year round (Columbus Circle, at Central Park); see bikenewyorkcity.com for details.

See also The Schooner Pioneer at South Street Seaport Museum, page 49, and the Staten Island Ferry, page 492.

New York Water Taxi and Circle Line Downtown (at 42nd Street)

Pier 83 (West 42nd Street and Twelfth Avenue)
(212) 563-3200
www.circleline42.com
Subway: A,C,E to 42nd Street-Port Authority; 1,2,3,L,S,N,Q,R to Times Square-42nd Street (optional: transfer to M42 and M50 bus lines along 42nd Street terminating at 42nd Street and Twelfth Avenue)
See www.circleline42.com/new-york-cruises/schedules.aspx for cruise schedules and pricing. Arrive 45 minutes prior to sailing time.

This classic boat ride appeals to tourists and children alike for its unparalleled views of Manhattan's geography and skyline. There are a number of cruises to choose from, including the Semi Circle Cruise (1.5 hours) and the Full Island Cruise (2.5 hours). The accompanying narrative, delivered by a tour guide, provides snippets and historic details about the sights in both the New York and New Jersey landscapes.

But this experience is, truly, all about getting a sense of the city from the water. In particular, the Full Island Cruise offers a unique opportunity to see Manhattan in 360 degrees, including from the narrow Bronx River at the north end. (The Semi Circle Cruise around the southern end of Manhattan turns north along the East River to about 42nd Street, and then returns via the same route.) Choose a beautiful day to set out; sit outside so that you don't have to see the views through windows and near the narrator where it's easiest to hear.

Circle Line offers several alternatives to the standard Semi Circle and Full Island Cruises. Many of them are seasonal only and all depart from piers other than Pier 83. Visit www.circlelinedowntown.com for details.

The Shark Speedboat Thrill Ride departs from Pier 16 (89 South Street, near South Street Seaport) and runs hourly during daylight hours June through August and on weekends in May. As you might guess, this boat speeds through New York harbor and offers close-up views of the Statue of Liberty and the Brooklyn Bridge. Notes: children must be at least 40" tall; pregnant women and people with heart or back problems should not ride this boat; wear sunscreen, and be prepared to get wet. The ride lasts about 30 minutes. Tickets are $24 (adults), $17 (children 3–12, subject to height requirement), and $22 (seniors).

The Statue by Night cruise is a one-hour night-time boat tour aboard a New York Water Taxi that departs from Pier 16 (at South Street Seaport). From it you'll enjoy dramatic views of the Statue of Liberty, the Brooklyn Bridge, the World Trade Center site, and the Empire State Building. Check www.circlelinedowntown.com/tours/statue-by-night for seasonal schedule. Tickets are $28 (adults), $17 (children 3–12 years), and $24 (seniors).

SEASONAL EVENTS

Spring
Cherry Blossoms at BBG (Brooklyn Botanic Garden)
Fleet Week
New York International Children's Film Festival

Summer
Bryant Park Summer Film Festival
Celebrate Brooklyn!
Central Park Conservancy Film Festival
Front/Row Cinema (South Street Seaport)
Harlem Week
Macy's Fourth of July Fireworks
The Mermaid Parade (Coney Island)

The Metropolitan Opera Summer Recital Series
Movies with a View (Brooklyn Bridge Park)
New York Philharmonic Concerts in the Parks
RiverFlicks (Hudson River Park)
SummerStage Festival
Summer on the Hudson (Riverside Park)
Warm Up (MoMA PS1)

Fall
Feast of San Gennaro (Little Italy)
New York Comic Con
The Annual Atlantic Antic (Brooklyn)
The Annual Columbus Day Parade
The New York City Marathon

Holiday Season
George Balanchine's *The Nutcracker*
Grand Central Terminal Holiday Train Show
Holiday Train Show (New York Botanical Garden)
Holiday store window displays
Macy's Thanksgiving Day Parade
New Year's Eve (Times Square)
Outdoor holiday markets
Radio City Christmas Spectacular

Winter
Lunar New Year (Chinatown)
Polar Bear Swim (Coney Island)
The Westminster Kennel Club Annual Dog Show

87th-A·····
Feast of
San Germano

SEPTEMBER 12 - 22, 2013

FIAT

ONE WAY

zzo
RISTO······
ITAL·····

COTTON CANDY
CANDY APPLES
POPCORN

ICE SKATING

Some of the most inviting rinks in Manhattan include:

Bryant Park

Sixth Avenue at 42nd Street

(212) 661-6640

Subway: 1,2,3,N,Q,R to Times Square-42nd Street; 4,5,6 to Grand Central-42nd Street; B,D,F,M to 42nd Street-Bryant Park; 7 to 5th Avenue

www.bryantpark.org

November–February: Sunday–Thursday 8am–10pm; Friday, Saturday 8am–midnight

Free; skate rental $14; lock rental $9

Lasker Rink

Central Park, near 110th Street and Malcolm X Boulevard/
Lenox Avenue
(917) 492-3856
Subway: 2,3 to Central Park North-110th Street;
B,C to Cathedral Parkway-110th Street
www.centralparknyc.org/visit/things-to-see/north-end/lasker.html
November–March: Monday–Thursday 10am–3:45pm;
Friday 10am–11pm; Saturday 1pm–11pm; Sunday 12:30pm–4:30pm
Adults $7.50; 12 and under $4; skate rental $6.50; lock rental
$3.25 plus deposit, cash only

The Rink at Brookfield Place

220 Vesey Street between West Street and North End Avenue
(718) 704-3867
Subway: E to World Trade Center
www.therinkatbrookfieldplacenyc.com
November 15–mid-March
Daily 10am–9:30pm
$15; skate rental $5

The Rink at Rockefeller Center

Rockefeller Center, Fifth Avenue between 49th and 50th Streets
(212) 332-7654
Subway: B,D,F,M to 47th-50th Streets-Rockefeller Center;
E to 5th Avenue-53rd Street; N,Q,R to 49th Street
www.patinagroup.com/restaurant.php?restaurants_id=74
Mid-October through April: 8:30am–midnight
Adults $27; under 11 $15; skate rental $12

Wollman Rink
East side of Central Park, between East 62nd and 63rd Streets
(212) 439-6900
Subway: F to 57th Street; N,Q,R to 5th Avenue-59th Street;
A,B,C,D,1 to 59th Street-Columbus Circle
www.centralparknyc.org/visit/things-to-see/south-end/wollman-rink.html
November–March: Monday–Tuesday 10am–2:30pm;
Wednesday–Thursday 10am–10pm; Friday–Saturday 10am–11pm;
Sunday 10am–9pm
Monday–Thursday: adults $11.25; 11 and under $6;
Friday–Sunday and holidays: adults $18; 11 and under $6.
Skate rental $8; lock rental $5 plus deposit, cash only

BABYSITTING SERVICES

Parents who want a night out in NYC without the children have a wide choice of babysitting services that can help make that a reality. Hotels can usually recommend sitters, but for parents who would like to deal directly with babysitters, rather than go through a concierge, these services will come in handy.

Some of these agencies operate in other large cities, some are small Manhattan- or Brooklyn-based services. They will send babysitters to stay with children in a hotel, and some provide sitters who will take children on excursions. Some provide artists who not only stay with children, but do craft projects with them (and they bring the supplies and clean up). Many agencies have babysitters who speak languages other than English. Other considerations when booking:

are babysitters CPR-certified? Have they undergone a background check? Does the agency require a booking fee, charge a cancellation fee, or require minimum hours? Check websites for details and to get a feel for the individual agency.

American Child Care Inc.
(212) 244-0200
www.americanchildcare.com

Artist Babysitting Agency
(646) 465-2829
www.artistbabysitting.com

Sitters Studio
(646) 246-6024
www.sittersstudio.com

Metropolitan Sitters
(917) 471-2015
metropolitansitters.com

The Babysitters' Guild
(212) 682-0227
babysittersguild.com

NY City Explorers/Bag of Tricks Babysitting
(718) 809-6486
www.nycityexplorers.com
www.bagoftricksbabysitting.com\new-york.htm

Easy Care Sitters
(347) 855-5437
www.easycaresitters.com/ny

Pinch Sitters Agency
(212) 260-6005
www.nypinchsitters.com

IF YOUR CHILD IS SICK

Emergency Phone Numbers
Police 911
Fire 911
Ambulances are dispatched by both police and fire departments;
call 911.

Poison Control
During normal business hours, call the New York City
(800) 222-1222, (212) POISONS

Medical Care
www.citymd.net is a designated urgent care practice offering a variety of pediatric (and adult) services, with seven locations throughout Manhattan. Common conditions treated at the facilities are earaches, asthma, allergies, sprains and fractures, vomiting and diarrhea, and more. CityMD accepts all major insurance.
(212) 772-3627

24-hour Pharmacies
Duane Reade has 24-hour pharmacies as well as Doctor on Premises locations with walk-in medical care (888) 535-6963. Customer service: (866) 375-6925, duanereade.com

CVS
(800) 746-7287
www.cvs.com

Walgreen's
(800) WALGREENS / (800) 925-4733
www.walgreens.com

Rite-Aid
(800) 748-3243
www.riteaid.com

PLAY

EAT

SHOP

For the nearest recommended shops, see Tribeca (page 97).

South Street Seaport & Lower Manhattan

PLAY

Imagination Playground at Burling Slip

John Street at Front Street
(866) 986-5551
Subway: 2,3 to Fulton Street; 4,5 to Wall Street; J to Broad Street; N,R to Whitehall Street
www.nycgovparks.org/parks/imaginationplayground
Daily 9am–5pm (later in good weather)

Spend a few minutes here with children and you'll witness the creativity that Imagination Playground is meant to nourish. Designed

by architect David Rockwell, this unique space may at first seem sparse: it's mainly an open area with few structures and little in the way of play equipment. On one end of the park is a sand area with a tube slide, on the other end is a water area with fountains. Scattered around—and this is how the park differs from others—are giant foam blocks, mats, wagons, and crates, all light enough for children to lift and build with. Having such a large number and variety of items to work with lets kids construct almost any fanciful structure they can envision, from a sprawling palace to a maze of canals below the waterspouts.

African Burial Ground National Monument
Museum: inside the Ted Weiss Federal Building
290 Broadway, between Duane and Reade Streets
(212) 637-2019
Subway: 1,2,3 to Chambers Street; 2,3 to Park Place;
4,5,6 to Brooklyn Bridge-City Hall; A,C to Chambers Street;
J to Chambers Street; N,R to City Hall
www.nps.gov/afbg
Tuesday–Saturday 10am–4pm
Outdoor Memorial: behind the Ted Weiss Federal Building
Duane Street and African Burial Ground Way/Elk Street
Daily 9am–5pm; closed in winter months
Free

In 1991, the construction of a Federal building in lower Manhattan came to an abrupt halt when the excavation uncovered a centuries-old cemetery. After maps from the colonial era were consulted, it was determined to be an African burial ground. The story of the controversy that ensued, the archaeological significance of the

discovery, and the story of the men, women, and children who were buried there (419 bodies were eventually exhumed) is the focus of this small but affecting museum.

Start by watching the 20-minute orientation film; part of it is a dramatization in which a young African-American girl, Amelia, sets off on an errand through the streets of colonial New Amsterdam. There's also a reenactment of a burial, as well as documentary footage of the excavation of the burial ground, the resulting protests, the ultimate re-interment of the bodies, and the consecration of the outdoor site near the museum. Within the limited space of the museum—only two or three galleries—are features that will hold the interest of children: dioramas, life-sized mannequins in a

tableau of the same burial portrayed in the film, drawers to open to examine reproductions of artifacts found at the site, and audio and video features.

After your visit to the exhibition space, walk around the corner to the somber black granite memorial and seven grassy mounds that cover the crypts containing the remains of these early New Yorkers.

The Anne Frank Center USA

44 Park Place, at Church Street
(212) 431-7993
Subway: A,C to Chambers Street; E to World Trade Center;
2,3 to Park Place; 4,5,6 to Brooklyn Bridge-City Hall; N,R to City Hall
www.annefrank.com
Tuesday–Saturday 10am–5pm; closed Sunday, Monday
Adults $8; students $5; 8 and under free

Small, simple, and spare, this space nonetheless manages to convey the story of Anne Frank in a very satisfying way. The story is well known: while hiding with her Jewish family in Amsterdam during the Nazi occupation, the young Anne began keeping a diary. Discovered after her death in a concentration camp, this memoir of hope and faith in mankind is regarded as one of the most powerful documents of the Holocaust. The short orientation film is very much worth the price of admission; it tells the story of Anne and her family, the Holocaust, and World War II.

Along one wall is a cutaway model of the building in which the Franks lived in the secret annex, a display of family photos, and a timeline starting with the end of World War I (1918) and ending in 1945, the year of Anne's death. A small circular space in the back is wallpapered with a large photo of Anne's bedroom; several listening posts with earphones and iPads are devoted to various subjects, including an interview with the woman who provided food and essentials for the family in hiding, the BBC broadcast of the Allied landing at Normandy, and—most striking—32 seconds of the only known film footage of Anne.

The museum shop is a simple bookcase filled with books on related subjects. A few postcards of the Anne Frank House in Amsterdam are for sale, but the souvenir to take home is undoubtedly a red diary ($20) with a band printed with the pattern of the cover of Anne's own.

National Museum of the American Indian

Alexander Hamilton U.S. Custom House
1 Bowling Green, at Broadway and Battery Place
(212) 514-3700
Subway: 4,5 to Bowling Green; 1 to Rector Street;
R to Whitehall Street; J,M to Broad Street
www.americanindian.si.edu
Daily 10am–5pm, Thursday until 8pm
Free

In terms of size, contents, and setting, there can hardly be a museum better suited to kids than the NMAI, part of the Smithsonian Institution, located in the monumental Customs House, a National Historic Landmark. Pick up a free Adventure Guide, available at the front desk in English and Spanish, which features objects in the exhibition. As you pass through the soaring elliptical rotunda, notice the gorgeous Reginald Marsh murals depicting ocean liners arriving at the port of New York.

Visitors are greeted at the entrance to the galleries by *Walrus Spirit* (Larry Beck, 1982), a mask-like sculpture made of hubcaps, tires, chair legs, and PVC plastic; it's clever, beautiful, and funny. Beyond, pieces from the permanent collection are displayed in the Infinity of Nations galleries. In these four manageable rooms are displayed objects that children relate to (dolls, shields, masks) made of materials that they find appealing (feathers, beads, shells). The abundance of animal motifs only heightens their interest.

The nearby Haudenosaunee Discovery Room (fourth- and fifth-grade level), houses displays on subjects such as wampum, Native American ironworkers, and cornhusk dolls. Seasonal events for children are held throughout the year, including a Day of the Dead crafts workshop, a children's festival in May, and an art market at Christmas.

The gift shop is filled with items mostly made by Native American craftspeople and artists. For children, you'll find the museum's T-shirts (with butterflies, or with petroglyphs and pictographs, $16), Navajo dolls ($8), leather pouches decorated with a feather ($12), a lovely array of sterling earrings (a tiny silver feather with a turquoise, $12.50), and more.

Note: Outside in front of the Custom House is a kiosk with brochures and tourist information, including information about the free shuttle bus that circulates around Lower Manhattan, operated by the Downtown Alliance. On the fence of Bowling Green, the city's oldest park, look for the plaque dedicated to Peregrine Falcons in New York City; it details the story of some unexpected residents of Wall Street.

New York City Police Museum
100 Old Slip, at Front Street
(212) 480-3100
Subway: N,R to Whitehall Street; 2,3 to Wall Street;
4,5 to Bowling Green; 1 to South Ferry; J to Broad Street
www.nycpolicemuseum.org

As of this printing, the New York City Police Museum is closed because of damage sustained during Hurricane Sandy. Please check the website for updated information and alternative location.

Schooner Pioneer at the South Street Seaport Museum

Pier 16, East River Esplanade, off South Street
(212) 748-8600
Subway: A,C, 2, 3, 4, 5, J, Z to Fulton Street
www.southstreetseaportmuseum.org
April–October, weather permitting
Adults $45; 3–12 $35
Schedule and reservations: www.nywatertaxi.com/tours/pioneer-historic-sailing-schooner

This is your chance to raise and lower the sails and help navigate a beautifully restored nineteenth-century schooner in New York Harbor. The historic schooner heads south and west from Pier 16 at the Seaport, and during the two-hour ride passes close by the Statue of Liberty and the Brooklyn and Manhattan shorelines before returning to port. A maximum of 40 passengers are allowed per excursion.

The Schooner Pioneer is operated by the South Street Seaport Museum, which also operates several other boats moored at Pier 16. As of this writing, both the Peking (a barque) and the Ambrose (a lightship) are open to the public. Call the museum for details.

Small Potatoes Animation Factory Tour

Little Airplane Productions
207 Front Street, near Beekman Street
(212) 965-8999
Subway: 2,3 to Fulton Street; 4,5,6 to Brooklyn Bridge-City Hall;
J to Chambers Street
www.littleairplane.com
Weekdays at various times; reservations required
$10 per person

This tour gives kids a behind-the-scenes look at how a working production studio creates animation. Tour-goers watch a professional illustrator bring an animated character to life from preliminary sketches to final form. After a demonstration of how voiceovers work, kids add their own voices to animated characters, and then watch and listen to their work on a monitor. Older kids interested in the technology and artistry behind animation will particularly enjoy the hour-long tour, but it has much to appeal to children as young as six.

South Street Seaport Museum

12 Fulton Street, between Front and South Streets
(917) 492-3379
Subway: 2,3 to Fulton Street; 4,5 to Fulton Street;
A,C to Fulton Street
www.southstreetseaport.com

As of this printing, the South Street Seaport Museum is closed because of damage sustained during Hurricane Sandy. Please check the website for updated information.

Adrienne's Pizzabar

54 Stone Street, between Hanover Square and Coenties Alley
(212) 248-3838
Subway: 2,3 to Wall Street; J to Broad Street; 4,5 to Bowling Green;
R to Whitehall Street
No website
Monday–Saturday 11:30am–midnight; Sunday 11:30am–10pm

In the warm weather months, Stone Street is closed to cars, and
the restaurants that line it bring out long tables for outdoor dining.
During weekdays and during happy hour they're packed with Wall
Street traders and financial district business types, but this short

cobblestone street is loveliest in the evening or on weekends when it somehow evokes a bit of the atmosphere of Colonial New York.

Adrienne's serves an increasingly popular style of pizza known as a "grandma pie"—the type of pizza your Italian grandma might make: thin crust with a crispy underside. At Adrienne's, the quality of what's on top, including fresh mozzarella, makes for a better grandma than those at most other places. The basic Old Fashioned Pizza is $19.50.

Cowgirl Seahorse

259 Front Street, at Pine Street
(212) 608-7873
Subway: 2,3 to Wall Street; J to Broad Street; 4,5 to Wall Street;
N,R to Whitehall Street
www.cowgirlseahorse.com
Monday–Thursday 11am–11pm; Friday 11am–midnight;
Saturday 10am–midnight; Sunday 10am–11pm

Eat at Cowgirl Seahorse for the food (it's far from gourmet, but
it's fun, and your kids will love it), for the drinks (legendary frozen
margaritas), and for its proximity to the South Street Seaport, Wall
Street, and other Lower Manhattan destinations. With rainbow flags
displayed in the window, and a bar that plays host to everyone from
Wall Street types and locals to tourists from around the world, everyone feels at home here.

The menu emphasizes Mexican, Creole, and American Southwestern flavors, including nachos, tacos, po' boys, and "rattlesnake bites" (bacon-wrapped jalapeños stuffed with grilled shrimp), all around $12–$18. The kids' menu includes fried chicken, a shrimp basket, and a burger, all well under $10.

The place is loud—classic rock blares over the speakers and voices are raised to compete with the music—but that also means it's a fine place for toddlers who sometimes forget to use their "inside voices."

SmorgasBar

Subway: 2,3,4,5,A,C,J to Fulton Street
www.brooklynflea.com/markets/smorgasbar-at-south-st-seaport
Daily 11am–10pm (seasonal)

This offshoot of two popular weekend foodie markets in Brooklyn arrived at the Seaport area just in the nick of time after Hurricane Sandy had devastated the neighborhood and left very few places to eat.

SmorgasBar's ten food vendors and two bars contribute some modern touches that the area's culinary scene had lacked: Blue Marble Ice Cream, made from milk from grass-fed cows; Red Hook Lobster Pound lobster rolls; and Asia Dog's fun and funky twists on New York's most popular street food. Kids love the grilled cheese sandwiches made by Milk Truck Grilled Cheese. Several choices are available; the basic Milk Truck Classic is $5.75. The shakes, especially the Crushed Malted Ball, are delicious ($5.75), as is the fresh lemonade.

Plenty of picnic tables line the block-long pedestrian street, alcohol is served by a couple of vendors, and on summer and autumn nights, it's possible to make an evening of it with free movies and other entertainment (for schedule check www.southstreetseaport.com or internet-search for "See/Change Front/Row Cinema").

SHOP

For the nearest recommended shops, see Tribeca (page 97).

PLAY

EAT

SHOP

PLAY

Also see "A Walk from the Battery through Battery Park City," page 70

Children's Room at Poets House
10 River Terrace, at Murray Street
(212) 431-7920
Subway: 1,2,3 to Chambers Street
www.poetshouse.org
Children's Room: Thursday–Saturday 11am–5pm
Free

This is a cozy and sunny book-filled space where children can curl up and read, or compose their own poetry at the vintage school desks, each equipped with an old-fashioned manual typewriter. Thursdays at 10am, Tiny Poets Time features songs and poetry readings for toddlers. Other special events for ages 4–10 might feature authors and illustrators, or craft and writing workshops. One event, Ships, Seas and Poetries!, taught kids "how to sing shanties like a sailor, write poetry like a pirate, and build model boats like a shipwright learning the trade" (check website for upcoming activities). Parents, peek into the second floor: at tables along the floor-to-ceiling windows overlooking the river, surrounded by a spectacular collection of poetry books, writers are quietly working at their craft.

Irish Hunger Memorial
Vesey Street at North End Avenue
www.batteryparkcity.org/new/Visit/Museums-And-Memorials/Irish-Hunger-Memorial.php

This unconventional memorial will engage children—who love to clamber up the path to the top—as well as adults interested in Irish heritage and the Great Irish Famine and Migration of 1845–52. One minute you're in Battery Park; the next minute you've walked through a tunnel and have emerged to find yourselves in a little plot of Ireland, in a reconstructed cottage donated by a family from

County Mayo in honor of forebears who emigrated to America. From the top, 25 feet above the promenade, are views, significantly, of the Statue of Liberty and Ellis Island beyond. (You won't find a better backdrop for a photo.) The soil with which the memorial was built and the native vegetation with which it was planted were transported from the western coast of Ireland. The stones were donated by each of the 32 counties of Ireland; each is engraved with its county's name. A free brochure at the end of the entry tunnel has a map showing the locations of each stone.

Museum of Jewish Heritage, a living memorial to the Holocaust

36 Battery Place, at First Place
(646) 437-4202
Subway: 4,5 to Bowling Green; R to Whitehall or Rector Street; 1 to Rector Street
www.mjhnyc.org
Sunday–Tuesday 10am–5:45pm; Wednesday 10am–8pm; Thursday 10am–5:45pm; Friday 10am–5pm (3pm in winter); closed Saturday
Adults $12; students $7; 12 and under free; Wednesday 4pm–8pm Free

There are two ways to see this museum with children, depending on their ages (the first and third floors are appropriate for children of all ages; for information about the second floor, see below).

At the front desk, pick up the free workbook for ages 7–11 that will lead children through the first-floor galleries, inviting them to be a "heritage detective," discover selected artifacts, and explore their own family's heritage and traditions. As you enter the galleries, first stop by the rotunda, where a short continuously running film explores, with both seriousness and humor, what it means to be Jewish. Next, wander through the first-floor spaces devoted to different aspects of Jewish life a century ago (topics include family life, education, names, seasons of the Jewish year, education, etc.); many of the displays are accompanied by videos. For children, the Steinberger Sukkah may be the highlight. Designed and decorated in 1920 by a Hungarian butcher to decorate his family's Sukkot tent, the richly detailed scenes are filled with charm.

The museum is designed so that parents with young children may continue their visit by going directly to the third floor of the museum. Before going to the second floor, The War Against the Jews, parents will want to consider their children's age and maturity. The museum advises that, in general, the sensitive material there, including documentary photographs and videos of the Holocaust, is appropriate only for children in the sixth grade and above. The Living in Terror display is accompanied by videotaped childhood reminiscences of survivors.

From the darkness of the second floor, visitors emerge into the light-flooded third floor, the Keeping History Center. The glass wall of the entrance hall overlooks Andy Goldsworthy's Garden of Stones, which is reached by nearby stairs; children will enjoy running around the large boulders from which trees are growing. At the Timekeeper monitor, visitors can view photos taken of the garden, with a time-lapse camera, every day since it was installed.

At the end of the passageway, the Voices of Liberty room has plenty of space for children to stretch their legs while taking in a spectacular panoramic view that stretches from the Verrazano-Narrows

Bridge to the Statue of Liberty, and up the Hudson River. Computers in the room allow users to access 2,500 video testimonies from the USC Shoah Foundation Institute for Visual History and Education. Listeners may search videos of refugees, Holocaust survivors, and others who immigrated to America by name or subject ("the trip," "lost in translation," "adapting") and may record their own stories to be added to the archives.

In the gift shop, there are all manner of Judaica from mezuzahs to mahjong sets. For kids, you'll find Yankees and Mets yarmulkes, Passover and Shabbat placemats and crayons, biblical stickers, dreidel erasers, lots of books including *The Cat in the Hat* in Yiddish, the board book *I can do a Mitzvah*, a sh'ma prayer bracelet, and much, much more.

If you're hungry, stop in The Heritage Café, which also overlooks New York Harbor, for a glatt kosher lunch or snack.

The museum's children's programs include free story times as well as arts and crafts workshops and musical performances. Check the website for specifics about upcoming events.

Leaving the museum, parents may want to point out the Battery Park City School across the street. Children from outside of New York City may be surprised to see that schools in the city can be in a high-rise, and that recess is held. . . on the roof.

The Skyscraper Museum

39 Battery Place, at First Place
(212) 968-1961
Subway: 1,N,R to Rector Street; 4,5 to Bowling Green
www.skyscraper.org
Wednesday–Sunday noon–6pm
Adults $5, students $2.50

The exhibitions in this one-room space aren't really aimed at children, so unless your child has a strong interest in architecture, and would find elevations, plans, and photographs intriguing, a visit should be planned only during one of the children's programs. Held weekly on Saturday mornings (some for 3- to 10-year-olds, some for 7 –14 year olds, some for all ages), the hands-on workshops ($5) guide kids as they build model skyscrapers and gargoyles, draw Mother's Day cards and sidewalk art, or design a Halloween costume based on a favorite skyscraper.

Statue of Liberty National Monument and Ellis Island

Liberty Island
(212) 363-3200
www.nps.gov/stli
Subway: 1 to South Ferry; 4,5 to Bowling Green; R to Whitehall
www.nps.gov/stli
Boat tickets to reach the island may be purchased from Statue Cruises (201) 604-2800; www.statuecruises.com or at the Castle Clinton National Monument in Battery Park.
Ellis Island, and Liberty Grounds and Pedestal: Adults $17; 4–12 $9; Ellis Island, and Liberty Grounds, Pedestal, and Crown: Adults $20; 4–12 $12. Children must be at least 4' tall to visit the Crown.

Boats depart throughout the day from Battery Park and make stops at Liberty Island and Ellis Island. Only 365 people per day are permitted to visit the Crown; Crown tickets can sell out months in advance so it's wise to reserve via the website. Expect airport-style security before boarding the boat, and again at the museum and Crown entrance.

When you disembark at Liberty Island, pick up a free self-guided audio tour available in both children's and adult programs and multiple languages. At the flagpole behind the Statue every hour on the hour, a National Park Service Ranger leads a free 30-minute tour around the grounds. Children may enjoy filling out the Statue of Liberty "Junior Ranger Activity Sheet," available in the Information Center beyond the flagpole. Those who complete it are awarded a Junior Ranger badge.

At the entrance are lockers ($2 for two hours, cash only) for storing items such as umbrellas and backpacks, which are not allowed in the museum or statue.

To get to the Pedestal level, either take the elevator or steps; to reach the Crown from the Pedestal level, you must climb up 162 steps on a steep and narrow spiral staircase (there are platforms on which to rest).

The Crown has space for only about ten people at a time. Because the number is so limited, the experience feels very intimate and privileged. Two park rangers not only allow lingering but are eager to share their vast knowledge, including how its design, which allows for a certain amount of sway, functioned as a prototype for the modern skyscraper. Touch the sides and feel the "two pennies-thick" wall

of the statue, look out the windows, spot Peregrine falcons, and relish the solitude.

The museum presents photographs and physical artifacts that trace the Statue's history, design, financing, and construction on Liberty Island. The museum is compact and succinct, and will likely interest children ages 6 and older.

Near the flagpole there's a cafe that has some stand-up seating indoors and tables and chairs on the outdoor terrace, perfect for nice days.

Ellis Island
www.nps.gov/elis

At the time of this writing, major sections of the Ellis Island Museum have been closed due to Hurricane Sandy.
For up-to-date information on the museum, visit its website, www.ellisisland.org/genealogy/ellis_island_visiting.asp
For details about the self-guided tour options, visit www.nps.gov/elis/forteachers/self-guided.htm

Located on the site of what was America's busiest immigration station from 1892–1924, this museum allows visitors to walk the same path as did roughly 12 million immigrants during that time period. (Ellis Island remained active, primarily as a center for the detention and deportation of illegal aliens, until 1954.)

In some areas of the museum, the artifacts on display, such as trunks and suitcases in the Baggage Room, make history a visual experience. In other areas, such as in the Registry Room (aka the "Great Hall"), the room itself speaks volumes about the crowds that once filled it.

A visitor's experience begins in the Baggage Room, the area where new arrivals had to deposit their luggage before heading upstairs for both physical and legal inspections before being allowed to enter the United States.

While there's much to absorb, plenty of the material is rudimentary enough for young children ages 5 and older to understand. In addition to the main areas of the museum, in side galleries are exhibits about Ellis Island and the history of immigration in America. Included are accounts of individuals and of groups of people, statistics (where immigrants came from, why they came, and—in plenty of instances—what became of them), large archival photographs with captions, preserved personal belongings and other artifacts, interactive displays, audio oral histories, and video footage.

Included with admission are self-guided tour options in several languages. Or, for a more personal experience, you can go on a free 30-minute Ranger Tour that begins hourly from the Information Desk in the Baggage Room. As at the Statue of Liberty, another National Parks–administered site, kids can request a Junior Ranger Activity Sheet, and earn a Junior Ranger Badge.

Visitors can also watch the enthralling 28-minute film, "Island of Hope—Island of Tears." It offers a narrated account, with archival

Over 12 million immigrants entered the United States through Ellis Island, the nation's chief gateway during the years 1892 to 1924. Today, over 100 million Americans can trace their ancestry to the immigrants who crossed this island before dispersing to points all over the country.

Following restoration in the 1980s, this building reopened as the Ellis Island Immigration Museum, a symbol of this nation's immigrant heritage. The museum exhibits chronicle Ellis Island's role in immigration history, and view it in the context of its time and the still broader context of four centuries of immigration to America.

The exhibits also portray and give voice to the immigrants themselves. Each of their stories is unique and bears witness to the courage and determination that enables men and women to leave their homes and seek new opportunities in an unknown land.

footage, of the immigrants' experience suitable for children 8 and older, also online at www.youtube.com/watch?v=qh5CWbTDsuQ.

If you'd like to locate the names of ancestors in ships' manifests, visit the American Family Immigration History Center (currently closed due to Hurricane Sandy). The database is also accessible at ellisisland.org.

A Walk from the Battery through Battery Park City

This walk takes you from the tip of Manhattan, where the Statue of Liberty/Ellis Island tour boats depart, along the Hudson River through spectacular Battery Park City to Tribeca. There are dozens of things for children and adults to do and see and good places to eat. The walk can take an hour or a day, depending on how long you spend at the museums, attractions, and playgrounds.

If you're getting off the Staten Island Ferry, or arriving at the South Ferry (1) or Whitehall (N/R) subway stations, walk toward State Street—look for the flagpole. A good start to the walk is to look at the three-dimensional bronze map depicting New Amsterdam in 1660. Ask your kids if they can find the windmill and the 12 cannons protecting the fort. Then walk west toward historic Battery Park. On the left is a small playground, newly renovated, but the main event here is the new SeaGlass carousel, with its spiral canopy recalling a chambered nautilus. Below, riders sit on 30 nine-foot-tall fiberglass fish that move up and down as the carousel rotates and a sound and light show plays. (As of this printing, hours and prices had not been determined.)

Continue west through the park, with majestic New York Harbor and the Statute of Liberty on the left. If you're hungry, the **Table Green** kiosk in the park serves local beer, hot dogs made from grass-fed beef, veggie chili, sandwiches, and snacks. If you want to take the cruise to the Statue of Liberty and Ellis Island, and you haven't bought advance tickets online (page 63), you can buy them at the Castle Clinton National Monument, which is straight ahead. Or, continue through the park, passing the Korean War memorial, Merchant Marine memorial, Emma Lazarus plaque, and eternal flame in honor of the victims of 9/11.

After you pass Historic Ferry Building A, bear left and walk a few steps through a small garden with a circular pond. You'll emerge in Robert F. Wagner Park, at the base of Battery Park City. The centerpiece of Wagner Park is a velvety green lawn with front-row views of the iconic harbor. It's an idyllic setting, and the Battery Park City Conservancy takes full advantage of it with activities like family concerts and dances, lawn games, and frequently scheduled art and nature activities (check the website, www.bpcparks.org/bpcp/events/events.php).

If it's a Monday, Wednesday, or Friday (10am to noon, May to October), you'll see dozens of babies and toddlers romping and rolling on the grassy expanse—the entire lawn is reserved for them at that time, with toys and climbing equipment provided. Both tourists and locals can hardly take their eyes off the delightful sight of the frolicking tots. On Fridays (7–8:30pm, May and June), Sunset Sing Circles are held. Last but not least, the park has large and clean **restrooms** (in the brick building with the arch). Before you continue on the walk, you may want to climb the stairs to the public viewing platform above the restaurant Giginio (page 78), where the entire breathtaking scene stretches before you.

Now head north on the riverside promenade. On your right, you'll see the sculpture, *Ape & Cat (At the Dance)* by Jim Dine, beloved by many New Yorkers who see in it a reflection of New York City's ideal: the peaceful, even blissful, embrace of diversity.

If you wish to visit the Museum of Jewish Heritage, bear to the right to enter on Battery Place (page 60).

Or, continue walking north following the walkway around a bend where you'll come across a structure of stairs, walkways, paths, a floating island platform, and a quay—all fun for kids to run around. If you're hungry or if you want to assemble a picnic to eat along the promenade before you continue north along the river, turn right and walk a block and pick up food to go at **Battery Place Market** (page 78).

Back on the esplanade, continue to North Cove, the large sailing marina. Right before you reach it, there's a family-friendly bistro on the right, **Merchants River House** (page 80).

As you pass the volleyball court, there's a small playground for toddlers, West Thames Park, up the stairs on your right. As you walk around the marina, don't miss the fence with the quotations celebrating New York by Walt Whitman and Frank O'Hara.

Inside the World Financial Center, in the 10-story glass pavilion Winter Garden, free public events are held. They're worth checking out online (brookfieldplaceny.com/arts-events). A friend once wandered in to find the New York City Public School Ballroom Dancing competition—you never know what performance or activity might surprise and delight you. There is seating, public restrooms, air conditioning, and Wi-Fi.

The World Financial Center, which towers over the plaza and marina, is filled with lots of **eating options** inside and, when the weather is good, outside (PJ Clarke's and, in the summer, stands selling grilled hot dogs, lobster rolls, hamburgers, and other food truck food—all good; see brookfieldplaceny.com/content/dining-27251.html).

Continuing around the marina, back toward the promenade, glance to the cul-de-sac on the right where **food trucks** regularly park. As you resume your walk, you'll pass the Mercantile Exchange. Inside is a small branch of the Tribeca toy store Boomerang (page 81), a good place to pick up sand toys or a ball. Now, continue along the promenade until you see the Irish Hunger Memorial—an unexpectedly delightful place for kids to play and a fabulous place to take a photo (page 59).

If you haven't yet eaten, and want a quick meal, there's a **Pain Quotidien** (page 429) across the way at River Terrace and North End Avenue and a **Shake Shack** (page 260) down the block (cross North End Avenue and walk down Murray Street).

Back at the promenade, stop a moment to let the children watch the paddling ducks and huge orange gliding koi fish in the large

lily pond just south of the playground. Adults will appreciate the poetry etched into the stone border, with poems by Seamus Heaney and Mark Strand.

Ready for more running around? Nelson A. Rockefeller Park playground—with its sandboxes and sand tables, slides and swings, swinging wooden walkways, pedal-powered carousel ride, picnic tables and benches—is a large and elaborate play area with lots of everything, for small to larger children.

Adjacent to the playground, slightly to the north, another lush grass lawn awaits; large balls and big foam toys are provided. The nearby kiosk, at Rockefeller Park House, loans board games, hula hoops, badminton sets, ping pong paddles and balls, and basketballs to use in the park; there are also kids books if you're ready to sit down for a moment (free; leave any form of ID, May through October). At the picnic tables north of Rockefeller Park House, free drop-in chess classes are conducted by an expert who will help kids 5–18 either learn chess or improve their game. Game boards and chess pieces are provided (3:30–5pm, May through the end of September). Free preschool art classes are held in Rockefeller Park on Thursday, 10:30am–noon, May–October).

Overlooking the playground, at 10 River Terrace, is Poets House, a serene and welcoming refuge for both children and adults. The Children's Room there is a good place to take some time out from active play and take advantage of the wonderful children's book collection and quiet activities provided (free; page 58). As you step out of Poets House, notice the quote by the architect Le Corbusier about New York City set into the sidewalk.

Behind Poets House is Teardrop Park. Tucked in the midst of four large apartment buildings, it is nonetheless a rugged 1.8 acres designed with water features, a children's slide, a reading area with rock seats, and places to "rock hop."

Continue north past the basketball courts to the seating area, the setting of Tom Otterness's sculptures, *The Real World*. Children are intrigued and adults entertained by the weird and wonderful little animals and creatures, pennies and footprints that decorate the ground, the walls, the chess tables. Look for the dog at the water fountain, who's looking at the cat, who's looking at the bird, who's looking at the worm.

If you're up for more fun and games, continue north to the contiguous Hudson River Park. Walk past another basketball court and skateboarding area on the right, and past a small harbor on the left to Pier 25 (page 84).

This is the conclusion of the walk. At one of the stoplights cross the Westside Highway into Tribeca, where the closest subway stops are the 1 at Franklin Street or the A,C,E at Canal Street.

EAT

Battery Place Market
77 Battery Place, at Third Place
(212) 786-0077
Subway: 1,N,R to Rector Street; 4,5 to Bowling Green
www.batteryplacemarkets.com
Monday–Friday 6:30am–10pm; Saturday–Sunday 6:30am–9pm

The first clue that this is not your basic deli: the sandwiches are served on bread from two top-notch local bakeries, Orwasher's and Sullivan Street. For a picnic lunch, choose among organic egg salad, smoked chicken breast, or the daily sandwich specials (red Thai poached curry on focaccia, hot Cuban sandwich on Texas toast, Philly cheese steak, lobster roll). Add a drink and dessert and you have all the fixin's for a gourmet picnic to take to Battery Park. If you want to eat inside, a window counter has eight seats. Another smaller BPM is at the north end of Battery Park City at 240 Murray Street; no seating.

Gigino at Wagner Park
20 Battery Place, at Esplanade (in Wagner Park)
(212) 528-2228
Subway: 1,N,R to Rector Street; 4,5 to Bowling Green
www.gigino-wagnerpark.com
Sunday–Thursday 11:30am–10pm; Friday, Saturday 11:30am–11pm

This casual restaurant serves regional Italian food, is welcoming to kids, and has a glorious view across New York Harbor. On a

beautiful summer evening, dining outside, there's nothing like it. The children's menu offers shrimp and zucchini, fried breaded chicken loin, tortellini with meatballs in tomato ragu, farfalle with pink cream sauce and cheese ($12, $13). Adult pasta dishes hover around $18, and a range of chicken and other entrees around $23.

Merchants River House

375 South End Avenue, between Liberty and Albany Streets
(212) 432-1451
Subway: 1 to Rector Street; A,E to World Trade Center
www.merchantsriverhouse.com
Monday–Friday noon–10pm; Saturday 11am–10pm;
Sunday 10:30am–10pm

The kids' menu at this American-style bistro on the Hudson River Esplanade offers a choice of chicken fingers, mac and cheese, burger with fries, pizza, or a corn dog, with milk, juice, or soda, for $9. The adult lunch and dinner menu includes steak sandwiches, pizzas, Cobb and Caesar salads, lobster rolls, and more popular standards, all moderately priced. The view of the busy Hudson River and the people-, dog-, bike-, and stroller-watching will keep everyone entertained.

SHOP

Boomerang Toys

1 North End Avenue (in the interior promenade of the New York
Mercantile Exchange building, across from the ferry terminal)
(212) 227-7271
Subway: 1,2,3,A,C to Chambers Street
www.boomerangtoys.com
Monday–Saturday 10am–6pm; Sunday 11am–5pm

This family-owned toyshop is perfectly located near the many Battery
Park City play areas. In addition to sand toys (a bucket, mold, rake,
and shovel set, made in the USA from 100% recycled milk jugs,
$22), you'll find kites, balls, foam baseball bats and balls, jump
ropes, Frisbees, and scooters. The larger store a few blocks away in
Tribeca at 119 W. Broadway (Duane & Reade Streets) is the U.S. flagship store for Bruder, the German toy manufacturer of beautifully
engineered, realistic, large, and functional toy construction vehicles.

Tribeca

PLAY

Washington Market Park

Chambers Street, between Greenwich and West Streets
1,2,3 to Chambers Street

This neighborhood park is a large and leafy expanse with an involved neighborhood "friends" group who keeps it in tip-top condition. In addition to play equipment, there's a gazebo and an expansive grassy lawn. Damaged in the attacks on the World Trade Center several blocks south, and used during that time as a parking lot for emergency vehicles and a power station, it has been restored to its former, verdant beauty.

Hudson River Park Play Area and Mini-Golf

Pier 25, Hudson River Park, on the Hudson River between Harrison and North Moore Streets
(212) 766-1104, ext. 228
Subway: 1 to Franklin Street
hudsonriverpark.org
Mini-Golf: Daily. In fair weather, official hours are noon–8pm, later if the weather is nice; as the season gets warmer the hours are extended to 10am–10pm
Adults $5; 13 and under $4

Pier 25 has now been repurposed to include a gorgeous playground with climbers, lots of equipment, and sand and water areas with overhead sprinklers. Past the playground and small marina there's an 18-hole miniature golf course with two working waterfalls. Beyond the golf course—you're out in the river now—are beach volleyball courts with lounge chairs for observers, another open lawn, and, at the end of the pier, a huge wooden deck with deck chairs, a spectacular perch from which you can see past the Statue of Liberty to the Verrazano-Narrows Bridge to the south, and up the Hudson to the north, and across to New Jersey. There are restrooms and seasonal food vendors on Pier 25.

Museum

Cortlandt Alley, between Franklin and White Streets
No telephone
Subway: J,Z,N,Q,R,6 to Canal Street
mmuseumm.com
Saturday, Sunday noon–6pm, or open 24 hours a day through viewing windows
Free

This is a museum unlike any you've ever seen, ever will see, or can even imagine: quirky, visionary, delightful. Housed in a formerly abandoned elevator shaft, at 60 square feet, this is the smallest museum in Manhattan. What it displays: weird and overlooked artifacts from around the world, such as the shoe allegedly thrown by an Iraqi journalist at President George W. Bush, a bag of bacon potato chips, a small piece of barbed-wire fence from Dachau, fake vomit. Andy Spade, the designer and artist, told *The New York Times*, "Look at this crazy stuff…they celebrate the awkward, the curious."

If Museum is "closed," you can still view the collection through the elevator car's window while you listen to an audio tour of each item (accessed by calling (888) 763–8839). The museum is not without amenities: there's a café (aka a Nespresso machine) and a gift shop (a shelf with T-shirts and postcards).

The National September 11 Memorial & Museum

Memorial Entrance: Corner of Greenwich and Albany Streets
Ticket pickup/ticket purchase: Preview Site, 20 Vesey Street,
between Church Street and Broadway
Visitor Center and Museum Store: 90 West Street, at Albany Street
(212) 227-7931
Subway: 2,3 to Park Place; A,C,J,Z,4,5 to Fulton Street;
E to World Trade Center; R to Cortlandt Street; 1 to Rector Street
www.911memorial.org
Hours are seasonal: www.911memorial.org/hours-operation
Reservations: for visitor's passes: www.911memorial.org/visitor-passes
Free ($2 per ticket processing charge if purchased online)

The 9/11 Memorial is appropriate for all ages, but children 6 and older are most likely to appreciate the beauty, solemnity, and symbolism of the site. The mammoth amount of water and the sound it makes as it falls, as well as the vast size of each of the two below-grade square pools (each is one square acre), render the large number of visitors barely noticeable. Each pool is built upon the footprint of one of the two Twin Towers and features along its perimeter the names of those who died on September 11, 2001, and February 26, 1993, the date of the first bombing of the World Trade Center. The water, after lingering atop an upper level, eventually vanishes downward into a dark square opening in the center, symbolizing a void that will never be filled.

Kids who max out on contemplation and families who need to rest or reset will find plenty of space to linger in the green spaces along the perimeters of the pools and in the tree-lined plazas.

Visits to the Memorial are timed so that the number of visitors at a given time is kept to an appropriate number for the space. To visit, you can reserve tickets online, print them yourself, and then bring them to the Memorial entrance; or you can purchase them at the Preview Site, in which case your entry time will be the next available time slot.

The 9/11 Memorial Museum is scheduled to open in Spring 2014.

Tribeca Performing Arts Center
Borough of Manhattan Community College
199 Chambers Street at West Street
(212) 220-1459; tickets (212) 220-1460
1,2,3,A,C,J, Z to Chambers Street; 4,5,6 to Brooklyn Bridge
www.tribecapac.org
Saturday and Sunday afternoons

Not all the great theater for kids is on Broadway. The Tribeca PAC offers family performances with guest theatrical companies staging shows that appeal to children as young as 3 (a puppet performance of Leo Lionni's children's books *Swimmy, Frederick,* and *Inch by Inch*). The organization has staged Theatreworks USA's presentation of Judith Viorst's *Alexander and the Terrible, Horrible, No Good, Very Bad Day,* Jim Henson's *Sid the Science Kid...Live!,* and *Bunnicula.* The line-up is always diverse, and might be a one-man circus comedy, a fairy tale adaptation, or a mystery, at ticket prices far below the Great White Way's.

EAT

Blaue Gans
139 Duane Street, between Church Street and Broadway
(212) 571-8880
Subway: 1,2,3 to Chambers Street (and Broadway);
A,C to Chambers Street (and Church)
www.kg-ny.com/blaue-gans
Daily 11am–midnight

Maybe this upscale restaurant isn't a place to take young kids late-ish on a Friday night—but plenty of families dine here, with infants through grade-schoolers, everyone feeling completely at home. The restaurant occupies a large loft space typical of Tribeca, with posters from now-famous art exhibitions adorning the walls, adding to the downtown ambience.

Parents will enjoy an excellent German-Austrian meal (wiener schnitzel $26, wursts $14) and an extensive list of German beers and specialty cocktails (Austrian Lemonade made with Chambord, raspberry schnapps, and lemon, or the White Cosmo, made with vodka, elderflower, and white cranberry juice). Blaue Gans is part of the restaurant group that includes top-notch Wallsé, so the menu isn't typical beer garden fare. The kids menu has wursts and schnitzel, as well as chicken and mac and cheese ($9). Between the cool setting and the local clientele, it's a great place to experience the Tribeca scene.

Duane Park Patisserie

179 Duane Street, between Greenwich and Hudson Streets
(212) 274-8447
Subway: 1,2,3 to Chambers Street (and Broadway);
A,C to Chambers Street (and Church)
www.duaneparkpatisserie.com
Monday–Saturday 8am–7pm; Sunday 9am–5pm

"Keep Calm and Bake On" says the poster on the wall of this quiet, shabby-chic little bakeshop where tiered cake stands festooned with crystals decorate the shelves. Sit at one of the three circa-1950s kitchen tables, and choose among classic baked goods (cupcakes, cookies, brownies) and more sophisticated sweets—a tiny orange panna cotta or a lemon passion fruit mousse topped with lemon curd and meringue.

Petite Abeille

134 West Broadway, between Duane and Thomas Streets
(212) 791-1360
Subway: 1,2,3 to Chambers Street (and Broadway)
www.petiteabeille.com
Monday–Saturday 8am–11pm; Sunday 8am–10pm

Moules marinieres (a pot of steamed mussels in a white wine broth) and Flemish beef stew with fries are favorites at this cozy Belgian café, which also has omelets, burgers, steak frites, and thick Belgian waffles slathered with whipped cream. Popular specials are Wednesday night's all-you-can-eat mussels and one Stella beer ($27) and Thursday's lobster night (a ¼-lb. lobster and Stella, $27). Omelets and waffles ($7–$12) are brunch favorites. On Monday, all

Belgian beers are half-price, and on Tuesday all bottles of wine are half-price. Prix fixe dinner 5–6:30pm, $30.

Additional locations: 410 East 20th Street (Union Square to Madison Square); 44 West 17th Street (Chelsea)

Sarabeth's

339 Greenwich Street, at Jay Street
(212) 966-0421
Subway: 1 to Franklin Street; 2,3 to Chambers Street
www.sarabeth.com
Monday–Thursday 8am–10:30pm; Friday, Saturday 8am–11pm;
Sunday 8am–10pm

For more than 30 years, New Yorkers have been devoted to the jams and baked goods first sold out of Sarabeth's tiny shop on the Upper West Side. Now there are Sarabeth's restaurants throughout the city, many serving full meals throughout the day. The brunch is legendary

for being one of the best in the city, and it's family-friendly to a fault—you'll see strollers galore at the Tribeca location—but dinner here, too, is an excellent meal for a reasonable price. While there's no kids' menu, there are plenty of choices that will appeal to children: mini cheeseburgers ($14), velvety cream of tomato soup, chicken pot pie, or maybe one of the bar snacks.

Additional locations: 75 Ninth Avenue (Chelsea Market); Sarabeth's at Lord & Taylor (page 320, Midtown), 381 Park Avenue South (Union Square to Madison Square), 40 Central Park South (Central Park), 1295 Madison Avenue (Upper East Side), 423 Amsterdam Avenue (Upper West Side)

Walker's

16 North Moore Street, at Varick Street
(212) 941-0142
Subway: 1 to Franklin Street; A,C,E to Canal Street
www.walkersnyc.com
Daily 11am–1am (food), 4am (drinks only)

Walker's nineteenth-century barroom is a perfectly unpretentious setting for Guinness, burgers, and well-executed basic food. With only steaks and an occasional fish entrée breaking the $20 barrier, Walker's prices are quite gentle, especially considering its chichi Tribeca location.

With children in tow, take a pass on the often-crowded front room and walk past the kitchen to one of two small backrooms. White paper atop white tablecloths functions as a perfect canvas for drawing, and crayons are provided.

There's a very good burger ($12), a grilled yellowfin tuna niçoise salad ($15.50), and a Friday fish and chips special ($16.50), accompanied by Sarson's, an authentic British malt vinegar. The kid's meal (burger with fries, pasta with butter or red sauce, grilled cheese, or chicken tenders, $7.50) comes with a small beverage and ice cream. If you'd rather have pizza, try Girello next door, under the same ownership.

Zucker's Bagels & Smoked Fish

146 Chambers Street, between Hudson and Greenwich Streets
(212) 608-5844
Subway: 1 to Chambers Street
www.zuckersbagels.com
Monday–Friday 6:30am–7pm; Saturday, Sunday 6:30am–6pm

The hand-rolled, fresh, kettle-boiled bagels, cream cheese, all sorts of schmears, smoked fish—along with the subway tiles on the walls, and the pressed tin ceiling—make New Yorkers feel right at home. In this sparkling and cheery bagelry, there are a few tables and chairs, and a counter with stools; you may want to take your bagels to nearby Washington Market Park or over to the Hudson River esplanade.

SHOP

Adeline Adeline
147 Reade Street, between Greenwich and Hudson Streets
(212) 227-1150; (888) 9X0-BIKE; (888) 996-2453
Subway: 1,2,3 to Chambers Street; A,C to Chambers Street
www.adelineadeline.com
Tuesday–Sunday 11:30am–6:30pm; closed Monday

Here, bicycles are taken seriously as both transportation and coveted design objects; anyone who cycles seriously will be wowed by the high-end British, Danish, and Italian models on display, many not sold elsewhere in the U.S. The bike accessories that have attracted the attention of *Vogue* and *Vanity Fair* are an inspired mix of kids things and adult things: bike bells hand-painted to look like peppermint candies, old-fashioned phone dials, or cupcakes ($19.50–$24); whimsical bike helmets for toddlers, including one that looks like a watermelon; stylish helmets for women covered with faux leopard or patterns inspired by vintage fabric; helmets for both men and women with changeable tartan, tweed, and herring-bone covers ($65–$150). Need a reflective helmet bow ($16)? You'll find it here, along with bicycle baskets made in Nantucket, New Hampshire, Ghana, and Britain; high-tech lights and locks; pumps and phone holders; and more.

Babesta Threads

66 West Broadway, between Murray and Warren Streets

(212) 608-4522

Subway: 1,2,3 to Chambers Street; A,C to Chambers Street

www.babesta.com/Threads

Monday–Friday 11am–7pm; Saturday, Sunday noon–6pm

This is a small store with quality merchandise that reflects the signature Tribeca look: cool, casual, and cutting edge. You'll find Che tanks, Ramones T-shirts, faux leather coats with wide lapels and brass snaps in small-fry sizes, "beast-free" yellow sneakers with sliding toggle closures, a girl's tiger-print bathing suit with a peplum.

A notebook on the counter is filled with iron-on transfers that can be applied while you wait to T-shirts (2–12 years) and onesies (3–24 months): Hillary Clinton ("For President"), Elmo ("Tickle me"), a double popsicle ("Let's stick together"), "My mom is the bomb," and many more ($25).

Koh's Kids

311 Greenwich Street, between Reade and Chambers Streets
(212) 791-6915
Subway: 1,2,3 to Chambers Street; A,C to Chambers Street
No website
Monday–Saturday 10am–7pm; Sunday 11am–6pm

This little shop is directly across from Washington Market Park and a hop, skip, and a jump from Battery Park. If the weather turns unexpectedly chilly—and it often does this close to the water—here you'll find a jacket, sweater, or hat for your little one. If the weather turns warm and your child wants to run through the sprinklers in the parks, you'll find a bathing suit and flip-flops. The store stocks European brands, as well as items from local designers (cotton dresses from Eye Spy in Brooklyn, headbands and knitted scarves made by a neighbor). Koh's Kids has been in business for almost 20 years; for much of that time it was the only children's clothing store in Tribeca. The owner has an eye for style, but first and foremost she makes sure the local kids are provided with all the basics, and that the working parents of the neighborhood are able to find what they need, when they need it.

Playing Mantis

32 North Moore Street, between Hudson and Varick Streets
(646) 484-6845
Subway: 1,2 to Franklin Street; 1 to Canal Street;
A,C,E to Canal Street
www.friendlymantis.com
Tuesday–Saturday 11am–7pm; Sunday 10am–6pm; closed Monday

"For the Hobbit lover" is how one Tribeca mom describes this large shop filled with handmade and mostly wooden toys. Most of the toys here are made by small family businesses, American and European. You'll find many beautifully crafted knights' shields, helmets, swords, and leather and "chain mail" tunics. For princesses, try Sarah's silk dresses ($87.95), cone hats, wings, and a billowing tent-like play canopy ($129.95). On the shelves are lap harps and xylophones from Sweden, spinning tops from Austria, puppets made from recycled sweaters ($30), a choice of wooden "runs" for marbles, disks, and balls—the balls travel over a xylophone with a pleasing tinkle—that you're unlikely to find elsewhere. Books are chosen for both their beautiful illustrations as well as their subject matter (fables, fairy tales, and folk tales). The holiday present of choice for Tribeca's toddlers in recent years has been Playing Mantis's handcrafted wooden kitchen with a refrigerator, stove, oven, stainless steel sink, and cupboards, and a pull-out cutting board ($399). Not much here is inexpensive, but everything is of heirloom quality.

Roberta Roller Rabbit

176 Duane Street, at Greenwich Street
(212) 966-0076
Subway: 1,2,3 to Franklin Street; A,C to Chambers Street
robertafreymann.com, robertarollerrabbit.com
Monday–Saturday 10am–6pm; Sunday 11am–5pm

There's a bit of a Lilly Pulitzer vibe here in the colorful printed beachy cotton clothing, but with a touch of bohemian St. Barts. Not A-line shifts, but caftan-like kurtas; not lime-green and pink, but azure-blue and white. RRR's full range of apparel for men and women and housewares are available here, as is the fetching line of children's clothing. You'll find sleeveless sundresses ($65), featherweight peasant tops for girls, shirts for boys, and pull-on pants for both ($50). The diminutive lacy jellie sandals are to die for. Shelves are filled with stacks of pima cotton knit baby pajama sets in monkey, hearts, and other happy prints ($55).

Additional location: 1019 Lexington Avenue (Upper East Side)

PLAY

EAT

SHOP

Chinatown

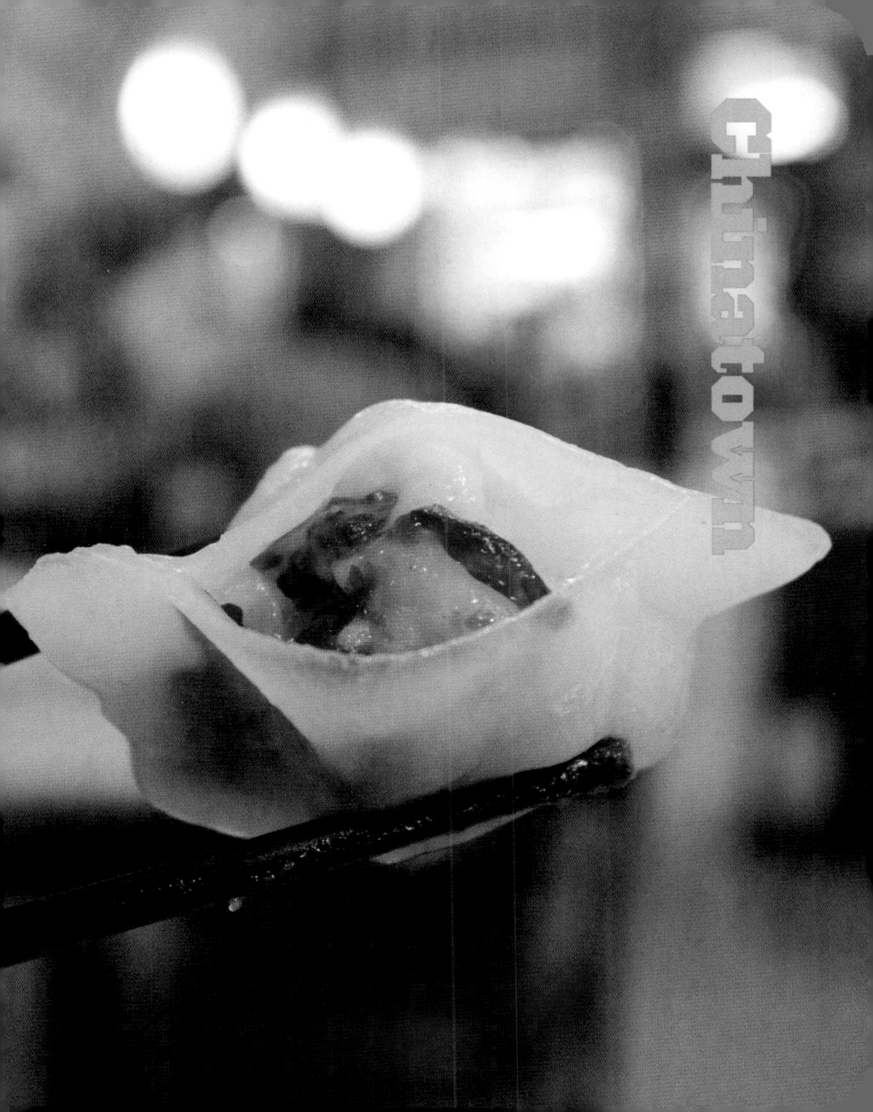

PLAY

Columbus Park
Between Bayard, Worth, Mulberry, and Baxter Streets and
Hogan Place
Subway: 6,N,Q,R to Canal Street; J to Canal Street or
Chambers Street

If you're in Chinatown or near the Manhattan side of the Brooklyn
Bridge, a visit to this park provides a quintessential neighborhood
experience. On a typical day, you'll find many elderly Chinese playing
cards and other games, as well as singers of Chinese opera and
musicians playing traditional instruments.

EAT

456 Shanghai Cuisine

69 Mott Street, between Canal and Bayard Streets
(212) 964-0003
Subway: 6,J,N,Q,R to Canal Street; B,D to Grand Street
www.456shanghaicuisine.com
Daily 11am–11pm

The endless array of eating options in Manhattan's Chinatown can be a challenge for visitors trying to decide where to dine. Part of the fun, of course, is eating unfamiliar and delicious foods for low prices. 456 Shanghai Cuisine fits the bill perfectly: the quality is high, and along with an emphasis on Shanghai preparations, the restaurant also offers many Americanized Chinese standards.

A favorite is soup dumplings (called Juicy Pork Buns, 8 for $5.25 on the menu). Allow the waiter to explain how to eat them without losing the soup or burning your tongue: the method involves using a spoon and chopsticks, with which you execute a puncture-and-slurp move. The ginger-laced dipping sauce adds an additional layer of complexity to that of the dumplings' rich meaty interior. Kids who normally default to chicken fingers or pasta will probably like the homemade lo mein, which can be ordered with chicken, pork, or shrimp ($6.95)—it puts standard lo mein to shame. You can take the safe route and order dishes you have had before, and they'll be great, or take advantage of the chance to sample Shanghai-style cuisine, which is relatively uncommon in the U.S. But be sure you try the soup dumplings.

Chinatown Ice Cream Factory

65 Bayard Street, between Mott and Elizabeth Streets
(212) 608-4170
Subway: J,N,Q,R,6 to Canal Street; B,D to Grand Street;
F to East Broadway
www.chinatownicecreamfactory.com
Daily 11am–10pm

Since 1999, the Chinatown Ice Cream Factory has delighted children
and adults with its Asian-centric selection of top-notch ice cream.
Here, the "standard" flavors are avocado, black sesame, lychee, and
taro, while chocolate, vanilla, and strawberry are considered "exotic."

You're allowed two sample tastes before making your selection, so even if you plan on choosing a familiar flavor, why not dip your tongue into unknown territory? Sorbet, sundaes, and milkshakes also are on the menu (single scoop $3.99, double $6.50, milkshakes $7.25).

Jing Fong

20 Elizabeth Street, between Canal and Bayard Streets
(212) 964-5256
Subway: J,N,Q,Z,6 to Canal Street; B,D to Grand Street;
F to East Broadway
www.jingfongny.com
Daily 9:30am–3pm and 5pm–10pm

Customers here ascend via escalator to arrive in a dining room that seems as big as half a football field. Unless your party has six or more people, be prepared to share a table with others, which of course is part of the fun. If you're new to the dim sum experience, you can watch, learn from, and ask your fellow tablemates about items you don't recognize.

Be adventurous. From the carts that circulate from table to table, order anything that looks good. The ladies pushing them usually know the English words for the main ingredients of the foods they offer. Be sure to head over to the side buffet, where there are many additional choices. Each time you opt for a dish, a server marks your ticket, so be sure to bring it with you to the buffet. There's also a printed menu. There are different types of servers in the dining room: in addition to the ladies pushing the carts, servers wearing

vests and ties, usually men, take orders for food on the menu, bring extra condiments and more tea, and tally the bill.

Favorite dim sum choices include shrimp har gow (a round dumpling filled with shrimp), jiu bao tai (water chestnuts, garlic greens, and shrimp filling in a green wrapper, fried on one side), and sia chang (long rice noodles filled with shrimp), and from the buffet, the clams with black bean sauce. Try anything; prices are low ($2.35–$5.95 per plate, $8.95 for "kitchen" items, and $10.95 for special items such as clams), so you can't go too wrong.

What your children will eat ultimately depends upon how adventurous they are. Many items are made with shrimp and/or pork, but there are vegetarian and non–seafood options as well. In any case, kids will love the energetic atmosphere of this place, where you'll see many Chinese families with kids.

Joe's Shanghai Restaurant

9 Pell Street, between Bowery and Doyers Street
(212) 233-8888
Subway: B,D to Grand Street; 1 to Houston Street; E to Canal Street
www.joeshanghairestaurants.com/chinatownstore_eng.html
Tuesday–Sunday 11am–11pm

Joe's Shanghai is famous for its soup dumplings—and they merit the acclaim—so it's unusual to find the restaurant without a line to get in. If you don't mind waiting, or if you've happened by on one of those rare times when there isn't a wait, try an order or two. Choose between pork (8 for $4.95) or pork and crab (8 for $6.95). Remember, the dumplings are filled with hot broth, so in order to avoid burning your mouth, eat them like this: bite off a tiny bit of the wrapper, allow the broth to drip onto a spoon or suck it out after it cools, and then eat the dumpling. Kids will like the regular dumplings (boiled or fried, without the soup), the beef with broccoli, and the fried rice with a choice of meat or vegetable. The menu has lots of choices (149 items, including two desserts), so there's sure to be something for everyone.

Nom Wah Tea Parlor

13 Doyers Street, near Bowery
(212) 962-6047
Subway: J to Chambers Street or Canal Street; N,Q,6 to Canal Street;
B,D to Grand Street; F to East Broadway
www.nomwah.com
Sunday–Thursday 10:30am–9pm; Friday–Saturday 10:30am–10pm

If you're looking for a dim sum experience that's low on chaos and
mystery and high on ease, Nom Wah is the perfect spot. It claims
to be "Chinatown's First Dim Sum Parlor" (it opened in 1927), and
the exquisitely preserved vintage tile floor, wooden cafe chairs, red
vinyl booths, and tin ceiling provide a more picturesque setting
than found at most other places in Chinatown. Even dim sum

aficionados with favorite dives of their own would agree that for atmosphere, Nom Wah can't be beat.

Unlike most dim sum restaurants in Chinatown, Nom Wah prepares food to order. This means you'll miss out on the entertaining (and chaotic) experience of circulating carts common at other places, but you don't have to wonder how long ago the food was actually cooked. This bodes especially well for fried items meant to be served crisp.

At Nom Wah, you also know exactly what you're ordering: the menu is in English, with photographs, and the servers speak English. Even the sauces on the table are labeled. Favorites include the shrimp and snow pea leaf dumplings ($4.50 for 4 pieces) with fresh and tender whole shrimp enclosed by a super-thin wrapper, the shrimp rice roll, and the stuffed eggplant, but you can hardly go wrong at Nom Wah.

Busiest at lunch on weekends, the wait can be long (up to an hour). Your best bet is to arrive at 10:30am when it opens, or on a weekday if possible. The restaurant will not seat incomplete parties.

Tai Pan Bakery

194 Canal Street, between Walker and Mulberry Streets
(212) 732-2222
Subway: 4,6,J,N,Q,Z to Canal Street; B,D to Grand Street
www.taipanbakeryonline.com
Daily 7:30am–8:30pm

The glass cases in this sometimes crowded and chaotic Chinese bakery hold sweet and savory confections, some familiar, and some not so familiar. Some beautiful fruit tarts would look at home in a

Parisian patisserie, but this is a place to sample curry beef buns, mango mochi, and other items that may provide a new culinary experience for a very reasonable price. Egg custards and the fluffy Cantonese barbecue pork buns are popular favorites. There is some seating, but much of it is taken by elderly residents of the neighborhood who use the bakery as an informal social club. If Tai Pan is packed, try Fay Da around the corner at 83 Mott Street.

Tasty Dumpling

54 Mulberry Street, between Bayard and Worth Streets
(212) 349-0070
Subway: J,N,Q,R,6 to Canal Street; 4,5 to Brooklyn Bridge;
1 to Franklin Street
Daily 9am–8:30pm
Cash only (ATM on premises)

Take a seat at one of the four tables at this no-frills, inexpensive dumpling shop across from Columbus Park (page 104) that serves homemade pork and chive dumplings (5 for $1.25). Douse them with both of the sauces provided: a soy-based one and a fairly tame red hot sauce. Other options, including homemade noodle soups, cost a little bit more ($3–$4.25), but are still inexpensive and all quite good. There's no bathroom.

Tasty Hand-Pulled Noodles

1 Doyers Street, between Pell Street and Bowery
(212) 791-1817
Subway: J to Chambers Street or Canal Street; N,Q,6 to Canal Street;
B,D to Grand Street; F to East Broadway
www.tastyhandpullednoodles.com
Daily 10:30am–10:30pm

Tasty Hand-Pulled Noodles, though as no-frills as it gets when it comes to atmosphere, is no lightweight in the food category. Everything is made from scratch: meat-based and vegetarian broths are made daily, tofu comes from a neighborhood purveyor, and noodles are hand-pulled to order.

Try to snag a table with a view into the kitchen so that your kids can watch the chef as he stretches noodles. He begins with a mound of dough, twists and stretches it, twists it again and again, then bunches it back into a mound. He then cuts it into a couple dozen two-inch segments, each of which will become a single portion of noodles. The process is absolutely mesmerizing.

Among the 22 options on the menu are noodles with vegetable and egg ($4), beef tendon ($5), or roast duck ($5.25). For each dish, choose a type of noodle (hand-pulled, knife-peeled, regular, skinny rice, or sticky) and a preparation (in soup or pan-fried). Standouts are the chicken and shrimp pan-fried noodles ($6). Note: the chicken and duck choices have bones.

Ten Ren's Tea Time

79 Mott Street, between Bayard and Canal Streets
(212) 732-7178
Subway: 4,6, J,N,Q,Z to Canal Street; B,D to Grand Street
www.tenrenusa.com
Sunday–Thursday 11am–9:30pm; Friday–Saturday 11am–10pm

Just a few doors down from the highly regarded Ten Ren tea store (established 1953) is the shop's new outpost, this one serving mainly pearl tapioca tea, known popularly as bubble tea. Think tea-based Asian-flavored smoothies. The drinks ($3 to $6) are divided into six categories on the menu: tapioca traditional iced tea (hibiscus, chrysanthemum, Jasmine Green Milk, Japanese Green Milk, Okinawa Green Milk, and more), tapioca fruit tea (lychee, kumquat lemon, star fruit, plum, and more), tapioca iced milk drink (taro milk, honeydew milk, black sesame milk, buckwheat green milk, and

more)…and on and on. And then there are toppings to choose among… Behind the counter, a young man pours the ingredients into what looks like a cocktail shaker, shakes them up, and pours the foamy result into a plastic cup. If all these choices are too over-whelming, traditional Chinese hot tea and black tea are available, as are small snacks: spring rolls, sticky rice, fried fish cake, udon, and green tea noodles, none more than $5, which can be eaten at the eight tables for two in the back.

SHOP

Aji Ichiban

37 Mott Street, at Pell Street
(212) 233-7650
Subway: 6,J,N,Q,R to Canal Street; 4,5 to Brooklyn Bridge-City Hall;
B,D to Grand Street
www.ajiichiban.com.hk/eng
Daily 10am–8pm

This cheerful outpost of a Hong Kong chain of confectionary stores,
whose name means "the best and superior" in Japanese, has an
enormous selection of mostly Asian candy and savory treats sold in

bulk. In the U.S., the kumquat is a rather uncelebrated fruit, but at Aji Ichiban it's the main ingredient in four confections: licorice, Japanese style, supreme salted, and preserved. If kumquats aren't your thing, choose among dried kiwi and guava, individually wrapped marshmallows (in blackberry, apple, strawberry, and chocolate; $5 per 1/4 pound), "rabbit creamy candy," and dozens of gummy candies. The savory items here include dried grouper, fruit-flavored beef jerky, dried squid, garlic-coated beans, crispy fried tiny crabs (eat them whole, $8.80 per bag)—the list goes on. Aji Ichiban offers free tastes of most items along the perimeter of the store, which include dried fruits, jerkies, seafood items, and plenty more, but not the gummy candies in the center of the shop.

Good Field Trading Company

74 Mott Street, between Bayard and Canal Streets
(212) 431-4263
Subway: 4,6,J,N,Q,Z to Canal Street; B,D to Grand Street
No website
Monday–Sunday 9:15am–7:30pm

For the neighborhood, this crowded shop serves as a newsstand and a stationery store, but pop in. The beautiful and inexpensive Chinese New Year's decorations might be used for any celebration: tissue paper garlands, scrolls, tassels, fans, and many sizes and shapes of paper lanterns. Almost everything in this tiny shop is red (the color associated with good luck) and gold, including an assortment of money envelopes with beautiful calligraphy. There are some inexpensive toys, including yo-yos, finger traps, and Spaldeens, up front, along with paperback workbooks to teach English ABCs, and others to teach how to write Chinese characters.

Kam Man Food

200 Canal Street, at Mulberry Street
(212) 571-0330
Subway: 6,J,M,N,Q,R,W,Z to Canal Street
www.newkamman.com
Daily 9am–8:30pm

Kam Man bills itself as "the destination for all things Asian," and that's not an exaggeration. The three-floor store itself retains the un-Westernized aspects we loved about the former location of Pearl River Mart (see page 185). You'll smell the strong odors of the carryout food stand as you walk in, and right away you'll be drawn in to the main floor with its array of packaged food (for kids, a bag of candy or a beautiful tin of tea would make a cool souvenir). Upstairs is filled with Hello Kitty everything, and some non-Kitty items, including cute erasers for $1 each, origami paper, and minia-ture fortune cat figurines ($7.95). Downstairs, foodie parents will be drawn to the aisles of inexpensive but beautiful Japanese bowls, teapots, plates, bento boxes, and trays. Kids will have fun choosing among the kids-sized chopsticks lacquered in aqua, pink, apple green, with small goldfish or cat motifs ($2.50) and the little porcelain chopstick rests in dozens of shapes (a little turtle, fan, fish; $3.50).

Pearl Paint

308 Canal Street, between Broadway and Mercer Street
(800) 451-7327, (212) 431-7932
Subway: 4,6,A,C,E,N,R to Canal Street
www.pearlpaint.com
Monday–Friday 9am–7pm; Saturday 10am–7pm; Sunday 10am–6pm

If you have an artistic or crafty kid, this landmark art supply store
will provide supplies beyond your wildest imagination. This is where
professional artists and artisans, as well as students at Parsons
School of Design, Pratt Institute, and F.I.T. shop. New Yorkers with a
DIY project know they can find everything they need here—Pearl is
the world's largest discount art supplier. The store's five floors have
aisle after aisle of colored pencils, glitter, clay, kits, specialty papers,
and on and on and on. There's a children's department on the first
floor, but that's not where the treasures are; definitely venture
upstairs.

Yunhong Chopsticks Shop

50 Mott Street, between Canal and Bayard Streets
(212) 566-8828
Subway: 4,6,J,N,Q to Canal Street
www.happychopsticks.com
Daily 10:30am–7:30pm

Walking along a typically crowded and chaotic Chinatown street,
this serene and narrow shop would be easy to overlook. Don't—
venturing inside might be an auspicious move. According to the
shop, in China chopsticks are considered the ideal gift for special
occasions, from weddings to housewarmings, baby showers, birth-

days, anniversaries, and even business events. They make an easily transportable souvenir, especially when paired with a ceramic chopstick rest in the shape of puppies, pandas, little birds on a twig, or butterflies (a steal at $2.99).

The exquisite utensils displayed here in "the first chopsticks boutique ever in the United States" include the practical (stainless steel, travel chopsticks with a case, children's "learner" chopsticks); the elegant (sandalwood chopsticks, silver-inlaid wood, hand-painted); and the lighthearted (a pair that looks like colored pencils). Prices range from less than $10 to more than $200, but there are many choices at every price level, and the packaging is unusually beautiful. Additional location: 235 Canal Street (Chinatown).

PLAY

EAT

SHOP

PLAY

DeSalvio Playground
Mulberry and Spring Streets
Subway: 6 to Spring Street; N,R to Prince Street;
B,D,F,M to Broadway-Lafayette Street; J,Z to Bowery

This old-school park has only the basics, but the authentic Little Italy setting makes up for its lack of opulence.

Lost Wax Studio Jewelry Making Classes
171 Elizabeth Street, between Spring and Kenmare Streets
(646) 485-1117
Subway: J to Bowery; 6 to Spring Street; N,R to Prince Street
www.lostwaxstudio.com
Most workshops are weekday evenings at 6pm or Saturday at noon; check online schedule.

If you have an older child—classes are for 10- to 12-year-olds and older—boy or girl, this could be a very cool activity and real "only in New York" experience. This hip jewelry boutique holds workshops in which a designer teaches how to make a piece of jewelry that doesn't require metalsmith skills. Past objects have been a gem-stone wire wrap nest ring, a double leather wrap bracelet, and a knotted shambala leather cord and bead bracelet. All projects are unisex and designed to be made without many tools, so after the 2-hour session, you'll not only take a piece of jewelry, but a skill, home with you. Fees are $150–$165 per person, depending on the workshop. Advance reservation is requested, but drop-in may be available. E-mail before 4pm on the day of evening workshops, or before 4pm the previous day for morning workshops.

EAT

Caffé Roma
385 Broome Street, between Mulberry and Mott Streets
(212) 226-8413
Subway: 4,6 to Spring Street; J to Bowery; N,R to Canal Street;
B,D to Grand Street
Daily 8am–midnight
Closed every year June 23–July 7

Hollywood couldn't have created a set as pitch-perfect authentic as this café and bakery: tin ceilings, original lighting fixtures, wood paneling, marble-topped tables, vintage tile floors. Since 1891, Caffe

Roma has been operating in the same location, run by the same family. You'll find gelato, cannoli, tiramisu, biscotti, sweet-ricotta sfogliatelle, amaretto Italian cheesecake, pignoli cookies, and all of the traditional Italian desserts, all made on the premises. Roma may or may not be packed with tourists, and the service may be rushed or not, but Roma has a gentler, more timeworn and authentic atmosphere than the nearby, modernized Ferrara.

Ceci Cela Patisserie

55 Spring Street, between Lafayette and Mulberry Streets
(212) 274-9179
Subway: 6 to Spring Street; N,R to Prince Street;
B,D,F,M to Broadway-Lafayette Street; J,Z to Bowery
www.cecicelanyc.com
Monday–Thursday 6:30am–8pm; Friday 6:30am–9pm;
Saturday 7am–9pm; Sunday 7am–8pm

Squeeze your way past the customers at the take-out counter and discover a hidden back dining room with eight tables, waitress service, and a menu of various croissants, pastries, baguette sandwiches, a quiche of the day, and croque monsieur. Ceci Cela's croissants—viewed by many critics as the best in New York—are the premier reason to come here: they're perfectly buttery and flaky, with crunchy ends. If you decide to eat in the little back area, employees are happy to help you stash a folded stroller somewhere. Kids' favorites include pain au chocolat and ham and brie on a baguette. Mini-croissants are also available for mini-appetites.

La Mela Ristorante

167 Mulberry Street, between Grand and Broome Streets
(212) 431-9493
Subway: B,D to Grand Street; 6 to Spring Street; J to Bowery
www.lamelarestaurant.com
Sunday–Thursday 11:30am–2am; Friday, Saturday 11:30am–3am

Le Mela is a family-friendly restaurant with lots of bargains. Top value is at lunch, where the $9.95 lunch special includes an entrée, pasta, green salad, and bread. The chicken parmigiana oozes fresh mozzarella; the rigatoni is perfectly al dente.

La Mela offers several family-style options: three-course ($22 per person), five-course ($35), and two seven-course options ($60, $75) with unlimited beverages, including alcohol. Each family-style option includes several dishes per course and, while La Mela has no kids menu, children 9 and under are allowed to eat free if the table has ordered family-style and the kids do not outnumber the adults. The a la carte menu is also reasonable (pastas $13–$26, chicken dishes $18, veal $21, shrimp $22).

Lombardi's

32 Spring Street at Mott Street
(212) 941-7994
Subway: 6 to Spring Street; N,R to Prince Street;
B,D,F,M to Broadway-Lafayette Street; J,Z to Bowery
www.firstpizza.com
Sunday–Thursday 11:30am–11pm; Friday–Saturday 11:30am–midnight

Lombardi's claims to be America's First Pizzeria; it dates back to the turn of the last century when Gennaro Lombardi, an immigrant baker from Naples, sold scraps of baked dough, topped with tomatoes and cheese, out of his Little Italy grocery shop.

You'll still find excellent pizza: Lombardi's makes its pizza with fresh mozzarella from a *latteria* in the neighborhood, San Marzano tomatoes, and dough baked in an enormous old coal-burning oven. The slight char on the crusts of these thin round pies contributes a hint of smokiness that may come as a surprise to people accustomed to pizza from gas-fueled ovens, but New Yorkers love it. Popular toppings are oven-roasted red peppers, crispy-edged pepperoni, and spinach sautéed with garlic. A plain pie is $17.50 for a 14" small and

$21.50 for an 18". The clam pie is topped with clams steamed in the coal oven, chopped, and baked on a dough with garlic, olive oil, and parsley ($30, small only). The menu also offers a small selection of salads and appetizers. The roomy restaurant itself could not be more child-friendly.

If your family is interested in New York's pizza, and Italian immigrant and food histories, Scott's Pizza Tour (www.scottspizzatours.com) is an exuberant walking-and-eating experience through Little Italy and the Village that stops at Lombardi's and other places.

Parisi Bakery Delicatessen
198 Mott Street, between Kenmare and Spring Streets
(212) 460-8750
Subway: 6 to Spring Street; N,R to Prince Street;
B,D,F,M to Broadway-Lafayette Street; J,Z to Bowery
www.parisibakery.com
Monday–Saturday 7am–5pm; closed Sunday

Parisi Bakery's sandwich shop pumps out classic New York hero and roll sandwiches that make for a perfect city picnic at nearby DeSalvio Playground. The stars of the kitchen are the hot sandwiches, which are made to order. Ample fresh mozzarella on delicious fresh heros make for extraordinary parm sandwiches (chicken, meatball, and eggplant, $8). Any time during the day, try one of the top-notch breakfast heros—potato and eggs, peppers and eggs, or cheese and eggs ($5.50). Toppings for the cold deli meat sandwiches include fresh and smoked mozzarella, sundried tomatoes, and basil spread.

Prince Street Pizza
27 Prince Street, between Mott and Elizabeth Streets
(212) 966-4100
Subway: N,R to Prince Street; B,D,F,M to Broadway-Lafayette Street;
6 to Spring Street; J to Bowery
www.princestpizza.com
Sunday–Wednesday 11:30am–midnight;
Thursday–Saturday 11:30am–2am

Established at this location in 1959, this pizzeria was originally
called Ray's, but is now under new ownership with a new name.
This is a great place to grab an inexpensive slice, or, better yet, a
"square" ($3–4), cut from a rectangular pie that, despite its thick-
ness, is surprisingly light. For a change of pace, be sure to try the
rice and prosciutto balls; they're salty, creamy, and delicious ($1.25).

Rubirosa

235 Mulberry Street, between Prince and Spring Streets
(212) 965-0500
Subway: 6 to Spring Street; N,R to Prince Street;
B,D,F,M to Broadway-Lafayette Street; J,Z to Bowery
www.rubirosanyc.com
Sunday–Wednesday 11:30am–4pm and 5pm–11pm;
Thursday–Saturday 11:30am–4pm and 5pm–midnight
(Every day between 4pm and 5pm pizza, but not the rest of the
menu, is available.)

You may not make it to Staten Island during your visit to New York, but that doesn't mean you can't experience a unique and good pie from one of Staten Island's most heralded pizzerias, Joe and Pat's. Rubirosa's pizza is made from the same recipe. Kids love this pizza because it's thin, naturally sweet, and easy to eat. And while Rubirosa is not a huge restaurant, there usually isn't a wait for a table. If the kids get fidgety, take them one at a time to the back, where pizzas are being made in an unusual rotating gas-fueled pizza oven.

Order a regular pie (the Classic, $16, $24) or the Fresca, with fresh mozzarella. The vodka pie, with its creamy tomato sauce and hint of vodka that cooks away, is also a fun choice; it's the pizza version of penne alla vodka. Other standouts are the fried calamari appetizer ($12) and the lasagna "for two" (big enough for more than two, $26).

SHOP

Cat Fish Greetings

219 Mulberry Street, between Prince and Spring Streets
(212) 625-1800
Subway: 6 to Spring Street; N,R to Prince Street;
B,D,F,M to Broadway-Lafayette Street; J,Z to Bowery
www.catfishgreetings.com
Monday–Saturday 11am–7pm; Sunday noon–6pm

This small shop sells simple and unique greeting cards and gifts for newborns. The owner, who has a background in design, believes that "it doesn't have to say 'I ♥ New York' to say 'I love New York.'" She's right: without "saying it," the items here are distinctly New York in feel. Specialties include onesies and bibs with matching "new baby" greeting cards. A bib that says, "Lunch is on me" is the store's top-selling item. Sizes run from 3 months to 3T; all of the clothes are 100% organic cotton and are made in Brooklyn.

Makerbot Store

298 Mulberry Street, between East Houston and Bleecker Streets
(347) 457-5758
Subway: 6 to Spring Street; B,D,F,M to Broadway-Lafayette Street;
N,R to Prince Street
www.makerbot.com
Monday–Saturday noon–7pm; Sunday noon–6pm

This store specializes in 3D printers with prices that start at $2,200 . . . but you don't have to be in the market for one of these hi-tech marvels in order to enjoy the store. Not only can you watch the floor models "print out" solid objects, but some low-cost souvenirs are available. One is a unique portrait molded in plastic: MakerBot's 3D Photo Booth snaps four photos from different angles that together make a three-dimensional computer rendering of the subject's head ($5). The files, which Makerbot will share via e-mail, are included in the price. If you'd like a "print" to keep, Makerbot will produce one for you. They're available in five colors and three sizes: two, three, and four inches tall ($20, $40, $60). Printing takes about two weeks. Pick up at the store is free; shipping is $5 additional.

The store's supersized "gumball" machine contains a number of knickknack items. Drop a special gold token into the machine to receive a 3D-printed "prize" ($5), which might be a 2-inch apple, cupcake, alien, or Elvis head (with windup walking legs to attach), a rocket ship, or a robot.

MakerBot also offers Saturday morning classes for children ($10 a session that lasts a little under an hour) during which the staff teaches kids to make a design using a drag-and-drop computer application. The design is then "sliced" (converted into printable layers), and while your child watches, it materializes—one layer at a time—in a 3D printer. Online sign-up at the MakerBot website is required for classes.

Piccolini
230 Mulberry Street, between Prince and Spring Streets
(212) 775-1118
Subway: 6 to Spring Street; N,R to Prince Street;
B,D,F,M to Broadway-Lafayette Street
www.lovepiccolini.com
Monday–Saturday noon–7pm; Sunday noon–5pm

It's a small but meaningful detail: the palette at Piccolini is based on
the seven-layer cookies served at the Little Italy bakery once owned

by the grandfather of the shop's young proprietress. Long gone, the bakery's sweet spirit lives on in this hip and happy boutique with lots of pink, green, and yellow. The "only in New York" gifts are exceptional. This is where to find a witty NYC hot dog and pretzel onesie; a city blocks stacking game; a knitted Metrocard, baseball, or taxi rattle; a New York Rangers sock monkey; a mustache pacifier. You'll also find books, backpacks, jewelry, and more. The inventory is girly and *très* cool.

PLAY

EAT

SHOP

Lower East Side

PLAY

First Park

East Houston Street, at 1st Street and First Avenue
Subway: F to 2nd Avenue; J,M to Essex Street; J to Bowery;
6 to Bleecker Street; B,D to Grand Street

Swings, jungle gym, and a kiosk-and-tables outpost of Mud Coffee
make this tiny strip of a park a worthwhile diversion if the kids (or
the parents) are in need of a reboot or an easy outdoor snack. Since
it's located within a stone's throw of Katz's Delicatessen (page 148),
it may well save the day if the crowds of that popular destination are
too much for the young ones. Mud Coffee's offerings include juices,
fruits, muffins, and bagels.

Lower East Side Tenement Museum

103 Orchard Street, between Delancey and Broome Streets
(212) 982-8420
Subway: B,D to Grand Street; F to Delancey Street;
J,M to Essex Street
www.tenement.org
Friday–Wednesday 10am–6pm; Thursday 10am–8:30pm
Tours: Adults $22; students $17; themed tours also offered,
check website

Storefronts on Manhattan's Lower East Side have changed through
the years, but above street level it still looks much like it did in 1900.
Narrow five- or six-story brick tenements decorated with ornate cor-
nices and curlicue iron fire escapes fill block after block. Their tiny

apartments were home to generations of immigrants; 23 million people arrived between 1896 and 1924. It's possible that your ancestors once lived in this neighborhood.

The building that houses the Tenement Museum was home to about 7,000 people in total between 1863 and 1935. It lay empty until 1988, when it was purchased by the co-founders, who wanted to build a museum to honor America's immigrants. The museum has recreated seven atmospheric apartments to tell the stories of families who once lived there, including an 1870s German dressmaker, an Irish couple who were Famine survivors, and an Italian family who scraped their way through the Great Depression. A complete list of tours and other programs is on the website and includes minimum age recommendations. The Meet Victoria Confino tour is suitable for children 5 and up, the Hard Times and Sweatshop Workers tours for those 8 and older, and the remainder for ages 12 and older.

To see the museum it's necessary to take a guided tour, and wise to reserve online well in advance. Tours are limited to 15 people. Pick up your tickets at the Visitors Center and watch the orientation video while waiting for the tour to start.

97 Orchard Street, the museum itself, is a pristine example of a mid-nineteenth-century tenement. The twenty-first century vanishes the instant the front door closes behind you. Rows of old mailboxes on the left sit on a wall ragged with names scratched into the plaster. Kids will enjoy the dark and spooky front hall, climbing the creaky stairs, and peering into the two old-fashioned toilet stalls that were shared by everyone who lived on that floor. Each tour covers a single floor. The first stop is a "ruin" apartment, preserved just as it was left in 1935, that shows how a place looks after being abandoned for

80 years—crumbling paint, torn wallpaper, and layers of worn linoleum.

Next come the apartments; each floor has one or two that have been fully restored to the appropriate date. They are shockingly small with only a cast iron stove for heat and crammed with clothes, pots and pans, and piles of bedding. Here kids will see what city life once was without electricity, running water, bathrooms, or even a bed to sleep in. The educator will tell about the families, show pictures of them or their descendants, and explain what people went through when they first came to America, the difficulties they faced, and how they worked so their children could have good lives and become citizens. For many, seeing tenement life is a memorable experience and even brings tears.

Geared especially to kids, the Meet the Residents tour introduces Victoria Confino, a 14-year-old girl played by a costumed interpreter, who welcomes you into her family's home. The Confinos were Sephardic Jews from what is now northern Greece who came to America in 1913 at the start of the First Balkan War. Kids pretend to be immigrants who have just arrived in America and aren't sure what to do. "Victoria" answers their questions and shows them how household chores were done, and what life was like in 1916.

Another highlight for children is a peek into the rear yard on Allen Street, with its four privies and a spigot that was the only water source in the nineteenth century for the entire building. Kids can imagine having to climb up and down three or four flight of stairs to haul water and use the privies. An explanation of the rear yard is included in the Irish Outsiders tour.

The Visitors Center includes an extensive museum shop with a large assortment of books for children and young adults, games and puzzles, inexpensive toys, and souvenirs.

There is no café onsite but the area is thick with restaurants; a list of recommended spots is available at the museum's ticket counter. The museum does offer food tours of the Lower East Side, which children may enjoy, with tastings of many different local treats. See www.tenement.org/tours.php for information.

Streit's Matzo Factory Tour

148–154 Rivington Street, at Suffolk Street
(212) 475-7000
Subway: F to Delancey Street; J,M to Essex Street;
B,D to Grand Street
www.streitsmatzos.com
Tours: Monday–Thursday 9am–3pm; must be scheduled in advance;
Free
Store: Monday–Thursday 8:30am–4:30pm (to purchase matzo goods)

In the late nineteenth through the mid-twentieth century, the Lower East Side teemed with Jewish immigrants and businesses that catered to their needs: synagogues, bakers, "appetizing" stores, knish shops, and Judaica stores. Over time, as most of the Jewish population moved away, many of those businesses closed. Of the few shops remaining, the most significant is Streit's Matzo, the only family-owned matzo factory left in the United States.

The free factory tour lasts about fifteen minutes and includes an abridged history of Streit's, facts about matzo making, and a bit of the history of the Lower East Side. The factory's two 72-foot long conveyer ovens crank out nearly four million boxes worth of matzo annually. The visual experience of this old factory, doing things the way they've always been done, will captivate both children and adults. Baskets carrying matzo emerge from a long oven, float by on gearing tracks, are inspected, and then ascend through an opening in the ceiling to another floor where they will be boxed and sealed for distribution. There's a Streit's store on the corner and, of course, you sample the matzo during the tour.

EAT

Doughnut Plant

379 Grand Street, between Essex and Norfolk Streets

(212) 505-3700

Subway: F to Delancey Street; J,M to Essex Street; B,D to Grand Street

doughnutplant.com

Daily 6:30am–8pm

Offerings at this organic-when-possible doughnut destination change daily. Favorites include the peanut butter and banana cream doughnut (the peanut butter and jams are made in-house), as well

as fresh blueberry, carrot cake, coconut lime, or pistachio versions. The Blackout is a chocolate cake doughnut filled with chocolate pudding, dipped in chocolate glaze, and sprinkled with chocolate cake crumbs. During the summer, the Plant makes ice cream, too. Try a scoop on its own, on a doughnut, or in the Italian manner, *affogato*: with a shot of espresso.

Additional location: Hotel Chelsea, 220 W. 23rd Street, Seventh and Eighth Avenues

Essex Street Market

120 Essex Street, between Delancey and Rivington Streets
Subway: F to Delancey Street; J,M to Essex Street;
B,D to Grand Street
www.essexstreetmarket.com
Different merchants have different hours; see website for details.

The Essex Street Market is a hybrid of past and present, built in 1940 as part of Mayor Fiorello La Guardia's initiative to clear the pushcarts from the Lower East Side's crowded streets to make room for cars. It served for decades as a no-frills food market for immigrant residents of the Lower East Side. Today, alongside old-style meat, fruit, and fish stores, and grocers specializing in Latin food, you will find shops such as Saxelby Cheesemongers, which features American-made artisanal cheeses, and on any given day, a selection of three to five grilled cheese sandwiches ($7–$9).

Seating in the market is limited, but there are some communal tables and chairs at the north end of the market. Some places with seating include Brooklyn Taco Company (a few stools), and the Tra La La Juice Bar, owned by the adjacent Rainbo's Fish, which serves excellent inexpensive grilled fish sandwiches ($5).

Katz's Delicatessen

205 East Houston Street, at Ludlow Street
(212) 254-2246 or (800) 4HOT-DOG
Subway: F to 2nd Avenue; J,M to Essex Street; J to Bowery;
6 to Bleecker Street; B,D to Grand Street
katzsdelicatessen.com
Monday–Wednesday 8am–10:45pm; Thursday 8am–2:45am;
Friday 8am–Sunday 10:45pm (24 hours Saturday)

Today, only a small handful of New York's original delicatessens

remain. Katz's, which happens to be the oldest of them—it opened in 1888—serves a pastrami sandwich that many consider the best in town. Because of its vintage ambiance and the food, Katz's has become *the* place for a true New York deli experience and is usually packed. Do not be deterred by the crowds: when navigated with strategy and calm, Katz's can be an absolute delight, and the most "New York" of experiences.

Upon entering you will be handed a small ticket printed with a grid of numbers. Years ago, those numbers represented prices (without decimals) and employees punched holes into the prices when a food item was chosen. For instance, a sandwich costing $1.60 would have been punched at "160" and "13," the tax, in cents. Today, an employee writes prices onto the backside of the ticket and keeps a running total. You'll need the tickets in order to pay as you leave, so don't lose them.

There are two options for ordering: waiter service or self-service, which involves visiting separate counters for different foods. Waiter service is offered at the tables along the left wall running toward the back of the restaurant. Waiter service is much easier but because it is offered only at a small portion of tables it often means a longer wait than self-service. Ask if a service table is available, or how long the wait is.

Self-service can be expedient, though, even with family in tow. It's all about strategy. First, know where everything is. Beginning at the far right, nearest to the entrance, are hot dogs, soups, knishes, beer, and, during breakfast, eggs. The area to the left, the most crowded, is where corned beef, pastrami, brisket, and roast turkey sandwiches are made ($15.95–$17.95). Many people bunch up into a single line to the far right, but each sandwich maker has his own line, so save yourself time and make your way past the group to the line with the fewest people. French fries and sodas are to the left of the sandwiches. Water and glasses are at a fountain station along the back wall of the restaurant.

If you've opted for self-service, the plan should be: figure out what everyone wants, and then one parent can grab the easy no-wait items (such as hot dogs, fries, and drinks) and go with the kids to find a table while the other orders the sandwiches and brings them to the table.

Kossar's Bialys
367 Grand Street, at Essex Street
(212) 253-2138; counter (212) 473-4810
Subway: B,D to Grand Street; F to Delancey Street;
J,M to Essex Street
www.kossarsbialys.com
Monday–Friday 6am–7pm; Saturday 6am–midnight;
Sunday 6am–7pm

The bialy, a traditional Jewish baked item, is a close cousin to the bagel—but instead of a hole in the center, there's a small depression in which a bit of fresh onion has been baked. Bagels are ubiquitous and bialys aren't, and you may wonder why when you walk into this bakery and are greeted by the irresistible aroma of these freshly

baked delicacies. In addition to bialys, Kossar's also makes bulkas (rolls), onion disks, pletzels (onion-and seed-covered crackers), sesame sticks, and—only since 1998—bagels.

Note: Kossar's has no seating. New Yorkers go there to pick up bialys and bagels to take home. You can eat one plain, as you walk, or pick up some cream cheese, grab a plastic knife, and picnic in Seward Park one block south on Essex Street.

The following table appears within the image:

	½ PINTS	PINTS	QUARTS	½ GALLONS	GALLONS			½ PINTS	PINTS
GREEK OLIVES	$3.00	$5.50	$10.50	$20.00		PEPPERONCINI		$3.00	$5.00
KALAMATA OLIVES	$3.75	$7.50	$13.50	$26.00		CELERY		$3.00	$5.00
WHOLE GREEN OLIVES	$3.00	$5.50	$10.00			KRAUT (SWEET OR SOUR)		$2.25	$3.75
PIMENTO OLIVES	$3.50	$6.00	$11.00			RELISH		$2.50	$3.50
JALAPENO OLIVES	$4.00	$7.50	$14.00			MUSTARD		N/A	$2.75
GARLIC OLIVES	$4.00	$7.50	$14.50			HORSERADISH		$3.00	
SPECIALTY OLIVES	$4.50	$8.00	$15.00						
MUSHROOMS	$4.00	$7.50	$14.50					HERRING $5.00	PICKLED
GIARDINIERA	$3.00	$5.00	$9.00						
SWEET GHERKINS	$2.75	$4.50							

Pickle Guys

49 Essex Street, between Grand and Hester Streets
(212) 656-9739
Subway: F to Delancey Street; J,M to Essex Street;
B,D to Grand Street
www.pickleguys.com
Sunday–Thursday 9am–6pm; Friday 9am–4pm; closed Saturday

This shop, although in business for only a few years, carries on the tradition of the many pickle shops that once catered to the immigrant populations on the Lower East Side. Owner Alan Kaufman makes many varieties in this garage-like store, scooping them out from forty-gallon barrels and filling up plastic containers of various sizes. Unlike pickles made by most commercial manufacturers, these are made without preservatives. At Pickle Guys, it's just water, salt, and spices. Options include "new pickles" (crunchy, not very sour), "sour pickles" (the biggest seller, not very crunchy), "half-sours" (crunchy and sour), and other variations. Other options include pickled tomatoes, tomatillos, peppers, olives, and okra. Pickles are 75 cents each, three for $2, $6.25 a quart, or $11.50 a half-gallon.

Schiller's Liquor Bar

131 Rivington Street, at Norfolk Street
(212) 260-4555
Subway: F to Delancey Street; J,M to Essex Street;
B,D to Grand Street
www.schillersny.com
Monday–Thursday 11am–1am; Friday 11am–3am;
Saturday 10am–3am; Sunday 10am–midnight

With its elegant oyster bar, black and white tiled floor, slow-turning ceiling fans, friendly staff, and the great kids' specials, the trendy yet laid-back Schiller's is the ideal place for a special meal if you're taking kids along. In addition to oysters, Schiller's has a great steak-frites ($25), French onion soup ($11), and moules frites ($19.50)—classic French bistro fare. You'll also find burgers (beef, tuna, or veggie, $13–$17), pork tacos, and, as a starter, Rhode Island-style fried oysters with tartar sauce. The children's menu includes a beverage, main course, and dessert for $12.50 (grilled cheese, macaroni and cheese, burger, grilled chicken breast with fries, and fish

and chips). Monday through Friday from 5pm to 7pm, one child eats for free for every adult entrée ordered.

Souvlaki GR

116 Stanton Street, between Essex and Ludlow Streets
(212) 777-0116
Subway: F to Delancey Street; J,M to Essex Street; B,D to Grand Street
www.souvlakigr.com
Sunday–Thursday 11am–11:30pm; Friday–Saturday 11am–midnight

The brief menu recalls that of a Greek diner, but the quality of the food here is reliably excellent and everything is made fresh. The SGR pita souvlaki with spicy feta sauce comes with fries (on the inside) and a choice of chicken, pork, or seasoned beef ($5.50–$7). The feta appetizer, baked with tomatoes, peppers, chopped scallions, and olive oil, is great for sharing. Children can try a skewer or two, and tzatziki, a yogurt dip made with cucumbers. Souvlaki GR's warm, light, crispy pita triangles are superior to the soft ones served at most other low-priced Greek restaurants. If you are four or fewer, grab a table on the "terrace," which is decorated like an outdoor balcony, with whitewashed walls and blue shutters and doors. Some of the restaurant's tables even have umbrellas, all in order to recall the look of a quaint village on a Greek island.

Vanessa's Dumpling House

118A Eldridge Street, between Broome and Grand Streets
(212) 625-8008
Subway: B,D to Grand Street; J to Bowery; F to Delancey Street;
M to Essex Street
www.vanessadumplings.com
Daily 7:30am–10:30pm

Delicious pork and chive dumplings cost four for $1 at this busy shop, and when it comes to captivating the kids, it's not just the dumplings that appeal. The highlight may be the view through the window in the back of the restaurant where children can watch the kitchen staff make dumplings from scratch throughout the day. Adults, too, are mesmerized by the speed and skill of these ladies. The chive and pork fried dumplings are a must.

At the front of the restaurant you can also watch employees make the bread used for the extraordinary sesame pancake sandwiches.

It's fried in a wok, then sliced in half horizontally and cut into wedges before being made into sandwiches with a variety of fillings. Vegetarians will appreciate #17 (cilantro, carrot, and cucumber) and #18 (an egg sandwich), both $1.75. If you eat meat, be sure to try the one made with Peking duck, scallion, and hoisin sauce ($2.50); it's a poor-man's version of a normally expensive restaurant dish.

Whole Foods

95 East Houston Street, between Bowery and Chrystie Street
(212) 420-1320
Subway: F to 2nd Avenue; B,D,M to Broadway-Lafayette Street;
6 to Bleecker Street; J to Bowery; N,R to Prince Street
www.wholefoodsmarket.com/stores/bowery
Daily 8am–11pm

Like every Whole Foods in NYC, this one offers plentiful seating and devotes substantial space to prepared foods—local families find that convenient, and you may, too. This location stands out, though, because of a partnership with Smorgasburg in Brooklyn, so in addition to the standard offerings, you'll find some very trendy "only in New York" options. Vendors change periodically, but you're sure to find some surprising, high-quality choices.

The regular offerings at Whole Foods, also found at other locations in the city, may include a Caribbean hot bar; a nachos bar; soups; salad bars; a selection of sushi; a burger bar; and pizza, panini, and rotisserie stations.

Other locations: 270 Greenwich Street (Tribeca), 4 Union Square South, 250 Seventh Avenue (Chelsea), 226 East 57th Street (Midtown/Upper East Side), 10 Columbus Circle (Midtown), 808 Columbus Avenue (Upper West Side)

SHOP

Economy Candy

108 Rivington Street, between Ludlow and Essex Streets

(212) 254-1531

Subway: F to Delancey Street; J,M to Essex Street;
B,D to Grand Street

www.economycandy.com

Monday 10am–6pm; Tuesday–Friday 9am–6pm;
Saturday 10am–5pm; Sunday 9am–6pm

Now in its third generation of single-family ownership, this shop, opened in 1937, is an overflowing cornucopia of candy. Fancy European chocolates and British imports share shelf space with old school American confections like candy necklaces, little cloth sacks of Gold Mine Nugget bubblegum, and Nik-L-Nips wax bottles filled with colorful syrup. There are penny candies as well as nonpareils, chocolate-covered orange peel, and chocolate-cashew patties hand-made in Brooklyn. When asked whether young children go too wack-adoodle here, the manager said, "No, the biggest problem is that they can't make a choice."

PLAY

EAT

SHOP

PLAY

Vesuvio Playground

Thompson Street, between Prince and Spring Streets
Subway: C,E to Spring Street

This much-loved playground, named for the nearby Italian bakery, now called Birdbath (page 172), has climbing equipment and swings for tots to school-aged children and is situated on one of the most picturesque streets in Soho. One parent can take a turn watching the kids while the other dips into the chic nearby shops or picks up a gourmet picnic lunch at Alidoro (page 170) or Once Upon a Tart (page 177). There are bathrooms and, in the summer, a mini-pool and sprinklers.

Children's Museum of the Arts

103 Charlton Street, between Hudson and Greenwich Streets
(212) 274-0986
Subway: 1 to Houston Street; C,E to Spring Street
www.cmany.org
Monday noon–5pm; Wednesday noon–5pm; Thursday, Friday noon–6pm; Saturday, Sunday 10am–5pm (closed Tuesday)

This attractive art-making mecca for children offers scheduled classes for neighborhood children and drop-in workshops for ages 1–15. Workshops are either coached by a teaching artist or self-guided (for instance, a self-portrait station at which kids face a mirror while drawing themselves without looking at the paper). Kids will like the array of choices that includes weaving, painting, Claymation, and drawing. Parents will appreciate the proactive involvement of

the teachers, the supplies and set-up, and the fact that they don't have to clean up the mess. During summer months CMA sets up a free art-making outpost in Nolan Park (Buildings 11 & 13) on Governors Island (page 482), Saturday and Sunday, 11am–3pm.

Film Forum Jr.

209 West Houston Street, between Sixth and Seventh Avenues
(212) 727-8110
Subway: 1 to Houston Street; A,C,E,B,D,F,M to West 4th Street
www.filmforum.org
Sunday 11am
$7

Wish your child could see the original *Miracle on 34th Street* on a big screen? Film Forum's weekly matinee series for kids screens classic

1921 Chaplin Dress-Alike contest
held in Bellingham, Washington

movies and gets the younger generation up to speed, cinematically. Films, most appropriate for 5 years and up, run the gamut from *David Copperfield* to the Marx Brothers, and are a bargain to boot: all tickets, for kids and adults, are $7. The participatory elements of the screenings are fun, too: a screaming contest at *Bride of Frankenstein*, a Charlie Chaplin look-alike contest, and more. Advance tickets are sold online and at the box office.

New York City Fire Museum

278 Spring Street, between Varick and Hudson Streets
(212) 691-1303
Subway: 1 to Houston Street; C,E to Spring Street
www.nycfiremuseum.org
Daily 10am–5pm (Closed New Year's Day, Easter Sunday, July 4th, Thanksgiving, and Christmas Day)
Adults $8; under 12 $5; under 2 free

The fire museum at first glance will appeal more to adults than children. The first floor is devoted to twentieth-century firefighting apparatus—several engines (no climbing allowed), vintage photos and maps, tools, helmets—things that only a child who is a real devotee will find interesting, but a continuously running video, "Brotherhood," might entertain a child while parents tour the exhibits that detail the history of the New York City water supply, the history of the fire hose, etc. There are several firefighters' jackets, in adult and child sizes, available to try on for a photo op. At the rear, a two-room 9/11 memorial honors the 343 of New York's Bravest, many of them from the neighborhood, who were killed during the terrorist attacks. Upstairs, equipment and artifacts from the *Gangs of New York* era are displayed.

A free *Official FDNY Fire Safety Activity Coloring Book* is given to children as part of admission, but if you want another souvenir (or two), the gift shop has an array of firefighter-related paraphernalia: the bestsellers, a junior firefighter jacket, bib overalls, and cap ($60); bright red boots with flames ($29); a *Fireman's Safety Hints* board book ($9); and walkie-talkies ($16).

Trapeze School New York

Hudson River Park, Pier 40
West Street, at West Houston Street and the West Side Highway
(212) 242-8769
Subway: 1 to Houston
newyork.trapezeschool.com
Class times vary, but include morning, afternoon, and evening hours, daily, weather permitting.
2-hour flying trapeze group class $50 (weekday mornings); $60 (weekday afternoons or evenings); $70 (weekends); with a one-time registration fee of $22 per group (not per individual)

New York is famous for its iconic skyscrapers, and they certainly can afford you memorable views, but there is an even more thrilling way to take in a bird's-eye view of the city: the New York Trapeze School gives you a stunning, high-flying perspective on things. And, yes, they will teach your child how to fly.

The First Time Flyers class will have your child (and you, if you choose) swinging from a 23' platform while strapped into suspension lines and with a full net below, and—if ready—executing a "catch." A helpful Welcome to First Time Flyers letter on TSNY's

website outlines exactly what happens in the class. The minimum age for classes is 6, but most young students who take a class are in their early teens or 'tweens. Drop by and watch a class; weekday classes typically don't fill to capacity so quickly that you couldn't watch a class one day and be registered for one the next. Classes accommodate 10 people, of mixed ages. Private classes are also available.

EAT

Alidoro

105 Sullivan Street, between Prince and Spring Streets

(212) 334-5179

Subway: C,E to Spring Street; 1 to Houston Street; N,R to Prince Street; B,D,F,M to Broadway-Lafayette Street; 6 to Spring Street

www.alidoronyc.com

Monday–Saturday 11:30am–4pm; closed Sunday

Alidoro does have some rules, and it's worth your while to follow them. Arrive at the front of the line without knowing what you want, or ask for mayo on your sandwich, and the owner's wife may reprimand you. No worries, the rules are simple: know what you want and don't ask for things Alidoro doesn't have. The reward is an excellent Italian sandwich. The owner handpicks each ingredient with great care. Each morning on his way to the shop from deep in Brooklyn, he makes four separate stops for bread, and another for fresh mozzarella.

The menu lists 40 different sandwiches, each one perfectly conceived. The Pinocchio, for example, has prosciutto, sweet soppressata, fresh mozzarella, roasted peppers, and olive paste ($12.25; prices range from $8.75–$13). There are no child-size sandwiches on the menu, so sharing makes sense.

If there are two adults in your group, we suggest one order the sandwiches (the line moves quickly) while the other takes the kids to Vesuvio Playground next door. If Alidoro's three tables are occupied, the playground has tables and park benches.

Birdbath Bakery

160 Prince Street, between Thompson Street and West Broadway
(646) 556-7720
Subway: C,E to Spring Street; N,R to Prince Street; 1 to Houston
Street; B,D,F,M to Broadway-Lafayette Street; 6 to Spring Street
www.thecitybakery.com/birdbath
Monday–Friday 8am–7pm; Saturday 9am–7pm; Sunday 10am–7pm

When City Bakery took over this spot, it preserved the vintage lettering and the awning of its predecessor, the venerable Vesuvio Bakery.
What's new is the eco-aesthetic of the place: organic and/or local
ingredients, recycled building materials, and baked goods delivered
via bicycle rickshaw from the company's flagship location, City

Bakery. On any given day you might find a delicious assortment of cookies, including chocolate chip (regular as well as a gluten-free version), oatmeal raisin, and a cocoa nib and a coconut cookie, each of which are vegan, as well as a few savory items such as sandwiches.

Additional locations: 35 Third Avenue (East Village); 200 Church Street (Tribeca); 518 Columbus Avenue (Upper West Side); 18 West 18th Street (Union Square to Madison Square), in Books of Wonder, page 265); 189 East 79th Street (Upper East Side)

Dig Inn

350 Hudson Street between King and Charlton Streets
(917) 720-1205
Subway: 1 to Houston Street
www.diginn.com
Monday–Thursday 8am–9pm; Friday 10:30am–9pm; Saturday, Sunday 11am–9pm

Dig Inn promises delicious, nutritious food, quickly—and it delivers. Working with local farmers means the produce is fresh and it's showcased in a variety of seasonal side dishes. There are soups, sandwiches, and salads—many, but not all, vegetarian—and proteins that include wild salmon, braised beef, lemon chicken, spicy meatballs, and more. Healthy shakes, including pomegranate pear and peanut butter, as well as cold pressed juices and desserts, round out the menu. Make your choice at the counter, then carry it to a table. The rustic farmhouse decor contributes to the laid-back and comfy vibe.

Additional locations: 150 East 52nd Street (Upper East Side); 40 West 55th Street (Midtown); 275 Madison Avenue (Midtown);

17 East 17th Street (Union Square to Madison Square); 80 Pine Street (South Street Seaport and Lower Manhattan)

Famous Ben's Pizza of Soho
177 Spring Street, at Thompson Street
(212) 966-4494
Subway: C,E to Spring Street; N,R to Prince Street; B,D,F,M to Broadway-Lafayette Street; 1 to Houston Street; 6 to Spring Street; A to Canal Street
www.famousbenspizzaofsoho.com
Monday–Thursday 11am–11:30pm; Friday–Saturday 11am–12:30am; Sunday noon–10:30pm

This classic slice joint in the heart of Soho is always busy. If you're in the neighborhood and looking for cheap eats or a good New York slice, Ben's will do you right. Try the Sicilian or the Palermo. Each is a thick-crusted rectangular slab of pan-cooked pizza, and in both cases, thick does not mean heavy. The Palermo, technically *sfincione*, not pizza, has a spongier crust and is traditionally made with tomato, caramelized onion, anchovy, and breadcrumbs (here, without anchovy); it's a rare find in Manhattan.

Hampton Chutney
68 Prince Street, between Lafayette and Crosby Streets
(212) 226-9996
Subway: 6 to Spring Street; N,R to Prince Street; B,D,F,M to Broadway-Lafayette Street
www.hamptonchutney.com
Daily 11am–9pm

Hampton Chutney puts its own spin on the traditional Indian dosa (a crispy rice crepe rolled and filled with potatoes, onions, and spices) and uttapam (a softer version of the same) that are perfect for lunch and for kids. Try the #7 (roasted butternut squash, portobello mushroom, arugula, and jack cheese, $10.95) and the #10 (potato masala with grilled chicken and spinach, $12.45). Kids like the cheese with avocado, eggs, turkey, or chicken ($5.45–$8.95). The kids' dosas are the same size as the regular ones but with less filling. Stools provide most of the seating, but there are a few chairs and a bench with a couple of little tables—enough space for four or five.

Additional location: 464 Amsterdam Avenue (Upper West Side)

Kelly and Ping

127 Greene Street, between West Houston and Spring Streets
(212) 228-1212
Subway: B,D,F,M to Broadway-Lafayette Street; N,R to Prince Street; 6 to Bleecker Street; C,E to Spring Street
www.kelleyandping.com
Daily 11:30am–5pm and 5:30pm–11pm

At this roomy under-the-radar pan-Asian restaurant, parents don't have to worry about kids being kids. It's a true locals place, busy with families, chic gallerists, and fashion models alike. During lunch there are no servers—order at the counter and carry your own meal to your table—and the restaurant provides crayons and drawing paper. The inexpensive menu has plenty of variety and flavor for grown-ups who like a bit of adventure, including three different curries ($9.50–$11), Korean Jap Chae (yam noodles with beef, $11), and

a good selection of rolls and dumplings. The children's menu includes tamer choices like Bowl of Sunshine (chicken noodle soup, $3.75) and Chicken Lollies (chicken skewers with peanut sauce, carrot slices, and sticky rice, $5). At 5:30pm, the restaurant switches to waiter service and a different menu (with similar items, entrées $12–$18), but children are still welcome—in fact, the kids' meals offered during lunch are free between 5:30pm and 7pm, one per adult entrée ordered.

Once Upon a Tart

135 Sullivan Street, between West Houston and Prince Streets
(212) 387-8869
Subway: C,E to Spring Street
www.onceuponatart.com
Monday–Friday 8am–7pm; Saturday 9am–7pm; Sunday 9am–6pm

This quaint little bakeshop and café serves mouthwatering home-made scones, muffins, sandwiches, salads, soups, and sweet and savory tarts. Eat at one of the handful of café tables inside, on the tiny terrace overlooking the picturesque street, or around the corner in Thompson Park. The pear ginger muffins are peerless; mac and cheese, chicken potpie, and tender vegetable quiches rise to the same standard. Pair them with a café au lait or strawberry lemonade. Sandwiches are served on crusty baguettes (grilled chicken with roasted red pepper, Swiss cheese, parsley mint pesto, and organic baby greens; roasted loin of pork with rosemary aioli and frisee; both $8.75). Don't miss the whimsical and witty window displays, and if you want a souvenir that says New York, but doesn't scream it, consider the tote bag imprinted with the shop's understated and beautiful tart-pan logo.

S'Nice

150 Sullivan Street, between West Houston and Prince Streets
(212) 253-5405
Subway: C,E to Spring Street; 1 to Houston Street;
N,R to Prince Street; B,D,F,M to Broadway-Lafayette Street
www.snicecafe.com
Monday–Saturday 7:30am–10pm; Sunday 7:30am–9pm

S'Nice rewards health-conscious diners with plenty of flavorful options. Everything S'Nice serves is vegetarian, and many, but not all, of its offerings are vegan. The tempeh Reuben (with Swiss or daiya vegan cheese) is a favorite, and if anything can convince cynics that seitan works instead of chicken in a General Tso's dish, the one here just might. All sandwiches are $9.25. Fresh fruit smoothies ($5.50) and two not-on-the menu sandwiches, PB and J and grilled cheese, are popular with kids; each is $5 and comes with two vegan sugar cookies. Homemade desserts include vegan cupcakes made with tofu cream cheese frosting, brownies, and apricot bars ($3).

Additional location: 45 Eighth Avenue (West Village)

The Taqueria at La Esquina

114 Kenmare Street, between Cleveland Place and Lafayette Street
(646) 613-7100 (press "3" for "delivery" to reach the Taqueria)
Subway: 6 to Spring Street; N,R to Prince Street; J to Prince Street;
B,D,F,M to Broadway-Lafayette Street
esquinanyc.com/menu_t.php
Daily noon–2am

La Esquina occupies a former 24/7 sandwich and coffee dive that catered mainly to taxi drivers and locals; the old spot's original neon signage survives. Since then, a trio of restaurants has been built in the space. The Taqueria, the cheapest and most informal of the three, functions as both a tiny luncheonette serving Mexican food and as a pathway for well-dressed customers heading to the underground brasserie, the most expensive of the three. The door to the third restaurant, called the café, is around the corner. It takes no reservations, but is a fine sit-down option for Mexican food. It's also, by the way, where the bathrooms are located. So, La Esquina is an unusual place.

Enter the Taqueria, throw your jackets over some stools facing the window, and head to the counter to place your order. Tacos ($3.25–$3.95) are served on fresh, soft corn tortillas. Standouts include char-grilled marinated steak, mushrooms and epazote with hominy, and stewed pulled chicken with avocado.

The Taqueria also offers quesadillas and the Plato Julia, which includes rice, beans, corn, pico de gallo, queso fresco, and avocado, with add-on options like rotisserie or shredded chicken, grilled steak or fish, and pulled pork. Sandwiches, soups, and salads are also available. Note: the Taqueria does not serve chips or guacamole.

Children and adults alike find the view and the people-watching one of the most enjoyable aspects of eating here. The panoramic windows look onto a small square bookended by two streets. Sitting here feels like watching a movie of New York life while eating excellent cheap tacos instead of popcorn.

Westville

333 Hudson Street, between Charlton and Vandam Streets
(212) 776-1404
Subway: 1 to Houston Street; C,E to Spring Street
www.westvillenyc.com
Monday–Friday 9am–11pm; Saturday, Sunday 10am–11pm

This is the perfect place for lunch or dinner if you're visiting the nearby Children's Museum of the Arts or the Film Forum. Simple comfort food, fresh ingredients, and reasonable prices keep the place busy and the diners happy (it can be packed at lunch, so try to arrive at an off time). The big draw here is the vegetable plate ($11, $15). The blackboard menu lists about a dozen fresh veggies prepared in a variety of ways: garlic or pesto mashed potatoes, cauliflower Dijonnaise, roasted beets, sautéed kale and shallots, Asian-style bok choy, grilled asparagus with lemon and parmesan, and more. There's a changing roster of quesadillas, chopped salads, burgers, frittatas, and scrambles, as well as fish, chicken, and steak entrées, a choice of three different hot dogs (classic Hebrew National, a no-nitrate/no-nitrite Niman Ranch Fearless Frank, or vegan), shakes, and classic New York egg creams.

Additional locations: 210 West 10th Street (West Village); 246 West 18th Street (Chelsea) and 173 Avenue A (East Village)

SHOP

Bundle

128 Thompson Street, between Prince and Houston Streets

(212) 982-9465

Subway: 1 to Houston Street; 4,6,N,R to Spring Street

www.bundlenyc.com

Monday–Saturday 11am–7pm; Sunday noon–6pm

In Soho, where prices for even basic children's clothing can soar into the stratosphere, this small independent shop manages to stay stylish yet reasonable. The boutique offers items for boys and girls, birth to age 6, that appeal to a wide range of tastes without losing any edge—whether you come from Brooklyn (hip) or the Upper East Side (classic), you can find something that fits your style. One of those things might be a limited edition little cotton skirt, trimmed with a handmade Liberty of London fabric flower, edged with velvet ribbon, and embellished with a tiny crystal—all sewn by hand. At Bundle, you can order a piece of custom baby art that illustrates important facts about your newborn: date and time of birth, parents' and siblings' names, doctor, first address (matted and framed, $150).

Jacques Torres Chocolate

350 Hudson Street, at King Street
(212) 414-2462
Subway: 1 to Houston Street
www.mrchocolate.com
Monday–Friday 8:30am–7pm; Saturday 9am–7pm;
Sunday 10:30am–6:30pm

If you're at the Children's Museum of the Arts or the New York Fire Museum, you may want to duck into the nearby factory/boutique/café of genial French chocolatier Jacques Torres and watch the chocolate being made on vintage equipment. At Easter time, three-foot-high bunny molds rotate slowly, as workers make chocolate-covered peeps and decorate giant eggs; the activity continues year 'round. Sweet treats range from traditional chocolate bars to chocolate-covered Cheerios, cookies (available at room temperature or warm), and just about everything that can be made of, dipped or rolled in, or sprinkled with chocolate. Sit down at the counter and order a dark hot chocolate, classic or "wicked" (with a hint of ancho and chipotle peppers) in a variety of flavors (orange, mocha, peanut butter, caramel); or coffee or tea. In the summer months, a sidewalk cart offers homemade ice cream.

Les Petits Chapelais

146 Sullivan Street, between Prince and Houston Streets
(212) 625-1023
Subway: C,E to Spring Street; N,R to Prince Street;
1 to Houston Street
www.facebook.com/pages/Les-Petits-Chapelais-
NYC/198481876863560
Monday–Saturday noon–7pm; Sunday 1pm–6pm

Les Petits Chapelais, named for the owner's family farm in France,
stocks lighthearted and playfully stylish garments for newborns to
age 12-ish. The girls' clothing—such as a little pink pointelle cardigan
with bright orange cuffs—looks girly but never saccharine. Here,

in the same garments, prints and stripes happily coexist, as do neon and pastels, and gingham and tulle. There's a vintage-y vibe that spans the twentieth century: a black cotton sun suit, with white polka dots, is ruched and edged with rickrack, calling to mind something a 3-year-old Veronica Lake might wear. Next to it, a mid-century modern-ish print slip of a cotton dress is spangled ever so slightly with apple green, orange, and hot pink sequins. If your child wants to put out a bit of a rocker vibe, try a lambswool sleeveless vest from Copenhagen. Things for little boys, too, are cute and cool: swim trunks in a modern Union Jack print; T-shirts with images of sea creatures. At the back of the store, a toddler-sized red leather sofa and armchair let kids be comfy while trying on shoes; this is the only place stateside where you'll find the French shoe line, Pomme d'api.

Makié

109 Thompson Street, between Prince and Spring Streets
(212) 625-3930
Subway: 1 to Houston Street; A,C,E to Spring Street;
N,R to Prince Street
www.makieclothier.com
Monday–Saturday 11am–7pm; closed Sunday

Everything about this baby and children's clothing boutique is refined and exquisite. The palette is mostly white, beige, gray, and navy; the fabrics are cottons and cashmere; the craftsmanship is of the highest order. The designs are quiet and understated: tiny dotted Swiss bibs hardly larger than a playing card; diminutive "fur" collars of organic cotton; cable knit alpaca berets; a silken cord with a tiny mother of pearl fish charm and a blue glass bead. There's a design called Simple Dress and one called Puffsleeve Blouse, in a range of colors from pale peach to indigo; floral print corduroy bonnets; smocked blouses. A small range of women's clothing has the same subtle aesthetic.

Pearl River Mart
477 Broadway, between Broome and Grand Streets
(212) 431-4770
Subway: N,R to Canal Street; 4,6 to Spring Street or Canal Street
www.pearlriver.com
Daily 10am–7:20pm

This huge general store spans three floors and is filled with lacquer trays and kimonos, bedding, lamps, tatami mats, teapots, chopstick

rests, and thousands of other Asian items. For children, all sorts of "stuff": cute lunch sacks, girls' traditional Chinese outfits in brocade or, for boys, embroidered with a dragon ($24–$30), butterfly and dragonfly kites, masks, wind chimes, little brocade change purses, mobiles. Paper garlands, rice paper daisies, paper parasols, paper balloon animals, and kites all make fun birthday party decorations and favors. You'll have trouble finding anything over $10, with many items around $2.50. Don't miss the trash cans shaped like Chinese take-out containers ($11.50) and—essential for kids en route to dim sum in Chinatown—a selection of practice chopsticks. Last but not least: there's a clean restroom on the lower level.

The Scholastic Store

557 Broadway, between Prince and Spring Streets (stroller entrance: 130 Mercer Street)
(212) 343-6166
Subway: N,R to Prince Street; 4,6 to Spring Street;
B,D,F,M to Broadway-Lafayette Street
www.scholastic.com/sohostore
Monday–Saturday 10am–7pm; Sunday 11am–6pm

Housed in the corporate headquarters of the children's book publisher, this loft-like store is filled with shelves and shelves of children's books and more, with complete selections of Scholastic's well-known lines (Harry Potter, Clifford the Dog, I Spy, etc.). Scholastic has resisted the temptation to stock only its own books and products, though, and has assembled a wide and appealing inventory of quality books, toys, and CDs from other companies,

too. The store has lots of elbow room and different play areas and stations (a Chuggington train table, a Magic School Bus video area, a 39 Clues interactive screen and keyboard). Books are arranged by age; there are also shelves devoted to Homework Help and Teaching Resources. The assortment of craft kits is especially strong.

PLAY

EAT

SHOP

PLAY

Tompkins Square Park
Between East 10th & 7th Streets and Avenues A and B
Subway: 6 to Astor Place; N,R to 8th Street-NYU; F to 2nd Avenue;
L to 1st Avenue

In the past, this park has been the scene of many protest demonstrations and cultural celebrations. In the mid-1800s New Yorkers demonstrated in the park over poor economic conditions; a century later it was a hotspot for clashes between police and area residents demonstrating on behalf of the homeless. The city's major renovation of the park in 1992 transformed it into the family-friendly place that it is today. It has several playgrounds, and the overall manicure of the paths and grassy areas makes it a respite from some of the East Village's lingering gritty "character."

Blue Man Group

The Astor Place Theatre
434 Lafayette Street, between East 4th Street and Astor Place
(800) BLUEMAN
Subway: 6 to Astor Place; N,R to 8th Street-NYU;
L,4,5 to 14th Street-Union Square
www.blueman.com
Performance times vary; no shows on Tuesday
Tickets range in price; discounted same-day seats are sold through
TKTS
Children must be 5 or older to attend.

They bang on drums and tubes and other homemade percussion instruments, and they splatter paint as they drum. They throw marshmallows and paint balls across the stage and land them in each other's mouths with nary a miss. They invite an audience member to join them for a romantic meal of Twinkies that hilariously ends a little awkwardly. Throughout the show, these three men painted blue have a grand time with each other and with the audience in a light and easy, non-verbal performance that will entertain people of all ages: kids will love the antics and grownups will appreciate how the show can veer toward social commentary, but without offending anybody.

Those in the front five rows are provided with plastic rain ponchos for protection from flying bits of food. Be sure to use the restroom before the show starts. The performance lasts about 100 minutes without an intermission. And don't be late; if you are, you will be called out for it in front of everyone.

Stomp

Orpheum Theatre
126 Second Avenue, near St. Mark's Place
www.stomponline.com
Subway: 6 to Astor Place; N,R to 8th Street-NYU; L to 3rd Avenue;
F to 2nd Avenue
Tuesday–Friday 8pm; Saturday 3pm and 8pm;
Sunday 2pm and 5:30pm
See website for ticket information.

This is a perfect show for children of any age (providing they are not sensitive to loud sounds). The engaging group of eight performers create percussion rhythms using a wide array of (mainly) common household objects, including newspapers, brooms, flip-top butane lighters, and corrugated plastic tubing. The show is divided into a series of skits where the rhythms build from single or simple sounds to complex ensembles. Not only is the music irresistible, but the playful rapport between the performers kept kids in the audience in stitches throughout a recent show.

The Quantum Eye

Theatre 80
80 St. Mark's Place, at First Avenue
(347) 294-0092
Subway: 6 to Astor Place; N,R to 8th Street-NYU; L to 3rd Avenue;
F to 2nd Avenue
www.thequantumeye.com; tickets www.brownpapertickets.com
Saturday 5pm
General Admission $53; front section assigned seats $83

This 85-minute "mentalism and magic" show features Sam Eaton, a performer who invites volunteers from the audience up onto the stage to read their minds. Children, and even skeptical adults, will be convinced of his talent—if not his powers—and they'll wonder how he knows what he knows.

Among the many "tricks" he performs: blindly identifying playing cards chosen from a deck, knowing what time of day audience members are thinking of, and, without looking, mirroring pictures being drawn by different audience members. If you or your kids wish to participate onstage, let Sam know before the show when he makes his way through the audience to greet everyone. It's no guarantee he'll choose you— but he may!

EAT

B&H Dairy

127 Second Avenue, between East 7th Street and St. Mark's Place
(212) 505-8065
Subway: 6 to Astor Place; N,R to 8th Street-NYU; F to 2nd Avenue;
L to 1st or 3rd Avenue
Monday–Friday 7am–11pm; Saturday, Sunday 7am–midnight

This Kosher luncheonette (dairy, no meat) is too small for big families, or even strollers, but if you can fit yourselves onto a few stools or at a table or two—and if you appreciate amazing soup with complimentary challah bread and service so friendly you'll feel like a regular after only a minute—then this narrow restaurant from the 1930s is easily worth a stop-in. Customers love the challah French toast ($6.50), the potato pierogies ($8 for 4 pieces, $11 for 8), the tuna melt, and the soups (mushroom barley, lentil, Yankee bean, and matzo ball, $4.50 for a cup, $5 for a bowl).

Café Orlin

41 St. Mark's Place, between First and Second Avenues
(212) 777-1447
Subway: 6 to Astor Place; N,R to 8th Street-NYU; F to 2nd Avenue;
L to 1st Avenue
www.cafeorlin.com
Monday–Thursday 9am–12:30am; Friday 9am–1:30am;
Saturday 8:30am–1:30am; Sunday 8:30am–12:30am

If you want to step up breakfast from over-easy to eggs Benedict,

Café Orlin is the spot. Breakfast, which remains the best meal of the day here, is served until 4pm, with a great breakfast special on the menu: two eggs, home fries, toast, fresh orange juice, and a cappuccino, all for $8.50. Home fries are perfect little wedges with crispy edges and just the right amount of salt, pepper, and rosemary. More, please! For children with a sweet tooth, there's French toast and pancakes. More for adults are millet pancakes served with homemade chicken-pistachio sausage and a beet and goat cheese salad. A number of menu items have Middle Eastern flavors. Adults who like to spice things up can ask for harissa sauce on the side, great with eggs. The Middle Eastern eggs are served with labne (yogurt cheese) and the hummus is spectacular.

Note: To discourage people from camping out, Orlin does not serve drip coffee or coffee refills. The cappuccino, however, is excellent.

Macaron Parlour

111 Saint Mark's Place, between First Avenue and Avenue A
(212) 387-9169
Subway: L to 1st Avenue or 3rd Avenue; F to 2nd Avenue
www.macaronparlour.com
Monday noon–8pm; Tuesday–Wednesday noon–10pm; Thursday noon–11pm; Friday-Saturday noon–midnight; Sunday 11am–8pm

You'll find delectable macarons here in all the classic flavors (the young co-owners were trained in Paris), but this pristine, immaculate little cafe will appeal to foodies interested in tasting something new and different. The *pâtissiers* have ventured beyond the buttercreams and ganaches of tradition to more contemporary interpretations, including candied bacon with maple cream cheese frosting, frozen macarons (black sesame with cookies-and-cream ice cream), as well as other more conventional versions such as s'mores and snickers. A portion of the sales of every lemon macaron is donated to Alex's Lemonade Stand, an organization committed to finding a cure for pediatric cancer.

Momofuku Noodle Bar

171 First Avenue, between East 10th and 11th Streets
(212) 777-7773
Subway: L to 1st Avenue; 6 to Astor Place; N,R to 8th Street-NYU
www.momofuku.com/new-york/noodle-bar
Monday–Thursday noon–4:30pm, 5:30pm–11pm; Friday
noon–4:30pm, 5:30pm–2am; Saturday noon–4pm, 5:30pm–2am;
Sunday noon–4pm, 5:30pm–11pm

Food connoisseurs line up here for a taste of superstar chef David Chang's pork belly dishes. You can have it in ramen soup or as the filling in one of the famous pork buns, one of the most popular things on the menu. Unlike garden-variety pork buns in Chinatown, these are soft buns folded over like tacos. Scallions, hoisin sauce, and cucumbers contribute to the perfection. If your kids aren't into buns, Momofuku offers a kid's portion of ramen noodles and house broth for $6 (it's not on the printed menu); add-ins such as vegetables, an egg, or a protein are options. With kids, it's easiest to come here for lunch, and you should arrive early. Note: the stools and chairs here have no backs, and there's no place for strollers.

Pommes Frites

123 Second Avenue, between East 7th Street and St. Mark's Place
(212) 674-1234
Subway: 6 to Astor Place; N,R to 8th Street-NYU; F to 2nd Avenue;
L to 1st or 3rd Avenue
www.pommesfrites.ws
Sunday–Thursday 11:30am–1am; Friday–Saturday 11:30am–3:30am

French fries: the food health-conscious people hate to love. If you
do, you'll want excellent ones like those at Pommes Frites. Pommes
Frites serves fries in a cone (three sizes, $4.50–$7.75), with a
selection of sauces. Freebies include standards such as ketchup,
mustard, malt vinegar, and mayonnaise; organic black truffle mayo,
cheddar cheese, and ketchup mixed with cilantro and jalapeños are
$1.50 more. Seating is outside—there are a couple of chairs and a
table with slots to hold the cones—or eat while continuing to
explore the East Village.

Puddin'

102 St. Mark's Place, between First Avenue and Avenue A
(212) 477-3537
Subway: L to 1st Avenue or 3rd Avenue; F to 2nd Avenue
www.puddinnyc.com
Sunday–Tuesday 10:30am–1am; Wednesday–Saturday 10:30am–2am

Pudding may be regarded as a homey little dessert, suited to nurser-
ies and convalescents. . . but not in the hands of the chef behind
Puddin'. No surprise considering the impressive credentials she
brings to her miniscule counter-and-two-tiny-tables operation:
trained at the Culinary Institute of America, she held internships at

APARTMENTS
FOR RENT
866-NYC-DWEL
102 st. marks place
puddinnyc.com
PUDDIN'
A

Boulud restaurants, and worked on the pastry team at Union Square Café. Purists can choose among chocolate, vanilla, banana, butterscotch, coffee, lemon, coconut, tapioca, or classic rice (in three sizes: $4, $6.50, $8.50), with or without toppings (caramel, fudge, house-made sprinkles), made with local, organic ingredients. There are more complex concoctions, too—pudding parfaits, with add-ons such as crushed cookies and whipped cream; or, perfect for summer in the city, pudding pops ($5).

S'Mac

345 East 12th Street, between First and Second Avenues
(212) 358-7917
Subway: 4,6 to Astor Place
www.smacnyc.com
Sunday–Thursday 11am–11pm; Friday, Saturday 11am–1am

S'Mac is small, and you may have to wait for a seat, but once the piping hot macaroni and cheese arrives in a skillet, you're in for a treat. First, choose a size (a nosh at $6.75 serves one easily; the largest portion is $44!). Next, choose up to two cheeses (American, blue, fresh mozzarella, goat cheese, pepper jack, muenster, brie, and more). Then, choose up to three mix-ins (meats, including slab bacon, ground beef, Andouille; vegetables; and more). If it's all too overwhelming, there are a dozen of the most popular combos on the menu, from Parisienne and Mediterranean to Buffalo Chicken. Gluten-free macaroni is an option, too.

Additional location: 157 East 33rd Street between Lexington and 3rd Avenues (Murray Hill).

Veselka

144 Second Avenue, at East 9th Street
(212) 228-9682
www.veselka.com
Subway: 6 to Astor Place; N,R to 8th Street-NYU; L to 3rd Avenue;
F to 2nd Avenue
Daily 24 hours

Of the many Ukrainian and Polish diners that have served inexpensive meals to countless people over the years, Veselka has long been the busiest and cheeriest of the bunch. Its multifaceted diner menu has burgers, homemade soups, sandwiches, and all things breakfast. A number of dishes reflect the original owners' roots, such as hot or cold borscht ($4.75 small, $6.75 large), bigos (a hearty hunter's-style stew with mashed potatoes and another side, $15.75), a Ukrainian "meatball" hero ($13.75), and boiled or fried varenyky (aka pierogies) with fillings that include potato, cheese, meat, spinach and cheese, and sauerkraut and mushroom ($6.95 for 4, $10.95 for 7).

Veselka is busy just about any time of day but especially during breakfast. When you enter you may have to give your name to the host, who is stationed inside the door on the 9th Street side of the restaurant. Don't worry: even when the place is packed, the list moves quickly because of how efficiently Veselka manages to prepare the orders—a definite plus if you've got hungry or antsy children. Kids gravitate toward the chocolate chip pancakes ($9) or, for those with a miniature appetite, a single pancake or piece of challah French toast ($3.50). Breakfast is served all day (and night) long.

SHOP

Alphabets

115 Avenue A, between St. Mark's Place and East 7th Street
(212) 475-7250
Subway: 6 to Astor Place; L to 1st Avenue; F to 2nd Avenue
www.alphabetsnyc.com
Daily noon–8pm

Alphabets is choc-a-block with gag gifts, stocking stuffers, party favors, and lots of fun toys with attitude. The remote control whoopee cushion you didn't know existed? It does, and it's here. Have you been searching for a waitress action figure or cupcake-flavored toothpaste? Seek no further. You'll find the cute (little rubber ducky whistles that quack) and the ridiculous (a headband that holds a basketball net on top of your head). Tucked in among the novelties are some really great toys and games, including old-fashioned metal safes with combination locks and a Super Mario Brothers chess set.

Forbidden Planet

832 Broadway, between East 12th and 13th Streets
(212) 473-1576
Subway: 4,5,6,N,Q,R to Union Square-14th Street
www.fpnyc.com
Sunday–Tuesday 9am–10pm; Wednesday 8am–midnight;
Thursday–Saturday 9am–midnight

This is one of New York's greatest comic book stores, filled with a collection that ranges from the biggest Marvel titles to the smallest mini-comics. The comics section is rife with opportunities for a proper introduction to great comics for 7 and older. Even if you're unsure of where to begin, the staff is friendly and is almost guaranteed to find your child something memorable. In addition to comics, there is a wide selection of toys, games, and DVDs, perfect in case you also have a young one along who isn't interested in sequential art.

Pink Olive

439 East 9th Street, between First Avenue and Avenue A
(212) 780-0036
Subway: 6 to Astor Place
www.pinkolive.com
Monday–Friday noon–8pm; Saturday noon–7pm; Sunday noon–6pm

This tiny sliver of a gift shop is perfectly situated on a picturesque block that is home to a men's haberdashery, vintage clothing shops, an antique store, a bakery, and a wine shop. Walk to the rear and, carefully displayed in front of the beautiful flamingo-pink flowered wallpaper, you'll find a small but exquisite selection of baby and children's gifts: gingham or seersucker bow ties and neckties ($22), feathered mini-angel wings and wands, pink or golden metallic ballet slippers for infants, little handmade felt hairclips ($10), and more. A small selection of thoughtfully chosen toys includes a little mouse peering out of a matchbox ($28) and a princess-and-the-pea tucked into her own wooden bed, atop a pile of brightly-colored mattresses.

Strand Book Store

828 Broadway, between East 12th and 13th Streets
(212) 473-1452
Subway: 4,5,6,L,N,Q,R to Union Square-14th Street
strandbooks.com
Monday–Saturday 9:30am–10:30pm; Sunday 11:00am–10:30pm

When visiting New York, the first stop for many out-of-towners is
The Strand, where they know that somewhere in the celebrated 18
miles of new, used, and rare books, they'll find the unexpected treasure, the unanticipated discovery. Kids, too, can discover the thrill
of browsing aisle after book-crammed aisle in their own department

on the second floor. It's well organized ("new adventure books," "favorite series"), and there are themed tables ("best of the best," "award winners"), so kids can easily navigate the space. And, in the great Strand tradition, there are just enough miscellaneous piles and smaller shelves with unalphabetized volumes to provide kids with the quintessential Strand experience: the joy of stumbling over something surprising. In the same space, you'll find "literary" plush animals (Dr. Seuss, Sesame Street), Strand T-shirts ($18.95), wooden model subway cars ($8.95), and other appealing toys. Thursdays at 3:30 there's a free story hour; check the website for the schedule of other kids' events.

Sustainable NYC

139 Avenue A, between East 9th and 10th Streets
(212) 254-5400
Subway: L to 1st Avenue; 6 to Astor Place
www.sustainable-nyc.com
Monday–Friday 8am–10pm; Saturday, Sunday 9am–10pm

This is the East Village version of a general store, filled with "local, organic, recycled, fair-trade, re-purposed, biodegradable products and gifts." For babies: knitted teethers, baby hats with peace symbols, onesies, pink sequined Tom's baby shoes; for parents: soy candles, totes, jewelry, organic nail polish and soy polish remover, housewares, skin care products, vegan cosmetics, and housewares. There's a small café in the back serving pastries, sandwiches, snacks, and beverages.

Toy Tokyo

91 Second Avenue, between East 5th and 6th Streets
(212) 673-5424
Subway: 6 to Astor Place; N,R to 8th Street-NYU;
L to 1st or 3rd Avenue
www.toytokyo.com
Sunday–Thursday 1pm–9pm; Friday, Saturday 12:30pm–9:00pm

Toy Tokyo specializes in character-driven vintage and reproduction toys of the 1960s and later. High-end collectibles include Hot Toys, Medicom, Takara Tomy, and Kotobukiya. So as to not disappoint younger collectors with not-very-deep pockets, the shop also carries popular and affordable toys including Hello Kitty (one Kitty is made up like a member of the rock band Kiss); reproduction Star Wars and Godzilla dolls, and action figures. On the shelves you'll find Smurfs, Speed Racer, and Marvel items; and of course, robots. Despite its name, not all toys at Toy Tokyo are from Japan, though many are.

PLAY

EAT

SHOP

PRIVATE
COURT
No Trespassing

PLAY

Washington Square Park
Bound by West 4th Street, MacDougal Street, Waverly Place, and University Place
Subway: A,B,C,D,E,F,M to West 4th Street; N,R to 8th Street-NYU
www.nycgovparks.org

Historic Washington Square Park has always been at the heart of the Village, geographically and spiritually. In colonial days it served as a potter's field and then a burial ground for yellow fever victims. By the time Henry James was born there in 1843, it was an elegant neighborhood that he later used as the backdrop for his novel of the

same name. In the 1950s and 1960s, it was the epicenter of the counterculture.

Today, the park generally serves three main populations: NYU students (the park is the center of the university's campus); tourists who want to soak up its long and colorful history; and neighborhood residents who take advantage of its amenities that include two dog runs, chess tables, and plenty of benches for people-watching. For families, a toddler-friendly fountain and a wading pool, grassy areas, and a children's playground are the main attractions, along with the street performers (tumblers, musicians, and the like) who appear on sunny days. Public **restrooms** are located within the park near its southern side, between Thompson and Sullivan Streets.

Bleecker Playground

Hudson Street, at Bleecker and West 11th Streets
Subway: A,C,E to 14th Street; L to Eighth Avenue;
1 to Christopher Street-Sheridan Square

For parents and children, this is *the* West Village destination: a big, always-crowded playground with sprinklers, swings, play equipment, and **bathrooms**. Parents may want to take turns watching the children in order to check out the uber-chic shopping on Bleecker Street (Marc Jacobs, Diptyque, Nars, and countless other upscale boutiques). The celebrity sightings are part of the experience at this playground; the neighborhood's leafy streets lined with nineteenth-century brownstones are home to dozens of TV and film stars, many of them parents with young children.

Marshall Chess Club

23 West 10th Street, between Fifth and Sixth Avenues
(212) 477-3716
Subway: 6 to Astor Place; 4,5,6,L,N,Q,R to Union Square-14th Street
www.marshallchessclub.org/chess-for-kids
Monday–Friday 1pm–midnight; Saturday, Sunday noon–midnight
Marshall Chess Academy: Individual lessons ($25); call or e-mail a
day or two in advance to schedule a session.

The Marshall Chess Club, founded in 1915 and housed in a nine-teenth-century brownstone on one of the most beautiful blocks in Greenwich Village, holds Saturday classes for players 14 years and younger who have basic chess skills but want to improve their game. It might be the perfect "only in New York" experience if you have a half-pint chess aficionado who would love to spend an hour or so playing and learning alongside other kids who, too, are thrilled by the game. The group classes are taught by a professional children's chess coach who teaches in public and private schools (drop-ins allowed). There are two class levels for novice players (one for those rated 1000 and under, the other for those rated 1500 and under). The classes were voted "Best of NY 2012" for Kids by *New York* magazine, because "Chess feels important here—not nerdy niche-y, just cool." If your child doesn't want to take a class, it's also fun just to stop by and watch. The club is active, so there will always be people of all ages playing. If you want to play, it's better to e-mail and call ahead.

West Fourth Street Basketball Courts
Sixth Avenue, between West 3rd and 4th Streets
Subway: A,C,E,B,D,F,M to West 4th Street

Aka "The Cage," this smaller-than-regulation public basketball court is a high-octane venue for amateur basketball tournaments, drawing some of the best and the toughest players from all five boroughs. Jayson Williams and Anthony Mason played in leagues here, commercials have been filmed here, and reputations made. The talent is impressive, the physical play is intense, and it's never less than thrilling to line up at the anchor fence (no seating here), watch the action, and try to spot the next NBA superstar. This stretch of Sixth Avenue is a little seamy, but if you're coming out of the West Fourth Street subway station, don't miss it.

Whitney Museum of American Art
The Whitney, located on the Upper East Side when this guide went to press, is scheduled to move to Washington and Gansevoort Streets in 2015 (page 368).

A Walk through the West Village

There aren't really any tourist attractions in the West Village—visiting this part of the city has always been about meandering through the winding cobblestone streets, many of which were originally cow paths from colonial times, and listening for echoes of its artistic and literary past. There are few tall buildings; many row houses date from the early nineteenth century. This short walk takes no more than half an hour, starts and ends with a playground, and in between, points out a few sites that adults—and hopefully children—will find interesting, and that convey the charm and character of the neighborhood.

Begin at the southwest corner of Seventh Avenue South and St. Luke's Place, also called Leroy Street. Walk half a block west and take a few minutes to let your children run around the playground at J. J. Walker Park. The space and play equipment is best suited for toddlers and young grade-schoolers. The larger park includes a baseball field (home to Greenwich Village Little League), a bocce ball court that harks back to the neighborhood's Italian roots, a handball court, an outdoor pool—look for the joyful Keith Haring mural—and a community recreation center. There's even a tiny branch of the New York Public Library at 66 Leroy Street, with a sweet children's room upstairs, with picture books and toys, open to the public.

Across the street is a block of nineteenth-century row houses, shaded by some of the largest gingko trees in the city; this is a quiet and picturesque "moment" in the West Village. For film buffs: the park was the setting for *Raging Bull* (Robert De Niro lived across the street at #14) and the soccer game in *Stuart Little*

II was filmed in the baseball field. The façade of #10 stood in for the Huxtable's house in *The Cosby Show.* Look for the busloads of tourists having their photos taken on the stoop.

Leaving the playground, walk west to Hudson Street, turn north, and walk two short blocks to Barrow Street. Turn right, walk to Commerce Street and bear to the right (you'll pass the little Cherry Lane Theatre). Walk to the end of the block and turn right; the second house from the corner, #75½, is less than ten feet wide, the narrowest house in the Village, and the former home of the writer Edna St. Vincent Millay.

Across the street, ask the children to find four stars on the front of 70 Bedford Street. After several decades, the facades of many brick houses built during the Federal period began to sag and buckle. They had to be stabilized with metal rods that ran from wall to wall, capped by iron plates. The early plates, which functioned like large washers, were made in plain shapes; by the end of the Civil War, however, they were made from melted-down cannonballs, and ironworkers began casting them in the shape of stars to honor the Republic. You'll find these beautiful symbols of our United States on brick walls throughout lower Manhattan and the Village.

Retrace your steps and at the corner of Commerce Street, you may want to walk the short block towards Seventh Avenue and have a snack at the tiny **Milk and Cookies** (page 234). If not, continue another block up Bedford Street. Turn right on Barrow Street and walk halfway down the block until you see the music school on the left. Even if there wasn't a sign, there are clues that

the building has musical associations. Ask the children to find them. (And across the street, see if they can find more stars.)

Back on Bedford Street, as you walk past #84, #86, and #88, find the doors, each with a window over it, next to the main doors of the houses. You'll see these narrow horse passageways through-out the Village—they originally led to the stables behind the houses.

Continue north a few steps to Grove Street and walk toward Hudson Street on the south side of Grove. Peek through the iron gate at Grove Court (between #10 and #12 Grove Street), an enclave of dollhouse-like houses that date from 1848. Continuing to Hudson, you'll pass a row of houses built from 1825 to 1834. Look on the second step from the bottom on the stoops of #6 and #8. On each, there is an opening in the railing shaped like a croquet hoop that you can put your foot through, and a flat piece of metal at the bottom. It's a boot scraper, in colonial times necessary for ladies and gentlemen to use before entering the house; until the streets of Manhattan were paved, rain meant mud.

At the end of the block, turn right onto Hudson Street. Cross Hudson and peek into the hidden, romantic, quiet garden of St. Luke's in the Fields, a good place to take a picnic or to sit on a bench and enjoy the quiet.

If you're hungry, nearby you'll see **Cowgirl Hall of Fame** (page 229) and **Sanpanino** (page 237). Or, continue the walk north up Hudson a few blocks to Charles Street, and walk west. Halfway down the block you'll see a white clapboard house (#121)—another dollhouse-like structure—that looks as if it was blown in from the countryside. It was, sort of. In 1967, it was moved from its original location uptown, on Cobble Court, where it was once the residence of Margaret Wise Brown, author of *Goodnight Moon*. Go back to Hudson Street, and walk five blocks north and spend some time at the popular Bleecker Playground, where there's a public **bathroom** (page 212). Within a block or so, you can find **food and drink** at Frankies Spuntino 570 (page 230), the Corner Bistro (page 227), La Bonbonniere (page 233) or Barbuto (page 222).

EAT

Arturo's Pizzeria

106 West Houston Street, at Thompson Street
(212) 677-3820
Subway: C,E to Spring Street; 1 to Houston Street; B,D,F,M to
Broadway-Lafayette Street; 6 to Bleecker Street; N,R to Prince Street
www.arturoscoaloven.com
Monday–Thursday 4pm–1am; Friday, Saturday 4pm–2am;
Sunday 3pm–midnight

Thankfully, this old-timer has survived, and continues two hallowed
Greenwich Village traditions: pizza made in a coal-burning oven
and live jazz. The musicians set up in the front barroom where there

are a few tables. There are two larger dining rooms in the back and sidewalk seating when the weather's good. Regardless of where you sit, you will be rewarded with pizza made the classic New York way. The coal oven renders the crust chewy and crispy at the same time (small $17, large $20, toppings $2–$4). Arturo's also offers a full menu of Italian-American items, including pastas and entrées such as veal, chicken, and eggplant parmigiana.

Barbuto

775 Washington Street, at West 12th Street
(212) 924-9700
Subway: 1,2,3 to 14th Street; A,C,E to 14th Street; L to 8th Avenue
www.barbutonyc.com
Monday–Wednesday noon–11pm; Thursday, Friday noon–midnight; Saturday noon–3:30pm, 5:30pm–midnight; Sunday noon–3:30pm, 5:30pm–10pm

Though it has a regular clientele of model types and upper-crust New Yorkers, at heart, Barbuto is a casual neighborhood spot. The roast chicken is Barbuto's masterpiece: several respected New York chefs have gone on record as saying it's their favorite meal to have on a day off. Crisp on the outside, with a juicy-not-dry herby interior, it's served with a warm salsa verde and rosemary- and pecorino-fried smashed potatoes ($19). For kids, the *bambino* meal is pasta with either tomato sauce or butter and cheese; it's not on the menu, but if you ask, the kitchen will whip it up in a minute ($9). The menu changes seasonally and even daily, but you'll always find the chicken, as well as pasta carbonara, bruschetta, mussels, and salads. There's also the option of having a four-course private "family dinner" for parties of 7–12, served either in the kitchen at the "chef's table" or in a private dining room. ($65 per person, not including beverages, tax, or gratuity; the charge per child depends on age and entrée; book 30 days in advance.)

Bareburger

535 Laguardia Place, between Bleecker and West 3rd Streets
(212) 477-8125
Subway: 4,6 to Bleecker Street; B,D,F,M to Broadway-Lafayette Street; N,R to Prince Street
bareburger.com
Daily 11am–11pm

The idea behind this sit-down burger chain is that organic or all-natural ingredients are not only healthiest, but also taste best. Customers also love the menu's vast array of options for buns, cheese, bacon, veggie toppings, and sauces that can be mixed-and-matched on any of 13 types of patties (beef, turkey, veggie quinoa, black bean, mushroom, buttermilk fried chicken, and jerk chicken, $8.45), as well as several premium options (lamb, wild boar, elk, bison, and ostrich). There's a list of well thought-out combo burgers for those who are overwhelmed by the options.

Kids can go for a Cubby Meal ($7.95)—choice of burger, chicken tenders, panini, or chicken or beef hot dog with French fries, carrot sticks, apple slices, and a drink.

In addition to burgers, there are also appetizers, entrée salads, sandwiches, and milkshakes—organic, of course. For curious eaters, there's an info card with FAQs, fat content, which ingredients are organic, cage-free, grass-fed, etc.

Additional locations: 514 Third Avenue (Midtown), 153 Eighth Avenue (Chelsea), 85 Second Avenue (East Village), 1370 First Avenue (Upper East Side), 366 West 46th Street (Midtown), 1681 First Avenue (Upper East Side)

Big Gay Ice Cream Shop

61 Grove Street (at Seventh Avenue South)
(212) 533-9333
Subway: 1 to Sheridan Square-NYU;
A,B,C,D,E,F,M to West 4th Street
www.biggayicecream.com
Monday–Friday 11am–midnight; Saturday, Sunday noon–midnight

BGIC elevates soft-serve chocolate and vanilla ice cream to premium heights; watch in awe as dulce de leche not only coats the outside but is injected into your swirl so that the thick caramel also permeates the interior. Most popular with kids is a chocolate or vanilla cup or cone topped with, appropriately, rainbow sprinkles. Chocolate dip is also an option. Adults and more adventurous youngsters will dig combinations such as the Bea Arthur (vanilla ice cream, dulce de leche, and crushed 'nilla wafers) or Mermaid (vanilla ice cream, key lime curd, crushed graham crackers, and whipped cream).

Additional location: 125 East 7th Street (East Village)

Blue Ribbon Bakery Kitchen

35 Downing Street, at Bedford Street
(212) 337-0404
Subway: 1 to Houston Street; A,C,E,B,D,F,M to West 4th Street
www.blueribbonrestaurants.com
Monday–Friday noon–3pm, 5pm–midnight;
Saturday 11am–midnight; Sunday 11am–10pm

The quality food, charming setting, and congenial vibe has never faded at this neighborhood favorite. The lunch menu offers a full array of sandwiches, from a Reuben to a grilled Portobello P.L.T., all around $15, served on bread baked downstairs in the 135-year-old brick oven (you can take the kids downstairs to watch the bakers). The floor-to-ceiling windows afford views of one of the sweetest lanes in the Village, a little diagonal street with a smattering of bars, cafés, and bistros tucked in among the row houses and apartment buildings. An early dinner here might be the best choice with kids, before the restaurant fills up.

The dinner menu has lots to appeal to children in addition to a hamburger—fried chicken, mashed potatoes, a luscious cream of tomato soup—and adults will be hard-pressed to choose among the appetizers that range from beef marrow, bacon bread, and onion marmalade ($18) to garlic shrimp and chorizo ($17), and entrées that include duck breast or lamb chops ($28, $36). Brunch here is one of the most popular in the city. The wait can be long since reservations are accepted only for parties of five or more, but worth it to taste French toast made the classic New York way, with challah.

Corner Bistro

331 West 4th Street, at Jane Street
(212) 242-9502
Subway: 1,2,3 to 14th Street; L to 8th Avenue
www.cornerbistrony.com
Monday–Saturday 11:30am–4am; Sunday noon–4am

Don't go after 5pm when the traders and other 9-to-5ers descend en masse and refuel on these oversized hamburgers, which are often rated at the top of "Best Burger in NYC" lists. But at lunch on a weekday, perhaps before a visit to the High Line (page 272), the following details can conspire to give you great joy: the sun's rays as

they filter through the side windows, the initials scratched into the old wood tabletops, the inexpensive McSorley's ale on draught, and, of course, the signature eight-ounce Bistro burger with bacon and cheese ($8).

The restaurant itself hasn't been updated for decades—it's an authentically run-down, bohemian-Village-of-days-gone-by kind of place—nor has the menu. A BLT, grilled cheese sandwich, chili, burger, fries—that's about it. The thin French fries taste like McDonald's fries of yore, probably because they share oil with frying strips of bacon. A burger here does get messy, especially if you order it rare or medium rare, but roll up your sleeves and go for it.

Cowgirl Hall of Fame

519 Hudson Street, between West 10th and Charles Streets

(212) 633-1133

Subway: 1 to Christopher Street; A,C,E,B,D,F,M to West 4th Street

www.cowgirlnyc.com

Monday–Thursday 11am–11pm; Friday 11am–midnight;
Saturday 10am–midnight; Sunday 10am–11pm (Saturday and
Sunday brunch 10am–4pm)

Even born-and-bred West Village kids who don't know from a rodeo
can't resist the corn dogs served up at this friendly Western-themed
eatery. It's always filled with office workers, singles, families, locals,

tourists—not packed, exactly, but plenty busy; there's always a congenial bunch hanging out. The menu, top to bottom, is so child-friendly the kids menu ($6) seems almost unnecessary. On the main menu: breakfast BLT, buttermilk flapjacks, Catfish po'boys, chips and black-eyed pea salsa, nachos, burritos, enchiladas, chili and veggie chili, salads, omelets, ribs, burgers, wings, chicken fried chicken or steak (Cowgirl's #1 seller, $16, $18.50). Parents will appreciate the reasonable prices, popular margaritas ($10–$12, also available by the pitcher), and extensive tequila menu. Kids will be tickled by "the #1 best dessert ever," which "looks like a baked potato, tastes like a hot fudge sundae," perfect for sharing ($7.95).

Frankies Spuntino 570

570 Hudson Street, at West 11th Street
(212) 924-0818
Subway: 1 to Christopher Street-Sheridan Square; 1,2,3 to 14th Street
www.frankiesspuntino.com
Sunday–Thursday 11am–11pm; Friday–Saturday 11am–midnight

Villagers were delighted when the much-loved Brooklyn Frankies opened a second restaurant in their neighborhood, a step away from Bleecker Playground (page 212). *Spuntino*, in Italian, means an informal meal or snack, or a casual eatery. That's Frankies: regional Italian specialties served in a laid-back atmosphere. It's also roomy by New York standards and the dining room is never crowded at lunch. Adults may be drawn to the sweet sausage, roasted red peppers, and onions over creamy polenta, or the house-made gnocchi. The meatballs and any plate of pasta served here will be sure to please the *bambini*. On the lighter side are the cheese or cured meat plates and vegetable antipasti. The ingredients are superb: the sandwiches are made on bread from nearby Sullivan Street Bakery, sausages come from Faicco's on Bleecker Street, local cheeses from Anne Saxelby's tiny stand in Essex Street Market; Frankies presses its own olive oil in Sicily. Weekends, from 11am to 3pm, are also a great time to go with kids, when classic brunch items with an Italian spin are served: Frankies breakfast—eggs any style, grilled sausage, polenta cake; buckwheat pancakes with roasted apples and cinnamon mascarpone ($12); seasonal vegetable frittata, in addition to the regular menu. Try them with a Benevento aperitif or Italian Fizz.

Joe's Pizza

7 Carmine Street, between Sixth Avenue and Bleecker Street
(212) 366-1182
Subway: A,C,E,B,D,F,M to West 4th Street
www.joespizzanyc.com
Sunday–Thursday 10am–4am; Friday–Saturday 10am–5am

The criteria for a good slice? Respectable ingredients, homemade dough, not too much cheese, a sauce made from tomatoes essentially left alone, and a baker who pays attention. Perhaps no place succeeds better at this than Joe's. Joe's is usually busy, but the line moves fast. As a result, pies are always fresh. Joe's provides no regular tables and chairs; the few stools pulled up to the counters and a couple of bar tables inside and out provide great people watching. If there's no room, Father Demo Square across the street has many park benches. Slices are $2.75 for plain cheese, $3.50 for fresh mozzarella, and $3 for a Sicilian square.

Additional location: 150 East 14th Street (Union Square)

John's of Bleecker Street

278 Bleecker Street, at Jones Street

(212) 243-1680

Subway: 1 to Christopher Street-Sheridan Square;
A,C,E,B,D,F,M to West 4th Street

www.johnsbrickovenpizza.com

Monday–Thursday 11:30am–11:30pm; Friday 11:30am–midnight;
Saturday 11:30am–12:30am; Sunday noon–11:30pm

Try to arrive at John's when it opens or during off hours (between lunch and dinner on a weekday) because otherwise you're likely to have a long wait. John's makes its pizzas in ovens that burn coal; one of its two ovens dates back to pre-1929. Though the pizza at John's is the star of the show, the vintage setting itself is certainly part of the fun. Besides pizza, John's also has pasta; a few salads, calzones, and that's about it. Pizzas are $14.50 for small and $16.50

for large. Toppings are $3 each. A salad for two is $6.50. And, as the awning outside famously announces, "No Slices."

La Bonbonniere
28 Eighth Avenue, between West 12th and Jane Streets
(212) 741-9266
Subway: A,C,E to 14th Street; L to Eighth Avenue;
1 to Christopher Street-Sheridan Square
Daily 7am–9:15pm

As with many twentieth-century American greasy spoons, La Bonbonniere has counter stools from which children and adults can admire the swift cooking skills of the short order cooks. There's seating at tables, too, where expedient waiters will refill your coffee as often as you require. The pancakes ($6.50) will surely make children happy; they're soft and buoyant, slightly sweet, and in our current world of multi-grain this and gluten-free that, these well-executed flapjacks from America's culinary past occupy an important place in our hearts. Other (all-day) breakfast choices include omelets, oatmeal, challah French toast, and fresh fruit. The lunch menu is not vast, but it does include a number of salads, burgers, and a long list of sandwiches ($3.50–$11.75).

Note: the bathroom is located down some rather treacherous stairs. Make sure you and your kids proceed with care.

Milk & Cookies Bakery
19 Commerce Street, between Seventh Avenue and Bedford Street
(212) 243-1640
Subway: 1 to Christopher Street-Sheridan Square
www.milkandcookiesbakery.com
Sunday–Thursday 11am–10pm; Friday–Saturday 11am–11pm

Just steps off busy Seventh Avenue South, on a leafy Village side street, this miniscule bakery serves homemade cookies and sweets. Choose among classic cookies ($2.50; 3 for $7; 6 for $13.50; Baker's Dozen $27), brownies, or ice cream sandwiches ($5.50). The delicious, over-the-top Bacon Smack is made with maple syrup, candied smoked bacon, dried cranberries, dark chocolate chunks, toffee, and graham cracker pieces.

Otto Enoteca Pizzeria
1 Fifth Avenue, between Washington Mews and 8th Street
(212) 995-9559
Subway: 4,6 to Astor Place; A,C,E,B,D,F,M to West 4th Street;
N,R to 8th Street-New York University
www.ottopizzeria.com
Daily 11:30am–midnight

Mario Batali's pizzeria and wine bar is a crowd pleaser, for good
reason. Large, casual, and noisy, it's filled with locals, lots of families,
NYU students and parents, enjoying superb pizza and an extensive
wine list with lots of choices at every price. The appetizers are perfect for sharing, so most tables assemble an array from the $5 veg-

etable appetizers, the $9 platters of house-made cured meats, artisanal cheeses, and other small plates. About a dozen pastas are on the menu, but many diners opt for the pizzas ($7–$14), that range from the sublimely simple (lardo or olive oil and sea salt) to the unusual (fennel and bottarga, or clam, topped with the *vongole* in their shells). The house-made gelato, including the olive oil flavor, has a devoted following.

Peanut Butter & Co.

240 Sullivan Street, between West 3rd and Bleecker Streets
(212) 677-3995
Subway: 1,2 to Houston Street; A,C,E,B,D,F,M to West 4th Street
www.ilovepeanutbutter.com
Sunday–Thursday 11am–9pm; Friday–Saturday 11am–10pm

When the ethnic delights of NYC leave your kids longing for some plain old American food, take them to Peanut Butter & Co. Here, they can kick it Old School (a plain PB&J), vintage (Fluffernutter), or southern style (the Elvis, grilled and stuffed with bananas and honey, bacon optional). Adults might want to try the Peanut Butter Sampler, served with crudities, or other non-pb classic sandwiches (all around $5 to $8). Desserts include cookies, brownies and a no-holds-barred selection of sundaes: Pretzel, Bananarama (graham crackers, fluff, whipped cream), Wafflewich, Death by Peanut Butter (three scoops of ice cream on a bed of peanut butter Cap'n Crunch, topped with peanut butter, whipped cream, Reese's pieces, peanut butter chips, and peanut butter sauce, $6). The shop's custom flavors of peanut butter are available by the jar to go.

Sanpanino

494 Hudson Street, between Grove and Christopher Streets
(212) 645-7228
Subway: 1 to Christopher Street-Sheridan Square;
A,C,E,B,D,F,M to West 4th Street
Daily 7am–7pm

We can't recommend Sanpanino at high noon or when school lets out in the afternoon—that's when so many kids from PS3 next door crowd into this diminutive café you won't be able to squeeze in the door. But any other time, perch on the banquette at one of the tiny tables and tuck into one of the toasty, melty paninis, a grilled Italian wrap, or a cup of soup accompanied by the homemade focaccia. At $1, the homemade chocolate chip or oatmeal raisin cookies are a bargain you won't often find in NYC.

Sweet Revenge

62 Carmine Street, between Bedford Street and Seventh Avenue
(212) 242-2240
Subway: 1 to Houston; A,C,E,B,D,F,M to West 4th Street
www.sweetrevengenyc.com
Monday–Thursday 7am–11pm; Friday 7am–12:30am;
Saturday 10:30am–12:30am; Sunday 10:30am–10pm

Sex and the City ushered in The Age of the Cupcake, and since then it's been easy to find these little indulgences throughout the city. But Sweet Revenge manages to put a spin on the trend that Carrie et al would surely approve: cupcake and wine and beer pairings. In the late afternoon, before the happy hour crowd arrives at around 5pm, a Fleur de Sel cupcake with a glass of Prosecco, a Dulce de Leche cupcake and Chardonnay, a Mayan Chocolate with pear cider from Sweden, or a Very Strawberry cupcake paired with a glass of stout is a unique treat you won't find elsewhere. This bright and casual café with a bar and a handful of tables also serves breakfast and weekend brunch (red velvet Belgian waffles, eggs benedict, breakfast burritos, all around $11) and lunch (burgers, savory bread pudding, salads).

If you do want to make the *Sex and the City* cupcake pilgrimage, Magnolia Bakery is not far away at 401 Bleecker Street (at West 11th Street), but be prepared to wait in a long long line.

The Original Sandwich Shoppe (T.O.S.S.)

58A Greenwich Avenue, between Sixth and Seventh Avenues
(212) 255-2237
Subway: 1,2,3 to 14th Street
www.deli-nyc.com
Monday–Saturday 7am–9pm; Sunday 9am–5pm

This is a basic no-frills spot, but frills are beside the point when Rudy's golden-brown fresh roasted turkey comes out of the oven. That's when the signature sandwiches start being made to order: dark or white meat, or a combo? Bread, hoagie roll, or baguette? Homemade herb mayo? (Say yes.) It's a memorable sandwich, and at $9.25, a bargain. The other classics on the menu are fresh and homemade: chicken, tuna, and egg salad ($7–$9); soup ($4.25); chicken parm ($9.25); homemade bread pudding, brownies, pound and carrot cakes. Everything is kid-friendly; you feel like you're at your own kitchen table.

Bleeker Street Culinary Walk

A,C,E,B,D,F,M to West 4th Street; 1 to Sheridan Square-NYU or Houston Street

Bleecker Street is a narrow, one-way street that crosses the heart of Greenwich Village. It starts on the Bowery, runs through the old beatnik neighborhood near NYU, to finally end at Abingdon Square in the West Village. The few blocks of Bleecker that run from Sixth Avenue and Carmine Street north to Seventh Avenue are packed with some of the most fun and child-friendly food venues in the city. Pop into one or more spots, order whatever takes your fancy, to eat there or to go—you're sure to have a bite of something incredible.

Food tours are regularly conducted along this stretch, and it's a zoo on the weekends, so try to avoid Saturday and Sunday. If you opt for carry-out rather than sit-down, you can eat on one of the benches at Father Demo Square (where Sixth Avenue, Bleecker, and Carmine Street intersect) or walk a few blocks north to the large Bleecker Playground (page 212), where you'll find benches and tables.

Start at the corner of Bleecker and Carmine Streets. In the short block of Carmine that stretches to Sixth Avenue, you can choose between two popular places for ice cream; there's a third a block away (see Cones, page 242). **Pop Bar** at 5 Carmine Street has gelato, sorbet, and frozen yogurt on a stick that can be dipped in chocolate coatings and toppings. In cooler weather, try Pop Bar's hot chocolate on a stick (a block of chocolate on a popsicle stick,

immersed in steamed milk).

The celebrated *gelateria* **GROM** is on the corner. Started in Turin, Italy, the home of Slow Food, GROM follows the movement's principles: the gelato is handmade, using organic ingredients. Try the Crema di Grom, with crushed cornmeal cookies and chocolate chips, the hazelnut and chocolate Gianduja, the lemon or coffee granita, or any of the vividly flavored *sorbetti*. One scoop is $5.25, but the quality matches the price.

Also on this block, **Joe's Pizza** at 7 Carmine Street is regarded by many as having the best slices in the city (page 231). If you only want a slice, this is where to get it; Kesté (page 241) and John's (page 232) sell only by the pie.

Walking north on Bleecker, you'll see Our Lady of Pompeii

church, where the 11am Sunday Mass is still said in Italian. You'll pass **Pasticceria Rocco** (at #243), serving traditional Italian pastries and coffee; it's one of the few old school bakeries where the cannoli are filled with cream when you order, not beforehand, so the shell is crisp, not soggy.

If you want to sit down while you eat some superb pizza, the choices are Kesté or John's. **Kesté Pizza & Vino** (at #271) hails from Naples, and offers an assortment of wood-fired pies (as well as gluten-free and vegan options). Consistently named the best or among the best pizzas in NYC, it was also listed as one of the top 25 best Pizza Places in the U.S. by *Food and Wine* magazine.

Across the street, **Amy's Bread** (at the corner of Leroy Street) has a few tables where you can eat one of the delicious sandwiches, muffins, cookies, or sweets. A picnic can be assembled next door at **Murray's Cheese**, which has, in addition to a dizzying array of cheese, charcuterie, antipasti, and made-to-order sandwiches. The next storefront is the old-fashioned pork store **Faicco's**, a pristinely clean establishment where the butchers make sand-wiches that have a devoted following. A few steps further, at the corner of Morton Street, check out the casual **Risotteria**, where you can sit and have a reasonably priced plate of the Milanese specialty, panini, and more, all gluten-free and with many veg-etarian options.

The awning at **John's of Bleecker Street** (at #278, page 232) reminds customers, "No Slices," and reservations aren't taken, so there's usually a line, but it is the undisputed Village classic, in business at the same spot since 1929.

If you've resisted the ice cream options so far, you may want to give in to your craving at **Cones** (#272). The gelato holds its own against GROM and comes in some flavors you won't find else-where (the surprisingly delicious corn).

By now you've reached busy Seventh Avenue. Cross it, continue north past the many upscale boutiques. The walk ends at the popular Bleecker Playground.

SHOP

Chess Forum

219 Thompson Street, between West 3rd and Bleecker Streets
(212) 475-2369
Subway: A,C,E,B,D,F,M to West 4th Street; 1 to Houston;
6 to Bleecker Street
chessforum.com
Daily 11am–midnight

A young chess player looking for a special chess set will be sure to find something in this little shop. In the window alone are chess sets with archangels, Egyptian mythology figures, American Civil war soldiers, and many more. Inside, time seems to have stood still. Between the old-fashioned lights and the vintage wooden fittings, the scene looks like a sepia-toned photograph. In the showcases, you'll see a malachite tribal chess set from Zimbabwe, an onyx set and board, sets made from rosewood and boxwood, as well as travel sets and backgammon boards. In the back room, several games are in progress, the elderly competitors hunched over the board in silent concentration. You can play a game of chess here with anyone who happens to be around (adults $5 an hour; kids free).

CuRious Candy

396 Bleecker Street, between West 11th and Perry Streets
(212) 675-4710
Subway: 1 to Christopher Street-Sheridan Square; 1,2,3 to 14th Street
www.curiouscandy.com
Monday–Saturday 11am–8pm; Sunday 11am–7pm

Walk into clothing designer Cynthia Rowley's candy shop on the posh upper stretch of Bleecker Street and it's anything but saccharine-as-usual. The shop has a Diana-Vreeland-meets-Tim-Burton vibe and the Rolling Stones on the audio system are singing, "You

Can't Always Get What You Want." Brightly colored gummies of every type fill the black bins and provide a Technicolor jolt along one wall. You'll find chocolate cake lollipops, cookies and cream popcorn, and a bracelet cuff with three huge rock candy "jewels." CuRious can throw a party for you during which you learn how to make the bracelets, as well as gummy worm bib necklaces, and more edgy and edible accessories. In fact, CuRious has everything you need to throw the coolest party ever: foil-fringed piñatas in electric colors, "grand surprise" cornucopias (the surprise ball concept, supersized), tubes of sparklers, graphic paper plates and napkins,

and more. A cotton candy machine in the store creates poufs of the confection in flavors of the week, spangled with edible glitter.

Little Marc Jacobs
298 West 4th Street, at Bank Street
(212) 206-6644
Subway: 1,2,3 to 14th Street; L to Eighth Avenue
www.marcjacobs.com
Daily noon–8pm

Marc Jacobs has established a small principality of shops in this idyllic part of the West Village. His children's line, in sizes 1 month to 14 years, is showcased in this sparkling corner boutique with a welcoming bench outside. You may find lighthearted hoodies and pea coats, striped rain boots with red laces, gingham backpacks, all with the Marc Jacobs quirkiness that infuses classic designs with joie de vivre. You'll also find toys and accessories, including tiny Moroccan ballet flats, encrusted with sequins, rhinestones, and embroidery ($15); a happy menagerie of plush animals; as well as key chains and soft rattles by the heritage German toymaker Steiff; Keith Haring wooden blocks; and vintage children's books. The full range of Marc Jacobs diaper bags are sold in the boutique; in case you think diaper bags are utilitarian millstones, think again ($298–$348).

NYC Firestore

17 Greenwich Avenue, between Christopher and West 10th Streets
(212) 226-3142; (800) 229-9258
Subway: N,R,W to 8th Street; A,C,E,B,D,F,M to West 4th Street;
1 to Christopher Street-Sheridan Square; 6 to Astor Place
www.nyfirestore.com
Monday–Thursday 11am–7pm; Friday, Saturday 11am–8pm;
Sunday noon–6pm

After 9/11, this neighborhood shop—then at another location, primarily providing items for a local firehouse—became a pilgrimage destination, with New Yorkers, out-of-towners, and tourists showing up to buy T-shirts and baseball caps with logos honoring the first responders. In the new location, this family-owned-and-operated shop has expanded its inventory and stocks everything to do with New York's Finest (NYPD) and New York's Bravest (NYFD). You'll find onesies, bibs, and T-shirts for infants and kids. In addition to classic navy tees with the police or fire department emblem are sweet little girls' tees in white with delicate navy or red ruffled edges.

Kids' firefighter and police uniforms and PJs are displayed along with toy ambulances, fire engines, squad cars, fire and police stations, walkie-talkies, teddy bears, and playing cards. For mom and dad: baseball caps, tees, hoodies, boxers, travel mugs, and more. NYPD and FDNY trademarks are licensed by the City of New York and proceeds from the sale of products bearing the logos benefit the city's police and firefighter foundations. In addition, since September 11, 2001, the store has donated more than $250,000 to charities benefiting NYC's Members-of-Service, most to the UFA Widows' and Children's Fund.

Yoya

636 Hudson Street, at Horatio Street
(646) 336-6844
Subway: 1,2,3 to 14th Street; L to 8th Avenue
www.yoyanyc.com
Monday–Friday 10am–6pm; Saturday 11am–7pm;
Sunday noon–5pm

Preschool It Girls: start building your wardrobe here. You'll find tiny crocheted bikinis in bright colors, peasant shirts, demure floral print thin-wale corduroy dresses; ballet flats, hand knits, neon-pink patent sandals. The vibe is a little Carnaby Street, a little South of France, a little Majorelle Gardens. Yoya's whimsical, design-forward jewelry for little girls will look great on moms, too. There are items for boys— fluorescent sneakers, hip T-shirts you won't find elsewhere—as well as high chairs and toys and quilts and accessories to decorate your hipster's crib. In fact, speaking of It Girls, Sienna Miller and Julianne Moore have been snapped toting Yoya shopping bags.

PLAY

EAT

SHOP

PLAY

Madison Square Park
Fifth Avenue and Broadway, at 23rd Street
Subway: 6,F,M,N,R to 23rd Street
madisonsquarepark.org

The site of the original Madison Square Garden, Madison Square Park offers many child-friendly amenities that make it a favorite among local families, including a well-maintained playground and open lawn, and kid-friendly concerts and festivals throughout the year. On a nice day, grab sandwiches from **Eisenberg's** (page 257), delicacies from **Eataly** (page 256), or burgers from the **Shake Shack** (page 260), and picnic in the park. Between 23rd and 24th Streets on the east side of the park, there is a public pay **toilet**. In May, and from mid-September to mid-October, two dozen curated **food vendors** set up in adjacent Worth Square; the outdoor tables provide front-row views of the iconic Flatiron Building. The N/R subway station art by Keith Goddard is an absolute delight: on the walls, mosaic "hats" of former celebrities associated with the neighborhood (P.T. Barnum, Isadora Duncan, Marie Curie, Winslow Homer, and others) are positioned, according to the documented height of the person; Col. Tom Thumb's hat is only a few feet from the ground.

The Museum of Mathematics

11 East 26th Street, between Fifth and Madison Avenues
(212) 542-0566
Subway: 6 to 23rd Street; F,M to 23rd Street; N,R to 23rd Street
momath.org
Daily 10am–5pm; first Wednesday of each month 10am–2:30pm
Adults $15; 3–12 $9; 2 and under free
Tickets are available at the museum (capacity permitting) or
in advance through the website.

MoMATH is set up less like a traditional museum and more as a
collection of interactive activities. Exhibits range from tricycles with
square wheels that somehow roll along a bumpy road, to a backlit
computer surface where the challenge is to arrange tiles of different
sizes in the smallest possible area. Though not everything here will
be a perfect fit for every child, there's plenty for any child interested
in math, puzzles, or games of logic. Thirty-four stations are spread
out in an open space on two floors. For a look at the different stations, see momath.org/about/exhibit-guide.

Union Square Greenmarket

Union Square, East 14th to East 17th Streets, Broadway to
Park Avenue South
(212) 788-7476
Subway: 4,5,6,N,Q,R to 14th Street-Union Square
grownyc.org
Monday, Wednesday, Friday, Saturday 8am–6pm

Through the years, Union Square has been a locus of radical politics—
the scene of demonstrations, rallies, marches—but, some would argue,

none as revolutionary as the establishment of the Greenmarket there in 1976. Suddenly, New Yorkers had fresh locally grown produce; small farmers were able to sell directly to the public; regional agriculture was revitalized; and chefs in checked trousers and toques lined up at the Greenmarket's stands to see what ingredients might be showcased on their daily menus. Greenmarket is now a huge citywide enterprise, with 54 markets supplied by 230 family farms and fishermen, but the crown jewel is Union Square on a Saturday, where the produce may even outshine the celebrities that wander through. If your stomach starts to growl, there are plenty of things to nosh as you walk: not only apples and pears, but cider donuts, pretzels, sweet and savory baked goods, fresh juice, and yogurt drinks. Assemble a picnic and sit down at the benches in the adjacent park. If the crowds are too much for the kids, one parent can take turns watching them in the Union Square playground while the other explores the market.

EAT

Beecher's Handmade Cheese

900 Broadway, between East 19th and 20th Streets
(212) 466-3340
Subway: 4,5,6,N,Q,R to 14th Street-Union Square
www.beechershandmadecheese.com
Café daily 11am–8pm; cheese counter 11am–9pm

Seattle's Beecher's Handmade Cheese has come to New York, and settled, appropriately for an artisanal enterprise, only a few blocks away from the Greenmarket. The two-story shop and café is a casual spot to grab a grilled cheese sandwich or mac and cheese. It's quick: order at the counter and carry your meal to a table in the small seating area upstairs or—even better with kids—plop down on one of the old-fashioned milk can stools along a small counter and, through the window, watch cheese being made in the huge kitchen. As you'd expect from cheese made by hand using traditional practices, no preservatives, enhancers, or coloring agents are added, and the milk used is from hormone-free local cows. Try to avoid peak lunchtime, though, when Beecher's can be absolutely packed. Downstairs in the cheese cave, the Cellar serves wine and spirits to accompany small plates. Beecher's contributes 1% of all sales to its Flagship Foundation's Pure Food Kids Workshop, which teaches kids to make smart, healthy eating choices.

Eataly

200 Fifth Avenue, at West 23rd Street

(212) 229-2560

Subway: 6, F,M N,R to 23rd Street

www.eataly.com

Monday–Sunday 10am–11pm

If you have any interest at all in food, chances are the impressive Italian food hall Eataly is on your Must See list; if you're taking children along, you should keep a few things in mind. This luxury megamarket and its restaurants can be as crowded as Times Square; so go when Eataly opens, when the fewest people are there. First, pick up a map—there are staffers handing them out—to help you navigate the floor plan. Identify the food stations you're interested in (including gelato, pastry, cheese, coffee), or which of the seven sit-down restaurants you may want to visit. Each of the restaurants has a different focus: fish, cheese, meat, vegetables, pizza, etc. No advance reservations are taken for the restaurants, so if it's mealtime, and you want to eat at one, find the central station and give the hostess your name when you arrive. If there's a wait, you can browse the store until you are seated. If your kids might be interested in watching fresh pasta or cheese being made, check out those areas. This is an astonishing place, with authentic products and an abundance, to say the least, of things to see and taste. There's a fantastic beer garden on the roof.

Eisenberg's Sandwich Shop

174 Fifth Avenue, between East 22nd and 23rd Streets
(212) 675-5096
Subway: N,R to 23rd Street; F,M to 23rd Street; 6 to 23rd Street
eisenbergsnyc.com
Monday–Friday 6:30am–8pm; Saturday 9am–6pm;
Sunday 9am–5pm

Since 1929, Eisenberg's Sandwich Shop has been serving top-notch
sandwiches, soups, and breakfast to generations of New Yorkers,
and from the look of things, not much has changed. It's an old-
school New York deli with Formica counters and stools. Eisenberg's:
Thank you for the reminder that bacon is a perfect complement for

egg or tuna salad on rye. Thank you for keeping egg creams and lime rickeys alive. Thank you for all of the many delicious bacon, egg, and cheese sandwiches you've made over the years (still $4), for serving breakfast all day, for the (not oversized) corned beef and pastrami sandwiches ($10), for roasting your own turkey and roast beef, and for making homemade matzoh ball soup ($4). And thank you for keeping your employees for so long.

Hill Country Chicken
1123 Broadway, at East 25th Street
(212) 257-6446
Subway: N,R to 23rd Street; 6 to 23rd Street; F,M to 23rd Street
www.hillcountrychicken.com
Monday–Friday 7:30am–10pm; Saturday, Sunday 9am–10pm

Finger-lickin' is required at this wide-open space with vintage diner décor. Chickens are meaty and juicy, fried "Classic, Southern Fried" or using "Mama Els' Recipe," a skinless version with a crunchy, cracker crust. On a recent Sunday afternoon, the cafeteria-style restaurant was crowded with families devouring chicken (breast $5.50, drumstick $2.25), Texas Tenders, sides (coleslaw, fried mashed potatoes, pimento mac and cheese, and "blistered" corn salad, $2.50–$6), as well as sandwiches, salads, shakes, and pie. The "Kid's Coop" meal includes two Texas Tenders, French fries, and a drink ($6.50). Beer and wine, Boylan's sodas, and fresh squeezed lemonade are available, too.

The restaurant is spacious, with plenty of seating, both upstairs where the food is served, and in Grandpa's Rec Room in the basement, where there's additional seating as well as board games, Lite Brite sets, and a foosball table for all to use.

L.A. Burdick Chocolate Shop and Café

5 East 20th Street between Fifth Avenue and Broadway
(212) 796-0143
Subway: 4,6 to 23rd Street; N,R to 23rd Street;
N,Q,R to 14th Street-Union Square
www.burdickchocolate.com
Monday–Saturday 8:30am–9pm; Sunday 10am–7pm

This small café and artisan chocolatier is storybook perfect. The chocolate mice bonbons, with their little silk tails, never fail to charm and delight. (There are penguin-, honey bee-, and bunny-shaped chocolates, too.) In addition to chocolates, beverages (coffees, lemonade, cider, and eggnog) are served, as well as chocolate

Courtesy L. A. Burdick Chocolate

drinks (iced or hot, the hot with kirsch, poire William, scotch, or rum options). The luscious array of pastries, the extensive tea menu, and chocolate tastings make this a perfect place for both children and adults to enjoy an afternoon treat.

Shake Shack

Southeast corner of Madison Square Park, near Madison Avenue and East 23rd Street
(212) 889-6600
Subway: N,R to 23rd Street; 6 to 23rd Street; F,M to 23rd Street
www.shakeshack.com
Daily 11am–11pm

This chain of New York burger shops owned by famous restaurateur Danny Meyer began in 2004 with this kiosk in Madison Square Park

and has expanded its location roster at a quick pace: uptown, downtown, D.C., South Beach, Dubai, London, Istanbul, and more. And here's the bottom line: Shake Shack makes people happy. Fresh ground "proprietary blended" beef burgers (about $4–$7); nitrate-, hormone-, and antibiotic-free beef and chicken hotdogs; crinkle cut fries; beer and wine for adults; and the incredible frozen custard shakes and the even thicker frozen custard in a bowl, laden with mix-ins, called "concretes." Vegetarians: try the delicious 'Shroom Burger, a deep-fried cheese-filled portobello mushroom on a bun.

Additional locations: 154 East 86th Street (Upper East Side); 366 Columbus Avenue (Upper West Side); Grand Central Terminal (Midtown); 215 Murray Street (Battery Park City); 691 Eighth Avenue (Midtown); 409 Fulton Street (Brooklyn); Citifield, during Mets baseball games (Queens)

SHOP

ABC Carpet and Home
888 Broadway, at East 19th Street
(212) 473-3000
Subway: 4,5,6,N,Q,R to 14th Street-Union Square
www.abchome.com
Monday–Wednesday, Friday, Saturday 10am–7pm;
Thursday 10am–8pm; Sunday 11am–6:30pm

This dazzling ten-story emporium of rugs, home furnishings, bed linens, and antiques has a babies and children's boutique tucked at the rear of the second floor. ABC's signature style—a unique mix of modern and farmhouse, vintage and fashion forward, simplicity and sophistication—is once again beautifully expressed in the exquisite children's clothing and accessories that leave the primary colors far, far behind. You'll find butterfly garlands and tutus; pajamas and pillows; sweaters and shoes—everything in infant through kids sizes. There's furniture, too, from cribs to pint-sized chairs (no, not little wooden chairs like you'd find in a preschool classroom, but mini Bertoia chairs, the transparent plastic Lou Lou chair by Kartell, as well as rustic willow rocking chairs). There are child-sized Moroccan poufs, silkscreened pillows, lanterns, and wall art. There's whimsy (simple felt booties, one embroidered with a horseshoe, the other with a grasshopper), romance (the palest gray dress with a bodice sprinkled with barely perceptible sparkles, an ethereal net skirt with a thin violet-colored sash), practicality (brightly striped yoga mats for kids), and indulgences (stuffed animals, including a life-sized fawn). A simple white cotton kurta embroidered with a brightly colored elephant hangs next to a toddler T-shirt printed with gold metallic ABCs. And, because this is ABC, the boutique stocks a wide array of sophisticated and whimsical crib linens, among them a soft cotton baby quilt embroidered with a poem.

Abracadabra NYC
19 West 21st Street, between Fifth and Sixth Avenues
(212) 627-5194
Subway: N,R to 23rd Street
www.abracadabrasuperstore.com
Monday–Saturday 11am–7pm; Sunday noon–5pm; extended hours near holidays

Be aware, since you have children in tow, that you'll see some ghoulish monster masks and paraphernalia here (Dracula, Headless Horseman,

Frankenstein, and the like), and maybe some racy outfits (Showgirl Marilyn, Red Sexy Girlfriend Robe, Playboy Mansion Mistress). In general, though, this mega emporium of costumes and accessories has many delights that will make your child's next Halloween an occasion to remember. Kids' costumes include the usual (firefighters, pirates) as well as less common: Marine Dress Blues, Class Nerd, deluxe Max (from *Where the Wild Things Are*). Come October, girls might want to consider the more traditional ladybug, cheerleader, or ragamuffin doll outfits, or break gender stereotypes as a Pink Ranger, Danielle Boone, Draculara, or Miss Vampire. The helpful, congenial staff reports that the most popular holidays for costumes are Halloween (natch), Easter, St. Patrick's Day, and Santacon, so expect a very busy and crowded store at those times.

Beads of Paradise

16 East 17th Street, between Fifth Avenue and Union Square West
(212) 620-0642
Subway: 4,5,6,N,Q,R,L to 14th Street-Union Square
beadsofparadisenyc.com
Monday–Saturday 11am–7:30pm; Sunday noon–6:30pm

Children love this shop, and it is indeed heaven for anyone who loves beads or beading. Professional jewelry makers shop here, as well as Etsy shop owners, and hobby crafters, but even if your talents are limited to sliding a bead on a cord you can still walk away with something exquisite. Beads are sold individually and by the strand and are sourced from around the world. They range from semi-precious to wooden, glass, metal, shell, and more; antique to contemporary; very reasonable to expensive. You'll find jewelry making supplies, too. If you're buying in bulk, ask for a discount. There

is a range of other treasures here, as well: jewelry, hand woven textiles, paintings, carvings, lacquer ware, and more.

Books of Wonder

18 West 18th Street, between Fifth and Sixth Avenues
(212) 989-3270
Subway: F,M to 14th Street; N,R to 23rd Street
www.booksofwonder.com
Monday–Saturday 11am–7pm; Sunday 11am–6pm

This bright and roomy independent children's bookstore stocks a wide and thoughtfully chosen inventory of classics and newly released children's books—board books, pop-up books, paperbacks, hardcovers, series, and countless treasures you'll never discover shopping online or in big chain stores. The young staff seems to have read everything in the store—you can just imagine them as

children, reading by flashlight with their head under the covers, long after bedtime. They are filled with suggestions, and ready to help match each customer with just the perfect read. There are banquettes where parents and kids can read together, and aisles wide enough for kids to plop right down on the floor.

Inside Books of Wonder is the Birdbath Neighborhood Green Bakery, serving organic, seasonal, local food—breakfast and lunch, desserts, and specialty drinks. Built from recycled, found, vintage, or sustainable materials, the bakery is wind-powered, food is delivered from the main kitchen by bicycle-powered rickshaws, and discounts are given to customers who arrive by bike or skateboard.

Courtesy Lucky Wang

Lucky Wang
82 Seventh Avenue, between East 15th and 16th Streets
(212) 229-2900
Subway: 1,2,3 to 14th Street; A,C,E to 14th Street
www.luckywang.com
Monday–Saturday 11am–7pm; Sunday noon–6pm

Everything in this little store is cute, but the cutest of all are the cotton kimono onesies for infants and the kimonos for little girls, in lighthearted prints, creatively packaged in sushi containers. For little boys, lightweight cotton short-sleeved collared shirts are cool in both senses of the word. A small cotton blanket with a detachable attached wooden ring is a practical and unusual item for a teething baby. Barrettes that look like puffy mini bow ties in miscellaneous prints are irresistible.

Additional locations: 799 Broadway (Washington Square); 1435 Lexington (Upper East Side)

Paragon Sports

867 Broadway, at East 18th Street
(800) 961-3030
Subway: L,N,Q,R,4,5,6 to 14th Street-Union Square;
F,M to 14th Street; 1 to 18th Street
www.paragonsports.com
Monday–Friday 10am–8:30pm; Saturday 10am–8pm;
Sunday 11am–7pm

If you or your kids participate in any sports—from archery, bocce ball, or darts to scuba diving, trekking, or hockey—you may want to stop in this megastore of top-notch merchandise for every athletic pursuit imaginable. With goods on three floors, Paragon has mid-range and upscale products in all categories, and an enhanced selection of seasonal items. Skateboards for 7-year-olds? Check. Tennis racquets for all ages? Of course! Size 1 soccer cleats? Yep. Swimsuits, skis and boots, snowshoes, snorkels, compasses, ping-pong balls? All of that and more.

The staff here knows their merchandise, and Paragon will beat competitors' prices, including those of internet shops, if you present the listing in print or on your device. At certain times during the year, especially around holidays, the store has sale prices that may even beat the competition's.

Space Kiddets

26 East 22nd Street, between Broadway and Park Avenue
(212) 420-9878
Subway: 4,6 to 23rd Street; N,R to 23rd Street;
4,5,6,N,Q,R to 14th Street-Union Square
www.spacekiddets.com
Monday, Tuesday, Friday, Saturday 10:30am–6pm;
Wednesday, Thursday 10:30am–7pm; Sunday 11am–5pm

There isn't one "look" represented at Space Kiddets: downtown moms and uptown moms, whose taste may be decidedly different, both find things here that make their hearts beat faster. Ditto West Siders and East Siders. The owner has a knack for finding irresistible items that travel the spectrum from edgy to classic for both girls and boys. Channeling Ziggy Stardust? There's a black playsuit with a rolled collar and three diagonal zippers. Going to luncheon at grandmother's? Consider the Liberty of London print pinafore. This is where to go to find something you won't find anywhere else: exclusive lines from Japanese designers that have a psychedelic, vintage feel, for example, or a tangerine coat with a Peter Pan collar that—if it weren't in a size four—looks like something Mrs. Don Draper would wear. There are patent leather Mary Janes with a bit of a Doc Marten vibe (in surprising green apple, burgundy, or orange patent) coexisting happily next to classic Greek sandals and ballet flats. A recent eye catcher was an A-line jumper solidly spangled in red sequins and scattered with gold snowflake sequins—maybe the ultimate dress for a holiday party. There are toys, too, that reflect the same inclusive aesthetic: some are wooden and traditional, some a little zanier (trick dudes action figures).

PLAY

EAT

SHOP

For the nearest recommended shops, see Washington Square & the West Village (page 243)

PLAY

The High Line

Gansevoort and Washington Streets to West 30th Street between Tenth and Eleventh Avenues. Access points are at both ends, as well as West 14th, 16th, 18th, 20th, 23rd, 26th, and 28th Streets. Elevators are at the Gansevoort, West 14th, 16th, 23rd, and 30th Street on/off points.

Subway: 1,2,3,A,C,E,L to stops between 14th Street and 34th Streets
7am–10pm Spring and Autumn; 7am–11pm Summer; 7am–7pm Winter.
www.thehighline.org

Since opening in 2009, the High Line has become one of New York's most beloved parks. Built upon an elevated rail viaduct not used for transport since 1980, it appeals simultaneously, but in different ways, to both adults and children. Adults will appreciate how the design integrates old track beds with planned-wild gardens and unique views of old and new New York. Kids will find an array of appealing features: the bleachers near the 16th Street entrance that, through a panoramic window, overlook Tenth Avenue and its seemingly endless stream of yellow cabs; the grassy 23rd Street Lawn and Seating Steps; and the food vendors, performers, and artists along the route. If you enter the park at the north or south end and walk the entire distance, the walk is about a half-mile long—the length of about twenty city blocks).

The third and final section of the High Line, scheduled to open in the autumn of 2014, runs between 30th and 34th Streets and Tenth and Twelfth Avenues.

Chelsea Piers

Pier 62
Hudson River Park, between West 17th and 23rd Streets
(212) 336-6500
Subway: 6, C,E, N,R to 23rd Street, then take the M23 bus west
across 23rd Street. It stops directly in front of Chelsea Piers.
www.chelseapiers.com
Check website for current hours for individual activities.

The spectacularly large 28-acre sports complex, built on four piers
on the Hudson River, was a game-changer for New Yorkers who are
chronically short on open space and athletic opportunities. While
visiting Manhattan, out-of-towners might not want to spend time
doing what they can do at home, but Chelsea Piers offers drop-in
activities that might appeal to families on a rainy day or when they
need a break from sightseeing.

Twin ice rinks that overlook the Hudson River are open year 'round
(two-hour general ice skating sessions, $10; skate rental, $5; helmet
rental, $4.25). The Field House, open seven days a week, has daily
drop-in soccer and basketball sessions, batting cages, and youth
rock climbing. Rock-N-Rolls is a 90-minute session, half the time
devoted to rock climbing, the other half to gymnastics (ages 5–16,
$30); Open Youth Rock Climbing sessions are open to ages 5–15
($30 for 50 minutes, preregistration required, (212) 336-6500). If
your young child is tired of being a tourist, try the Little Athletes
Exploration Center, an indoor play area for ages 6 months to 4 years
($12 per 2½- to 4-hour session, with adult caregiver). There are also
bowling lanes within the complex. Adults used to traditional golf
courses may marvel at the NYC version: a multi-tiered driving range

that extends into the Hudson River. Moms: let the others play, and book a spa treatment at the Paul Labrecque Salon and Spa (212) 988-7816.

Museum at the Fashion Institute of Technology

Seventh Avenue at West 27th Street
(212) 217-7999
Subway: A,C,E,F,M to 23rd Street; 1,N,R to 28th Street
www.fitnyc.edu
Tuesday–Friday noon–8pm; Saturday 10am–5pm;
closed Sunday, Monday
Free

Remember Isaac Mizrahi's mother, in *Unzipped*, recalling her son's interest in fashion at a very young age? If you have a precocious designer in your family, you may want to check out the exhibition schedule. If the show appeals to you, duck into the museum; it's free, it's small, and the shows provide an extraordinary glimpse of glamour and creativity, whether the subject is shoes or evening gowns. And make sure to notice what the students are wearing as they walk around the urban campus of this world-renowned school, portfolios tucked under their arms: it's a sneak peek of what's about to be *au courant*.

Rubin Museum of Art

150 West 17th Street at Seventh Avenue

(212) 620-5000

Subway: 2,3 to 14th Street; 4,5,6 to 14th Street; A,C,E to 14th Street;
N,Q,R to 14th Street; 1 to 18th Street

rmanyc.org

Monday, Thursday 11am–5pm; Wednesday 11am–7pm;
Friday 11am–10pm; Saturday, Sunday 11am–6pm; closed Tuesday

Adults $10; 13 and up $5; under 12 free; Friday 6pm–10pm free

Family workshops, ages 2–4 with adult, $10; movement workshops,
ages 3–5, $10; art workshops, ages 5 and up, $16; family days and
festivals, $10 per child, adults pay regular admission

Though the front desk loans "yak packs," with a few child-friendly
activities for kids to do as they walk through the galleries, this
serene museum isn't a natural for children—it's devoted to art of
the Himalayas, and is exceptionally quiet. But the hour-long drop-in
family workshops that combine free play, story time, a gallery visit,
or an arts and crafts project seem beautifully designed to engage
children and provide an entry point to the museum's collection;
recent projects have included creating a mask, a sand mandala, or a
royal costume. Movement workshops are also offered. Family days
and festivals (check website for dates) also provide a fun way for
kids to get to know the museum and its art.

The museum's café is roomy enough to accommodate families,
even strollers, and though the menu has lots of Indian accents
(lentils, cumin, dal, garam masala), there's also basmati rice and
steamed vegetables, and an apple crisp for a teatime snack (open
during museum hours, except Friday 4:30pm–6pm).

TADA! Youth Theater

15 West 28th Street, between Fifth Avenue and Broadway
(212) 252-1619
Subway: N,R to 28th Street
www.tadatheater.com
Daily 8am–8pm
Adults $20; 14 and under $8

At TADA! kids 8 to 18 star in original musicals performed for family audiences. Three productions are staged each year; the directors and choreographers are professionals and a live band provides the music. Shows have included *Sleepover, Everything About Camp (Almost), The Gumball Gang: Crime-Solving Kids, Princess Phooey,* and other kid-centric productions, each about one hour long. At the theater, Bench Seats provide front-row seating for kids 10 and under, with guardians seated directly behind or near their children (request in advance). TADA! also runs classes in musical drama and summer and vacation programs.

EAT

Brass Monkey

55 Little West 12th Street, between Tenth Avenue and
Washington Street
(212) 675-6686
Subway: 1,2,3 to 14th Street; A,C,E to 14th Street
brassmonkeynyc.com
Irish music session: Sunday, about 5pm

Once a week, this low-key bar (an anomaly in the trendy Meat-
packing District) hosts an Irish "session," an informal gathering of
musicians who come together for an unscripted few hours to play
traditional music. The musicians—usually five or six of them—take
their place not on a stage, but around a table. One of the most
charming aspects of these evenings is that children who come with
their parents have the run of the place, wandering over to watch the
musicians up close, dancing to the jigs and reels, perhaps wandering
back to their table to grab a French fry. The food is classic pub grub
with plenty of items that kids will like. There's a rooftop beer garden
and an extensive menu of international and craft beers. At about
8pm, the musicians move on to another venue across town.

Chelsea Market

75 Ninth Avenue, between West 15th and 16th Streets (additional
entrance on Tenth Avenue between West 15th and 16th Streets)
(212) 652-2110
Subway: A,C,E to 14th Street; L to 8th Avenue
www.chelseamarket.com
Monday–Saturday 7am–10pm; Sunday 8am–9pm

Chelsea Market is a block-long passageway lined principally with food vendors and some other shops. One thing's for sure: you will be in the company of many food-loving New Yorkers, including those who work for or appear on the Food Network, which has offices and studios in the building. If you're looking for provisions for a picnic on the nearby High Line (page 272), Chelsea Market is perfect. It may not be the best option if you're seeking a place to have a stress-free sit-down meal with children—many of the shops have no seating and there is very little communal seating in the common area.

If you have time and you aren't totally famished, first walk through to assess the choices, though if you first happen upon a place that will please everyone, and a nearby table, by all means snag it. The best food choices for the family are: LOS TACOS #1, perhaps the best value of all at Chelsea Market (tacos $2.50–$3.50); Bar Suzette Crêperie; and Dickson's Farmstand, an upscale butcher shop with sandwiches and house-made hot dogs ($5). There's also Friedman's Lunch, an upscale diner with an unprinted kids' grilled cheese sandwich special, served with fries; default cheese is gruyere, but they'll do cheddar if you ask ($5).

At The Lobster Place, whole lobsters are steamed to order priced per pound at market prices. A lobster roll is available a la carte or as part of a picnic box, which includes chips, soda, and a cookie. The menu is much longer, and includes oysters on the half shell.

Ronnybrook Dairy, run by a third-generation family organic dairy in the Hudson Valley, is a fun place to have a milkshake, ice cream, a healthy sandwich, or breakfast. There's a kids menu and counter seating.

If you want a gift or souvenir, stop in Eleni's New York, known for its impressive decorated cookies. The "New York, New York" cookie gift set features 11 hand-iced cookies, each in the shape of a different city icon (a Metrocard, the Empire State Building, a yellow taxi cab, etc.; $37.50); *Sex and the City* T-shirt cookies "say," "I'm a Carrie/Miranda/Charlotte/Samantha."

The Frying Pan
Pier 66, Hudson River Park at West 26th Street
(212) 989-6363
Subway: 1 to 23rd Street; C,E to 23rd Street
www.pier66maritime.com
Daily noon–midnight

This is no ordinary bar, but a retired lightship parked on a barge floating in the Hudson River. If you pick your time wisely, it can be lots of fun for a family meal. If you opt for dinner rather than lunch, go early; it can be swamped at Happy Hour, with a long line to get in and nowhere to sit when you finally do get on board. Tables on the top deck have arguably the most magnificent view in NYC, a panoramic sweep from the Verrazano-Narrows Bridge, New York Harbor, and the Statue of Liberty on the south, to the George Washington Bridge on the north, but with the breeze and the bobbing, there's not a bad seat in the house. And on the river itself, the kayaks, speedboats, sailboats, ferries, tugboats, and helicopters and planes overhead, make it a setting straight out of a Richard Scarry book. There is no table service; place your order at the bar (steamed mussels and littlenecks, crab cakes, burgers, wraps, salads, corn on the cob, Old Bay garlic fries, craft beers, and sangria) and take it back to your table. Grab a quick meal or a drink and glory in the surroundings.

More for kids: Next to *The Frying Pan* is the fireboat *John J. Harvey*, one of the most powerful fireboats ever in service. Built in 1931, she served the FDNY until her retirement in 1994. She was reactivated on September 11, 2001, and pumped water for 80 hours until water mains were restored. Bring a copy of *Fireboat, The Heroic Adventures of the John J. Harvey* by Maira Kalman with you so your kids can read the inspiring NYC story while looking at many of the buildings (Empire State Building), structures (George Washington Bridge), and scenes pictured in the story—not the least of which is the fireboat itself.

The Meatball Shop

200 Ninth Avenue, between West 22nd and 23rd Streets
(212) 257-4363
Subway: 1 to 23rd Street; C,E to 23rd Street
www.themeatballshop.com
Sunday–Thursday 11:30am–midnight; Friday–Saturday 11:30am–2am

This mini-chain has a flexible menu of various meatballs, sauces, sizes, breads, salads, and specials. First, choose the type of meatball (beef, spicy pork, chicken, vegetable). Next, the sauce (tomato, spicy meat sauce, mushroom gravy, Parmesan cheese, or pesto). Finally, a size (sliders to hero, $3–$10). The beer and wine prices are fair, and there's a kids menu. Kids love the ordering system—check off the items you want to order on a dry erase menu, then hand it to the server.

Additional locations: 63 Greenwich Avenue (West Village), 1462 Second Avenue (Upper East Side), 84 Stanton Street (Lower East Side)

Sullivan Street Bakery

236 Ninth Avenue, between West 24th and 25th Streets
(212) 929-5900
Subway: C,E to 23rd Street; 1 to 23rd Street
www.sullivanstreetbakery.com
Daily 7:30am–9pm

Inspired by a style of light pan pizza popular in Rome, the baker-owner has created a selection, sold by the square, with crispy bottoms and simple refined toppings, that is eaten at room temperature. An option for young eaters is the Pizza Pomodoro ($3), with a simple topping of tomato puree mixed with olive oil and salt. Pizzas change daily, but usually include potato made with olive oil, rosemary, and pepper; zucchini with gruyere and bread crumbs; and mushroom, with onions, thyme, and olive oil. In addition to pizza, Sullivan Street sells sandwiches made on its homemade bread. For something truly delectable and different, try a Canotto Salato, a brioche loaf split in half and baked with prosciutto and mascarpone. For dessert, be sure to pick up a *bomboloni* or three. These Italian-style doughnuts are filled with custard, jam, or chocolate ($3.50). The Chelsea location offers a wider selection that includes salads and breakfast items and has more seating (stools at the bar and eight small tables suitable for kids).

Additional location: 533 West 47th Street (Midtown)

SHOP

For the nearest recommended shops, see Washington Square & the West Village (page 243) or Union Square to Madison Square (page 262).

PLAY

EAT

SHOP

MIDTOWN

PLAY

Bryant Park

West 40th–42nd Streets from Fifth–Sixth Avenues
Subway: B,D,F,M to 42nd Street-Bryant Park; 7 to 5th Avenue
bryantpark.org

Bryant Park seems like a verdant magic carpet that has softly landed in Midtown. Surrounded by sparkling silver skyscrapers on three sides, and the New York Public Library on the fourth, it's an idyllic stop for children and parents. Benches and café chairs and tables provide one of the scarcest resources in New York City: a place to sit down. There's a "reading room" stocked with periodicals for adults and books for children, free board games on loan, and quoits (a tossing game similar to horseshoes). Chess and backgammon boards are available for a small fee. In the summer, a *pétanque* court is built where children can learn the classic French bowling game using child-sized *boules*. Or, check out balls and paddles for free and play a game of ping-pong. There's a picture-perfect carousel, designed with the Beaux Arts setting in mind ($2 per ride or $10 for 15 rides, year round except January, weather permitting) and a putting green with free equipment available for public use. An imaginative mix of activities is on offer throughout the year: 20-minute tours around the park for birdwatchers; performances by jugglers, artists-in-residence, a pianist; concerts, open-air movies, and more. Check the website for updated listings.

From the end of October to March, a 170' x 100' ice skating rink is built in the park, with free admission; rental skates are available

(page 34). From the end of October through New Year's, more than 100 boutiques are set up in the park, offering jewelry, decorative items, clothing, food, and other gifts for holiday shopping.

Beverages, sandwiches, soups, and snacks are available at the **'wichcraft** kiosks in the park. Adjoining the park, The Bryant Park Grill is a bit too fancy for kids, but the outdoor **Bryant Park Café** is more informal and is open from mid-April to November. Reservations aren't required: (212) 840-6500.

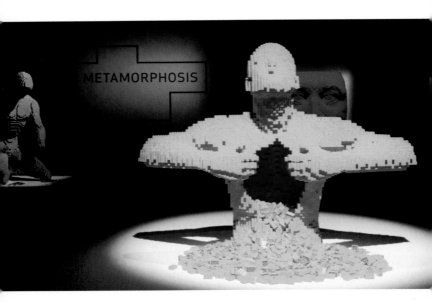

Discovery Times Square

226 West 44th Street, between Seventh and Eighth Avenues
(866) 987-9692
Subway: A,C,E to Port Authority-42nd Street; 1,2,3,7,N,R,S to
Times Square-42nd Street; B,D,M,F to 42nd Street-Bryant Park;
N,R to 49th Street
www.discoverytsx.com
Hours change seasonally; check website
Adults about $20–$27 for individual shows; 4–12 about $15–$20;
discounts available if you wish to see more than one show
Note: strollers, baby back carriers, and backpacks are not permitted
inside the galleries, but may be checked for free.

This venue hosts changing blockbuster exhibitions about "the greatest human stories ever told." Current and past exhibitions have included "Shipwreck!," "The Art of the Brick" (the LEGO extravaganza), "King Tut," "Harry Potter," "Pompeii," "The Dead Sea Scrolls," and "Leonardo DaVinci's Workshop." All are designed to have a wide appeal but not all are appropriate for children (in particular, "Body Worlds," which exhibits plastinated, skinless cadavers, both male and female; DTS's website suggests that parents view the materials on www.bodyworlds.com before deciding to attend with children). There's a DC Cupcake Café, an outpost of the famous Georgetown Cupcakes, in the building (11am–7pm).

Empire State Building Observation Decks

350 Fifth Avenue, between West 33th and 34th Streets

(212) 736-3100

Subway: B,D,F,M,N,Q,R to 34th Street-Herald Square;
6 to 33rd Street; 1,2,3,A,C,E to 34th Street-Penn Station

www.esbnyc.com

Daily 8am–2am

Main Observation Deck, 82nd floor: adults $27; 6–12 $21; under 6 free

Express tickets, which allow you to skip to the front of the elevator and security lines: 6 and older $50

Top Deck, 102nd floor, including Main Observation Deck: $44 for adults, ages 6–12 $38, under 6 free

Express tickets, both decks: 6 and older $67

The easiest and quickest way to buy tickets is through the website. (The site also contains a useful FAQs section.) Everyone must go through a security screening similar to those in airports. The lines for the elevators and security, which can be long, but move fast, may be avoided if you're willing to pay a premium and buy an Express ticket.

The ESB has two observation decks, one on the 82nd floor, and a smaller, enclosed Top Deck on the 102nd floor. If you buy a ticket in advance for the Main Observation Deck only, and, once you've arrived, decide you'd like to visit the Top Deck, you can buy the additional ticket there.

Once you make it up to one of the decks, the views make the lines and the crowds worth it. From each of the Main Deck's four sides are unobstructed views of the entire New York region. Be sure to

bring some quarters for the coin-operated binoculars (25 cents for 1–2 minutes of viewing time). While there are signs that offer basic information on the views ("Hudson River" and "Chrysler Building"), if you want more detailed information about the cityscape, opt for the self-guided audio tour (available on the second floor, $10). The best times to beat the crowds are in the morning between 8 and 9am, and in the evenings after 10pm.

Intrepid Sea, Air & Space Museum

Pier 86, West 46th Street & Twelfth Avenue

(212) 245-0072

Subway: A,C,E,to 42nd Street-Port Authority; N,R,S,1,2,3,7 train to
Times-Square-42nd Street, then walk or take the M-42 bus west to
the Hudson River (Twelfth Avenue) and walk north to the Intrepid
www.intrepidmuseum.org

Monday–Friday 10am–5pm; Saturday, Sunday, holidays 10am–6pm
General Admission (*Intrepid* only, including submarine *Growler*):
adults $24; 7–17 $19; 3–6 $12; under 3 free
Admission with Space Shuttle Pavilion: adults $31; 7–17 $24; 3–6 $17;
under 3 free
All Access Pass (access to the *Intrepid*, Space Shuttle Pavilion,
submarine *Growler*, any one simulator ride, and audio tour rental):
adults $42; 7–17 $35; 3–6 $28; under 3 free
Under the age of 16 must be accompanied by an adult.
Also see Operation Slumber (page 418)

Decommissioned in 1974, and opened to the public as a museum
in 1982, the aircraft carrier *Intrepid* is a National Historic Landmark
and a destination loaded with fantastic adventures for kids and
adults. Everything about the *Intrepid* is dramatic: the scale, the
history, the G-Force simulator ride, even the names of the aircraft:
Fury, *Saber*, *Avenger*, *Skyknight*. The descriptions of how things work
aboard are mind-boggling. A visit here is absorbing and thrilling,
all in a setting so vast that you don't feel rushed or crowded.

Be ready for a long stay; there is a lot to take in, and to see everything the *Intrepid* has to offer will take a few hours with a lot of
walking. (The *Intrepid* is only slightly smaller than the *Titanic,* and

the Chrysler Building laid on its side is about the same length.) A knowledgeable and friendly staffer every few steps or so will answer questions and help if you lose your bearings in the huge spaces.

Note: "photo op" stations throughout the *Intrepid* are staffed by a professional photographer—and you'll be given the chance to buy the photos when you leave the museum—but there's no pressure; when a visitor said, "we'll pass," the response was, "no problem at all." There are many places, too, to take your own photos in fun settings (upside-down in a space capsule, balancing on a rocking lifeboat, and more).

If you want a structured visit, the museum offers audio and guided tours on a variety of subjects and features within the *Intrepid*, which range in length from 45 to 90 minutes, and are recommended for ages 6-, 8-, and 10-and-up (adults $20; 3–7 $15). If you opt to go it alone, begin at the submarine *Growler* (to enter, you must be able to climb through an oval opening that reproduces many of similar size inside the sub, and the sub is not stroller or wheelchair accessible; those with claustrophobia issues are cautioned not to enter). Upon entering, a staffer tells a bit about life on board and the stress of a 3-month tour of duty. Visitors walk through a tunnel-like passage the length of the vessel, looking right and left into the tight sleeping, eating, service, and technical areas.

Emerging from the *Growler*, cross over the Hangar Deck and enter the interior exhibit hall, which is filled with aircraft, "rides," interactive exhibits, and videos that bring to life the history of the ship, from its service in World War II and Vietnam to its involvement in the Space Race. *Kamikaze: Day of Darkness, Day of Light* is a video that plays every 15 minutes. When the viewing starts, five screens lower from the ceiling and the story of two suicide planes striking the *Intrepid* in 1944 and 1945 begins. (A sign cautions that the footage may be too intense for small children.) The video is augmented by red flashing lights, loud audio, and a smoke feature. If you want to see it, get there a few minutes before the film starts; there's bench seating for about six people and everyone else has to stand or sit on the concrete floor.

Past more exhibits, visitors enter a zone called the Exploreum, a fun area filled with high-tech features (a 4D Motion Ride Theater [must be 38 inches tall to ride] and a G-Force Encounter [minimum 48 inches tall to ride] that simulates piloting a supersonic jet); some mid-tech features (climb into a reproduction space capsule, a cockpit, and aboard a lifeboat tossed by simulated waves); and some low-tech (put your hands in the space gloves worn by astronauts, and try to perform the tasks they did). Look for the astonishing 22-foot, 550-pound model of the *Intrepid* assembled by artist Ed Diment out of 250,000 LEGO® bricks.

The Flight Deck, packed with planes (including the F-14 Tomcat featured in *Top Gun*) and helicopters, is the level where aircraft were launched, using steam pipe catapults that operated much like slingshots. The mammoth aircraft elevator uses the same technology as the stage at Radio City Music Hall. Inside the Space Shuttle Pavilion is housed the *Enterprise*.

There's also a chance to go up in the bridge of the ship, but be wary: although there are elevators throughout the rest of the museum, the bridge is inaccessible to strollers and wheelchairs, and climbing the stairs to the bridge can be tricky for kids.

There's also a Flight Simulator on Pier 86 near the *Concorde* (must be 38 inches tall to ride); the *Concorde* was closed except for private tours as of this writing.

Each weekend, families are invited to drop by the Discovery Deck for arts, crafts, and experiments. Activities are free with museum admission.

Note: as of this writing, because of damage sustained during Hurricane Sandy, the only place to eat on the *Intrepid* was a small Au Bon Pain on the Third Deck.

MoMA, The Museum of Modern Art

11 West 53rd Street between Fifth and Sixth Avenues
(212) 708-9400
Subway: 1 to 50th Street; B,D,F,M to 47-50th Streets-Rockefeller Center; E to 5th Avenue-53rd Street
www.moma.org
Daily 10:30am–5:30pm; Friday 10:30am–8pm
Adults $25; 16 and under free; Friday 4pm–8pm free
Audio tours for kids and teens

Modern and contemporary art can be challenging for children (and parents), but MoMA offers an array of materials to help families enjoy their visit to this spectacular museum. Pick them up at the front desk and at the 2nd floor Education and Family Information desk near the escalators. You're set to go.

MoMA's manageable size and the number of masterpieces in close proximity to one another make a visit easy, but with a lot of impact. No walking great distances through centuries: go directly to the fifth-floor Painting and Sculpture Galleries I and you'll be rewarded with viewing what will be sure to interest and excite children: Van Gogh's *The Starry Night*, Monet's *Water Lilies*, Matisse's *Dance (I)*. Animal lovers will delight in Frida Kahlo's *Fulang-Chang and I* (the artist with her pet monkey) and the gentle lion in Rousseau's *The Sleeping Gypsy*. Alongside these paintings are countless others, all within a few galleries of each other, that children will remember throughout their lives.

Before or after visiting the galleries, stop by MoMA Art Lab (open mid-October through August), a hands-on space with art projects

and interactive activities. Themes change annually; consult MoMA.org/momaartlab for updated information. (To get to the MoMA Art Lab from the general galleries, walk past Café 2 on the second floor, then take the stairs down one flight to the first floor of The Lewis B. and Dorothy Cullman Education and Research Building.)

MoMA offers a number of excellent free programs for children ages 4 to 14. The programs not only suggest to youngsters different ways to appreciate art, but provide parents with strategic visiting tools that can be helpful when visiting any museum. Check the website for updated schedules.

Family Gallery Talks are held nearly every weekend during the fall and spring and include: Tours for Fours (for 4-year-olds and their adult(s); younger siblings permitted); A Closer Look for Kids (for 5- to 10-year-olds and their adult(s); and Tours for Tweens (for 11- to 14-year-olds and their adult(s). Tours for Fours and A Closer Look for Kids are available on a first-come, first-served basis; Tours for Tweens requires advanced registration through the website, MoMA.org/familyregistration.

MoMA's Family Art Workshops offer kids an opportunity to look at works of art, and then create their own in a studio within the museum; pre-registration through the website is required. MoMA also screens and conducts educator-led discussions about short films throughout the year. Admission to Family Films is free; tickets are first-come, first-serve. See www.moma.org/learn/kids_families/films for dates and details.

New Victory Theater
209 West 42nd Street between Seventh and Eighth Avenues
(646) 223-3010
Subway: 1,2,3,7,N,Q,R to Times Square;
B,D,F,M to 42nd Street-Bryant Park
newvictory.org
Balcony seats start at $14

This off-Broadway theater is the recipient of a special Drama Desk Award that recognized the high level of children's entertainment it provides. Maurice Sendak, Julie Taymor, and Tony Kushner have chosen the New Vic to present their works, as have the Guthrie Theatre, Steppenwolf Theatre Company, the Royal Opera House, and the

National Theatre of Scotland. Shows range from *Baby Rave* ("Bring your binky and your blankie and get ready to blast a move" while a DJ spins) to performances by Australia's contemporary circus company Casus, to Shakespeare plays. Last but not least, the theatre itself is a beauty; the oldest operating theatre in New York, it was built by Oscar Hammerstein.

New York Public Library Children's Center at 42nd Street

Fifth Avenue at West 42nd Street, Ground Floor, Room 84
(212) 621-0208
Subway: 1,2,3,N,Q,R to Times Square-42nd Street; 4,5,6 to Grand Central-42nd Street; A,C to 42nd Street-Port Authority; B,D,F,M to 42nd Street-Bryant Park; 7 to 5th Avenue
www.nypl.org
Monday, Thursday–Saturday 10am–6pm; Tuesday and Wednesday 10am–8pm; closed Sunday

The large children's circulating library on the lower level of the magnificent NYPL will be useful if you and your children need a place to sit down and regroup in Midtown. It's always filled with children and their adults happily making good use of the large collection of children's books on the shelves. The original Winnie-the-Pooh, as well as Eeyore, Piglet, Kanga, and Tigger are usually in residence here, in a glass case.

Check the NYPL website to see what exhibition is currently on view on the main floor. The recent "The ABC of It: Why Children's Books Matter" was a delight for adults and kids alike. One wall recreated the great green room of *Goodnight Moon*. Nearby, visitors peered through a cutout of Max framing a quote from *Where The Wild Things Are*.

If you're thirsty, there's a **small snack kiosk** on the main level. Next to it, don't miss the Readers and Writers Shop, one of the most interesting and best-curated museum stores in the city. Books, souvenirs, gifts, and reading-related items are all chosen for their quality, design, and humor. A NYPL lion tote bag for $1 is an easily transportable and useful souvenir.

If you're lucky, you'll visit the library on a day when the lions guarding the entrance, the much-loved Patience and Fortitude, are dressed up. If there's a subway series underway, one will be sporting a Mets baseball cap, the other a Yankees hat. At holiday time, they'll be wearing festive wreath necklaces; at other times of the year, you may catch them wearing top hats or graduation caps.

Radio City Music Hall Stage Door Tour

1260 Sixth Avenue, at West 50th Street
(212) 247-4777, (800) 745-3000
Subway: 1 to 50th Street; B,D,F,M to 47th-50th Streets–Rockefeller Center; N,Q,R to 49th Street
www.radiocity.com/tours/stage-door-tour.html
Daily 11am–3pm
Adults $19.95; 12 and under $15 (tickets are sold at the Radio City Sweets & Gifts Shop on Sixth Avenue between East 50th and 51st Streets). The Radio City combo package includes admission to three Rockefeller Plaza attractions: the Radio City Music Hall Stage Door Tour, the NBC Studio Tour, and the Top of the Rock observation deck (page 307); tickets are valid for 30 days.

New York City school children often take this tour, which seems surprising: how many kids are interested in Art Deco architecture? But, once there, it's hard not to be impressed—even if you're 8 years old—by the stunning interiors of this landmarked national treasure. Radio City was built to be thrilling, and it is. Standing on stage is exciting; walking around backstage feels very insider-ish. The facts alone grab the attention of young and old: the stage curtain weighs 6,000 pounds, for starters. The guide points out a corner backstage where a woodworking shop is set up for the moment; when the Christmas Spectacular is running, however, the area is turned into stables for the mules and sheep that star in the show. Camels have a separate "dressing room" and reindeer reside in their own climate-controlled lodgings. (Every morning during that season, the guide explains, many New Yorkers on their way to work are startled to see the animals getting a bit of fresh air and exercise outside on the street.) It's fun to peek into the costume room (and physical therapy room—being a Rockette is in many ways like being a professional athlete) and then to wind up the hour with a video and a Q&A with a Rockette. Everyone on the tour is photographed with her and there's a chance to buy the photo at the exit but, graciously, there's no pressure to buy. There are lots of stairs to climb as you visit the various areas of the building, but if you, your young child, or a stroller, can't manage them, elevators are easily called.

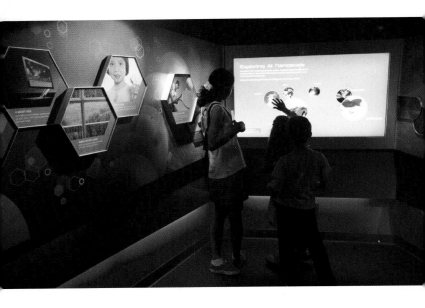

Sony Wonder Technology Lab

550 Madison Avenue, enter on East 56th Street

(212) 833-8100

Subway: F to 57th Street; E,M to 5th Avenue-53rd Street; N,Q,R to 5th Avenue-59th Street; 4,5,6 to 59th Street; B,D,E to 7th Avenue

www.sonywondertechlab.com

Tuesday–Saturday 9:30am–5:30pm

Admission is free but reservations are strongly recommended.

This mecca of hands-on tech-heavy activities on four floors is more than a backup plan for a rainy day. Rather, it's downright fun! Your visit begins with the creation of personalized "FeliCa" cards, which

will link you child's name and photo to the exhibits in which he/she participates. The card operates on a Radio Frequency Identification Device (RFID) system; its purpose is to personalize the experience of visitors. When it's time to go, a final swipe of the card will generate a printout to remind you of everything your child has done at the Lab.

A child could easily spend 90 fun-packed minutes, or longer, here. Activities include a movie trailer editing station; a live HD television production studio where kids and parents can assume various roles associated with television production (options include director, cameraman, reporter, field producer, and technical director);

creating an HD broadcast of a weather news report taping; and the rather challenging Virtual Surgery station, where haptic technology allows a user to "feel" the sensations a surgeon would experience while performing open heart surgery.

The Morgan Library & Museum

225 Madison Avenue, at East 36th Street
(212) 685-0008
Subway: 4,5,6, S to Grand Central-42nd Street
www.themorgan.org
Tuesday–Thursday 10:30am–5pm; Friday 10:30am–9pm;
Saturday 10am–6pm; Sunday 11am–6pm
Adults $18; 13–16 $12; 12 and under free;
Fridays 7pm–9pm free

This tranquil and beautiful museum houses Old Master drawings, medieval and renaissance manuscripts, and books and manuscripts important to the history of printing—not necessarily collections of interest to children, unless the Beatrix Potter manuscript letters from the permanent collection, with her drawings of Peter Rabbit et al, are on exhibit. (Check the website; the Morgan has mounted occasional shows related to children's books, Babar for example.) Sunday Storytime in Mr. Morgan's Library, though, is a sweet intro-duction to the Potter characters; the one-hour drop-in program is free with museum admission, and is held every Sunday at 11:30am and 2:30pm. Check the website for current family programs.

But because it's just a short walk away from the Empire State Building, the museum's gorgeous cafe is a real find for families. Large and airy, it's beautifully located in a soaring glass-enclosed court, and is elegant yet casual. Among menu items are burgers ($15.50); a soup, sandwich, and garden greens lunch ($16); deviled eggs ($7.50); and desserts. (Tuesday–Thursday 11 am–3pm, Friday 11am–8pm, Saturday–Sunday 11am–4pm)

The museum shop stocks books, games, puzzles, Peter Rabbit toys, posters from the Morgan's 2008 exhibition of Babar drawings ($20), and Beatrix Potter Tea sets ($100).

Top of the Rock

30 Rockefeller Plaza (entrance on 50th Street between Fifth and Sixth Avenues)
(212) 698-2000
Subway: 1 to 50th Street; B,D,F,M to 47th-50th Streets-Rockefeller Center; N,Q,R to 49th Street
www.topoftherocknyc.com
Daily 8am–midnight (last elevator up at 11pm); check website for extended holiday hours
Adults $27; 6–12 $17; for other packages see website

If you're trying to decide whether to visit Top of the Rock or the Empire State Building, take this into consideration: Top of the Rock offers a breathtaking view that the Empire State Building does not—the Empire State Building itself. In addition, the wider observation deck at Top of the Rock provides a more enjoyable overall experience. Rather than competing for space on the much narrower Empire State Building walkway (or paying an additional fee to access the less-crowded upper deck), Top of the Rockers may wander mostly unimpeded among viewpoints.

Purchase tickets in advance; time slots can quickly fill up. You then are assigned a 15-minute window for deck access. Daytime visits offer clearer views, but watching the city light up at night is an experience like no other. If possible, try to make it up for the sunset and take in both. For those interested, the Top of the Rock mobile app, available on Android and Apple platforms, offers a "Virtual Viewfinder" and audio tour that will help you identify and learn about iconic NYC landmarks.

The fun starts at the mezzanine level, where en route to the elevator you'll walk through a collection of photographs, artifacts, and short film screenings that provide a fascinating crash course on the history of Top of the Rock and Rockefeller Center. The entertainment continues in the Sky Shuttle to the top. In what feels like a Willy Wonka-inspired high-speed glass elevator, complete with a neon-lit elevator shaft, video sequences of important moments in Rockefeller Center history are projected on the ceiling. Once at the top, you'll find a dazzling panoramic view of the city. Don't be so distracted by the views on the first floor of the observation deck that you miss the easily overlooked signs guiding you to the deck's upper level (no additional cost). Here you'll find a 360-degree view of the city—the lower level doesn't have a view West—that has the added bonus of being less crowded than downstairs.

Before arriving, make sure to prepare for the elements. Dress appropriately during the fall and winter (it's windy up there!) and pack sunscreen as necessary. Don't arrive hungry or thirsty—there are no concessions at the Top, although there is a restroom.

If you're hungry and want a quick snack, duck into Thomas Keller's Bouchon Bakery at 1 Rockefeller Plaza. In warm weather, outdoor tables provide front-row seating on thrilling, busy Rockefeller Plaza; inside, counters with bar-height chairs line the windows. The baked goods are delectable, as are the salads, quiches, and sandwiches on excellent bread (Monday–Saturday 7am–8pm, Sunday 8am–7pm).

United Nations Children's Tour

First Avenue, at East 47th Street
(212) 963-8687
Subway: 4,5,6,7,S to Grand Central-42nd Street;
E,M to Lexington Avenue-53rd Street
www.un.org/wcm/content/site/visitors/home/to_see_and_do/
guided/children
Thursdays at 4:15pm; arrive by 3:45pm
Advance ticket purchase required, see website. Adults $16; ages 5–12 $9; students 13 and up with ID $11; children under 5 not permitted on tour

Once a week, the United Nations offers a tour that is especially geared toward children, with an emphasis on the organization's efforts to help children in countries around the world. Lasting just about an hour, the tour takes the group to several different sections of the UN and involves a fair amount of walking. Stops include the Security Council and the General Assembly, which may be in session. Kids will be interested in the translating devices. Topics discussed are disarmament, land mines, poverty, world health issues, the Arms Trade Treaty, and other subjects related to international politics and peace. The tour ends at the gift shop, which sells postcards, UN branded items, magnets, snow globes, flags from nations around the world, teddy bears, and more. Note: the Visitor's Center is scheduled to relocate in 2015.

EAT

Becco

355 West 46th Street, between Eighth and Ninth Avenues

(212) 397-7597

Subway: 1,2,3,N,Q,R to Times Square-42nd Street;

A,C,E to 42nd Street-Port Authority

becco-nyc.com

Lunch: Monday, Tuesday, Thursday, Friday, Sunday noon–3pm;

Wednesday, Saturday 11:30am–2:30pm

Dinner: Monday 5pm–10pm; Tuesday, Thursday 4:30pm–midnight;

Friday 5pm–midnight; Sunday 3pm–10pm

Reservations are recommended to avoid a wait, especially for

pre-theater meals on Wednesday and Saturday.

An all-you-can-eat pasta option conjures up images of warmed-up school cafeteria food, but Becco delivers the quality one would expect from a Lidia and Joe Bastianich restaurant. In addition to the unlimited trio of pastas—at $23, the most popular entrée on the menu—are appetizers that include house-made mozzarella, steamed mussels, and, if you want to pass on pasta, grilled and roasted fish, chicken, and meat. The kids' all-you-can-eat pasta option is $12 (butter and cheese or tomato are the only sauce choices). The $25 wine list is a brilliant idea for New York City, where restaurant wine lists usually have a hefty markup.

Café Un Deux Trois

123 W. 44th Street, between Sixth Avenue and Broadway
(212) 354-4148
Subway: B,D,F,M to Bryant Park-42nd Street;
1,2,3,N,Q,R to Times Square-42nd Street
www.cafeundeuxtrois.com
Daily 7am–midnight

The sparkling, cavernous, and bustling 1-2-3 is modeled on a French brasserie with menus written on mirrors, sparkling chandeliers, and dark wood. It's a festive place to have a pre-theater brunch, lunch, or dinner. In business since 1977, over the years it has changed little, in a good way: steak frites; French onion soup, chocolate mousse, and all the classics remain on the menu, solidly executed. Savory and dessert crepes and small plates are recent additions, so it's possible to have a reasonably priced dinner here. Many of the items on the regular menu will appeal to kids, and there is a children's menu, too, with customary choices as well as a Hot Dog Française (two hot dogs topped with Swiss cheese on baguette served with French fries, $13); vanilla ice cream with Un Deux Trois's chocolate sauce is included. For adults, a prix fixe dinner, available from 3pm to midnight, has a choice of appetizer, entrée, and dessert (paté de campagne, chicken cordon bleu, and chocolate mousse is a substantial meal for $29.50, and a bargain for the Times Square neighborhood). A bottle of the house Chardonnay is $37. At Christmas time, the staff has been known to engage diners in an impromptu sing-along of The Twelve Days of Christmas; it's a lot of fun.

El Centro

824 Ninth Avenue, between West 54th and 55th Streets
(646) 763-6585
Subway: A,C,E to 50th Street; 1,2,A,C,B,D to 59th Street-Columbus
Circle; N,Q,R to 57th Street-7th Avenue
www.elcentro-nyc.com
Monday–Wednesday 11:30am–11pm; Thursday 11:30am–midnight;
Friday 11:30am–1am; Saturday 11am–1am; Sunday 11am–11pm

We tend to think of Hell's Kitchen as being a hike from most tourist
attractions, but El Centro is just a couple of blocks away from the
southwest corner of Central Park. This is a fun place to end up for

dinner, starting with pomegranate margaritas or other South of the Border–inspired cocktails for the grown-ups, while everyone munches on chips and salsa or the addictive fried plantains. Diners can stay in their comfort zone with all the traditional choices, or get a little adventurous and follow the lead of the chef, who grew up on a farm in Mexico and who uses his family recipes as the basis of an updated cuisine: Sea Scallop Ceviche with Avocado and Radish Salsa on a Guajillo Tostada, Long Island Duck Breast with Sautéed Arugula and Pineapple Mole, Charred Sirloin with Sweet Potato Fries and Endive-Pasilla Sauce. There's no kids menu, but it's not needed with food this appealing and affordable. The decor is as cheerful as the flavors and prices: banquettes covered with fruit-patterned oilcloth, a chandelier made of Corona bottles, and a wall on which dozens of brightly colored tin ornaments are displayed.

IchiUmi Japanese Restaurant

6 East 32nd Street, between Fifth and Madison Avenues
(212) 725-1333
Subway: 6 to 33rd Street; B,D,F,M to 34th Street-Herald Square
www.ichiumi.com
Daily 11:45am–3pm and 5:30pm–10pm
Monday–Thursday, lunch $18.95, dinner $31.95; Friday, Sunday, and holidays lunch $24.95, dinner $34.95
Children are charged by how tall they are: 4'6" and under half-price; 3'6" and under lunch $7.95, dinner $12.95. Children under 2'6" are not allowed to serve themselves from the buffet.

This huge buffet displays a glistening assortment of impeccably fresh, beautifully made sushi, more than a dozen types each of gunkan, nigiri, and maki. There are hot entrées, too: fish, vegetable, chicken, pork, beef, and tofu yakitori, as well as a huge assortment of traditional Asian dishes such as crab soup, fried oysters, chicken teriyaki, black sea bass, fried rice, tofu, and much more—truly something for everyone. IchiUmi avoids the downside of most all-you-can-eat buffets—reheated food of so-so quality prepared earlier in the day—by having a dozen or more chefs constantly preparing dishes on the spot in the immaculate open kitchen. The stylish Asian-modern dining room is large, roomy, and welcoming to children.

Junior's Most Fabulous Cheesecake and Desserts

West 45th Street between Broadway and Eighth Avenue
(212) 302-2000
Subway: A,C,E to 42nd Street-Port Authority; 1,2,3,7,S to Times Square-42nd Street; B,D,F,M to 47th-50th Streets-Rockefeller Center
www.juniorscheesecake.com
Monday–Thursday 6:30am–midnight; Friday, Saturday 6:30am–1am; Sunday 6:30am–11pm

Smack in the middle of the Theater District and across the street from the popular Marriott Marquis hotel is this large and friendly branch of an old school Brooklyn diner famous for its cheesecake. While the atmosphere here is reminiscent of American chain-type restaurants, Junior's really is a New York classic.

Though cheesecake is its claim to fame, the food menu provides an easy family meal. Sandwiches range from $12.50 for pastrami, brisket, or turkey, to $14.50 for a Reuben, to $21.95 for a lobster roll on challah. Soups, salads, potato pancakes, and a number of different entrées make Junior's a definite crowd-pleaser, especially as a convenient pre-theater dinner option. There is a kids menu ($7.95).

Courtesy Laurent Tourondel

LT Bar & Grill
8 West 40th Street, between Fifth and Sixth Avenues
(212) 582-8200
Subway: B,D,F,M to 42nd Street-Bryant Park;
1,2,3,N,Q,R,S to Times Square-42nd Street; 7 to 5th Avenue
www.ltburger.com
Monday–Saturday 11:30am–10pm; closed Sunday

If you're at the Empire State building, Top of the Rock, Bryant Park, or nearby, do not miss Chef Laurent Tourondel's brilliant burger joint. You'll find American classics such as the LT Backyard Burger ($12) with grilled hickory-smoked bacon, American cheese, and LT sauce, a Kobe Hot Dog, Apple Smoked BBQ Baby Back Ribs, Kickass Wings! (12 pieces, $15), and a variety of salads. Sides include Smoked Gouda Curly Cheese Fries ($4.50) and Kosher Fried Dill Pickles served with smoked buttermilk-ranch dressing. Vegetarians can feast on the Green Curried Lentil Soup, Roasted Tomato Soup, 12 Veg Salad, and the Veggie Burger. Twelve milkshakes include macaron with almond gelato and marzipan, American Puff with vanilla ice cream, and Cocoa Puffs® and Reese's® Peanut Butter Cup (about $8), as well as a selection of spiked "Rated R" shakes and floats ($11). More than a dozen beers are on tap. There's a long bar along one side of the restaurant, half-circle leather banquettes around tables opposite, some smaller tables in the back, and more upstairs.

Margon Restaurant

136 West 46th Street, between Sixth and Seventh Avenues
(212) 354-5013
Subway: B,D,F,M to 47th-50th Streets-Rockefeller Center;
N,Q,R to 49th Street; 1,2,3,7,S to Times Square-42nd Street
margonnyc.com
Monday–Friday 6am–5pm, Saturday 7am–3pm

Only half a block away from the crowds and national-chain-restaurant vibe of Times Square is Margon, a family-run and mucho friendly Cuban/Dominican restaurant with a small menu of great

sandwiches and plenty of daily specials. The prices are as low as can be, but the quality of the food is home-style good.

The palomilla steak sandwich is a marinated and grilled thinly cut steak dressed with onions, lettuce, tomato, and American cheese on a Cuban-style roll, heated on a sandwich press ($7.50). The pressed Cuban sandwich has roast pork, Swiss cheese, salami, pickles, lemon-garlic olive oil, mustard, mayonnaise, and a dash of hot sauce ($7). Both are delicious, as are the shrimp ceviche and octopus salad.

Kids will gravitate toward straight-up black beans and rice ($4 for a small, $6 for regular size), a ham & cheese sandwich ($4.25), and the tropical shakes ($4). If anyone in your group is not sure what they want, the friendly staff (most of whom are family) offers tastes of just about anything.

Melt Shop

601 Lexington Avenue, at East 53rd Street

(212) 759-6358

Subway: 6 to 51st Street; E,M to Lexington Avenue-53rd Street

meltshopnyc.com

Monday–Friday 8am–9pm; Saturday, Sunday 11:30am–8pm

Melt Shop is a quick and inexpensive place to grab breakfast, lunch, dinner, or a snack (and more about the food below), but the real story here is the larger setting. With or without children, whether you're a New Yorker or visitor, the Citicorp atrium is an address to remember. It's a food court, but a high-quality one, a couple of blocks from MoMA and other Midtown attractions. Equally important, there's lots of indoor and outdoor seating, invaluable when you need a place to sit down and warm up or cool down, and refuel without spending a fortune.

Melt Shop is at the northeast corner of Lexington and 53rd down the stairs in the outdoor plaza. A testimony to its appeal is that on a day when the mercury was closing in on 100 degrees, there was a long (but fast-moving) line. Think a grilled cheese sandwich can't be improved upon? Check out the Three Cheese, the Dirty (with jalapeños), and the Buffalo Blue (chicken tenders, pepper jack, crumbled blue cheese, and homemade Buffalo sauce). There's a Truffle Melt, another version with pulled pork, and many many more (all around $8). Not in the mood for grilled cheese? Opt for homemade tomato soup, or several versions of tater tots, "hand spun" milkshakes, floats, and homemade ice cream sandwiches.

Additional locations: 135 West 50th Street (Midtown); 55 West 26th Street (Chelsea)

Pio Pio

604 Tenth Avenue, between West 42nd and 43rd Streets
(212) 459-2929
Subway: A,C,E to 42nd Street-Port Authority
www.piopio.com
Sunday–Thursday 11am–11pm; Friday, Saturday 11am–midnight

What began as a humble little Peruvian chicken restaurant far out in Queens has grown over the years into a chain of eight restaurants in New York City, each with the same basic menu but with variations in decor and atmosphere. The growth has been due, in no small part, to the inexpensive prices, delicious chicken, homemade green hot sauce, and the welcoming atmosphere.

The chicken is marinated in cumin and other spices; it's spicy but not fiery ($16 for a whole chicken, half- and quarter-chicken also available). Kids love the salchipapa, a sliced hot dog atop crisp French fries ($5). Adults: dip the fries (or anything) into the addictive green sauce. Vegetarian options include two kinds of plantains (maduros and tostones, $4), a refreshing salad with avocado ($8), and rice and beans.

Additional locations: 702 Amsterdam Avenue (Upper West Side); 210 East 34th Street (Midtown); 1746 First Avenue (Upper East Side)

Sarabeth's at Lord & Taylor

Lord & Taylor
424 Fifth Avenue, at West 39th Street
Subway: 1,2,3,N,Q,R to Times Square-42nd Street; 4,5,6 to
Grand Central-42nd Street; B,D,F,M to 42nd Street-Bryant Park
www.sarabeth.com/Menu—Restaurant-at-Lord-Taylor_ep_63.html
Fifth floor restaurant
(212) 827-5068
Sixth floor café
(212) 391-3015

Sarabeth's has both a restaurant and a café within Lord & Taylor.
The fifth floor restaurant has table service and offers breakfast all
day; sandwiches, and salads, warm plates (all about $15), desserts,
wine. The sixth floor café is self-serve, offering beverages, baked
goods, sandwiches and salads (around $9). (For a full description
of Sarabeth's, see page 93.)

Stella 34 Trattoria

in Macy's Herald Square
151 West 34th Street, Sixth floor (express elevator from the Broadway
and 35th Street entrance)
(212) 967-9251
Subway: 1,2,3 to 34th Street-Penn Station;
B,D,F,M to 34th Street-Herald Square
www.Stella34.com
Daily 11:30am–4pm; Monday–Saturday 4pm-9:30pm;
Sunday 4pm–9pm

Diners with the highest standards will be thrilled by this superb restaurant in, of all the unlikely places, Macy's. You'll find sublime food in a sophisticated setting where children are easily accommodated. The cityscape out the window is pure *Kavalier and Clay*: faded advertising signs from an earlier era painted on the sides of buildings, rooftop wooden water towers, beautiful architecture, clouds floating by as dusk falls and the Empire State Building begins to glow; yes, you have a front-row seat on the New York icon. Running along the other side of the dining room is an impressive 240-foot marble bar. The food is Neapolitan; pizza is made in three wood-burning ovens. The seasonal Frutta di Stagione pizza is topped with thinly sliced, just-slightly-pickled local plums, arugula, gorgonzola dolce, and

Parmigiano-Reggiano, with a few drops of vincotto ($18). The far-rotto (favas, asparagus, and English peas from the greenmarket, with farro, pecorino, and mint, $9) is a vegetarian starter that delighted the entire table, as did the crispy white baitfish served with lemon-garlic aioli ($7). A seasonal pasta, ricotta gnudi made with New Jersey sweet corn, peeky toe crab, chives, Calabrian chili, and breadcrumbs ($24) rivaled the roast suckling pig porchetta, served with bitter greens, peach chutney, gorgonzola dolce, candied almonds, and a bacon-sherry vinaigrette, as a favorite entrée. The excellent all-Italian wine list and the gelato made here, in the first outpost of the Florentine gelateria Vivoli, complete the perfection.

As befitting Macy's, the setting for *Miracle on 34th Street*, Stella 34 is open for **Santa Claus breakfasts** in the weeks between Thanksgiving and Christmas. An Italian breakfast feast is served (along with complimentary bellinis for adults), as kids have their photos taken with Santa and the elves make an appearance. (Ages 3–5 $35; adults $50). The restaurant group also hosts a Breakfast with Santa at Rock Center Cafe (212) 332-7620 and the Sea Grill (212) 332-7610), which includes skating time on The Rink at Rockefeller Center.

Uncle Nick's Greek Restaurant

747 Ninth Avenue, between West 50th and 51st Streets
(212) 245-7992
Subway: 1 to 50th Street; C,E to 50th Street
www.unclenicksgreekcuisine.com
Daily 11:30am–11pm

If you need a restaurant in the Times Square area, you'll find many independently owned family-friendly restaurants that are popular with New Yorkers only a few blocks away in Hell's Kitchen (Ninth Avenue between 34th and 57th Streets). One place that's been there for years is Uncle Nick's, a Greek restaurant serving both diner–style Greek food (souvlaki, kebabs, dips, and pita) and an array of grilled or fried seafood items, including red snapper, octopus, and skewered shrimp. Uncle Nick's prepares most of its fish simply, with only lemon and olive oil, in order to let the freshness shine through. Try the saganaki, a flaming cheese appetizer that is sure to wow the kids, and split a horiatiki (Greek country salad). Standout dips include tzatziki (yogurt, cucumber, and garlic, $7) and scordalia (potato and garlic, $7).

Additional location: 382 Eighth Avenue (Chelsea)

Virgil's Real Barbecue
152 West 44th Street, between Sixth and Seventh Avenues
(212) 921-9494
Subway: 1,2,3,N,Q,R,S to Times Square-42nd Street;
B,D,F,M to 42nd Street-Bryant Park
www.virgilsbbq.com
Monday 11:30am–11pm; Tuesday–Friday 11:30am–midnight;
Saturday 11am–midnight; Sunday 11am–11pm

This is an American barbecue joint that borrows from traditions from the Carolinas to Texas, with Caribbean and Cajun accents. Add roadhouse decor and big screens, and you've got a fun place with a staff used to getting people out the door in time for a Broadway play. Start with Trainwreck fries or BBQ wings, move on to platters with two sides, including collards, biscuits, rice, and pickled beets. There are salads, sandwiches (melts, clubs, and po'boys), fresh squeezed lemonade, and a full bar. In short, something for everyone.

SHOP

American Girl Place

609 Fifth Avenue, at East 49th Street
(877) 247-5223
Subway: B,D,F,M to 47th-50th Streets-Rockefeller Center;
4,5,6 to 59th Street; E,M to 5th Avenue-53rd Street; 6 to 51st Street
www.americangirl.com
Monday–Thursday 10am–7pm; Friday 10am–9pm;
Saturday 9am–9pm; Sunday 9am–7pm

Besides presenting plenty of opportunities to buy dolls, and outfits and accessories for them, American Girl Place also offers a number of other activities. On the second floor in the Creativi-Tees area, shoppers can accessorize their dolls, and themselves, with matching outfits (T-shirts are $10 for dolls, $24 for children). In the Doll Hair Salon, girls can schedule a "stylist" appointment for some serious doll pampering, including hair braids, ear piercing, and nail decals ($10–$25).

On the third floor, girls can pose with their dolls for a magazine cover photo shoot ($24.95 for an 8x10 in a frame), visit the souvenir shop, or stop in with their dolls (doll booster seats provided) at the American Girl Cafe for brunch, lunch, afternoon tea, or dinner. Cafe seating is only at certain times and reservations are strongly suggested (reserve via website, telephone, or with concierge at store entrance; price ranges from $20–$26 per person, plus tax and gratuity).

Books Kinokuniya

1073 Sixth Avenue, between West 40th and 41st Streets
(212) 869-1700
Subway: B,D,F,M to 42nd Street-Bryant Park; N,Q,R to
34th Street-Herald Square; 4,5,6 to Grand Central-42nd Street
www.kinokuniya.com
Monday–Saturday 10am–8pm; Sunday 11am–7:30pm

This is a large and impressive Japanese bookstore where children who love paper folding will be amazed at the wide assortment of origami books and paper; adults may be interested in the Japanese cookbooks in English. The downstairs stationery department is the real find, though—it has hundreds of cute (really, really cute) and affordable items for children. There are dozens and dozens of whimsical erasers, shiny and sparkly stickers, plastic folders printed with kittens and flowers or robots, and earbuds in the shape of ladybugs or frogs. Adults will find gorgeous notebooks, an irresistible array of stationery, endless pens and pencils, and all manner of related items. The small third-floor café has Japanese and American pastries and snacks.

Disney Store

1540 Broadway, between West 45th and 46th Streets
(212) 626-2910
Subway: N,Q,R to 49th Street; B,D,F,M to 47th-50th Streets-
Rockefeller Center
www.disneystore.com
Daily 10am–midnight

Here you'll find a vast selection of Disney merch (PJs, boxers, backpacks, sippy cups, mugs, onesies, and much, much more). For souvenirs, take home a "I (Mickey Mouse silhouette) NY" t-shirt or choose from a selection of Minnie-as-the-Statue-of-Liberty products (a plush toy, a Christmas tree ornament, each $16.50). An impressive array of glittery/iridescent/sparkly Disney princess dresses/slippers/wands/hairbands are generously embellished with bows/butterflies/flowers. In a small pavilion on the second floor, rotating Disney movies play on a not-very-large flat screen; there are a few child-sized chairs for kids and benches around the periphery for parents.

Hyman Hendler

21 West 38th Street, between Fifth and Sixth Avenues
(212) 840-8393
Subway: B,D,F,M to 42nd Street-Bryant Park;
N,Q,R to Times Square-42nd Street; 4,5,6 to Grand Central-42nd Street
www.hymanhendler.com
Monday–Friday 9am–5pm

Sometimes a party frock needs...an exquisite hair ribbon. Not gros-grain, or even velvet, but something really exceptional. This is where to find it. In business since 1900—it began as a pushcart on the Lower East Side—the shop is filled with shelves of rolls upon rolls of ribbons, ranging in price from a couple of dollars a yard to much, much more. You'll find the sweetly simple to the extravagant and opulent, much of it vintage and no longer manufactured. There are *bleu*, *blanc*, and *rouge* striped ribbons gamine enough for Gigi; wide cornflower-blue checked silk for your small Alice in Wonderland. Those twin red taffeta bows Olivia wears on her ears for special occasions? They may very well have come from Hyman Hendler.

M&M's World

1600 Broadway, between West 48th and 49th Streets
(212) 295-3850
Subway: 1 to 50th Street; C,E to 50th Street; B,D,F,M to 47th-50th Streets-Rockefeller Center; N,Q,R to 49th Street
www.mymms.com
Daily 10–midnight
Children under 13 must be accompanied by an adult.
Monday–Thursday 10am–midnight; Friday–Sunday 9am–midnight

Attendants handing out large shopping baskets give you a clue what to expect here: you'll be collecting lots of loot, including T-shirts, plush toys, backpacks, golf balls, sequined coin purses, sticker books, snap-on bracelets, some New York City–themed products, a range of M&M kitchen utensils, and candy dispensers in the shape of hot rods or slot machines. The special edition M&Ms stored in huge canisters are the main event on the first floor. Customers fill up containers with their own mix of the many colors, or choose among the custom mixes offered: a 22-color mix, a raspberry mix, the Shimmer collection (gold, silver, and white M&Ms), the Mother's Day mix (purple, lavender, rose, pink, and white). Also on the floor is a commemorative coin machine into which a penny is inserted, then flattened and embossed with an M&M image (51 cents); a counter at which to get an ID bracelet made; and a photo booth (2 photo strips or a 4x6 postcard, $5). One of the busiest areas is the Color Mood Analyzer. A customer steps in front of a screen, a computer voice announces, "Prepare for a candy scan," and an image of an M&M in "your color" pops up, along with an explanation of why that color appeared. One young girl was told her color was pink because "you are sweet and charming, qualities that will take you far—like chocolate and peanuts!"

Upstairs, customers can personalize their own M&M mix by choosing up to three colors of M&Ms, then clip art and/or lettering, and packaging; astonishingly, within a minute the custom mix is ready.

Another store devoted to candy is the nearby Hershey's Chocolate World Times Square (Broadway and 48th Street, (212) 581-9100, daily 9am to midnight, www.hersheys.com).

The Compleat Strategist
11 East 33rd Street, between Madison and Fifth Avenues
(212) 685-3880
Subway: 4,6 to 33rd Street; B,D,F,M,N,Q,R to
34th Street-Herald Square
www.thecompleatstrategist.com
Monday–Wednesday, Friday, Saturday 10:30am–6pm;
Thursday 10:30am–9pm

Gamers rejoice! In this small, packed store lies a treasure trove of board games, figurines, role-playing games, and more. The selection caters mainly to an older, more serious board game and role-playing game type, but there is plenty to choose from for kids of all ages at the back of the store. Classic board games abound, along with newer games geared toward younger gamers. Whether you just want to play Monopoly or interest your child in the world of D&D, you'll likely find what you need amidst overflowing shelves that are sure to inspire wonder in the hearts of young game enthusiasts. Thursday nights and all day Saturday you'll find gamers doing their thing; call the store to find out which games are being played, and when.

The Lego Store
620 Fifth Avenue, between West 49th and 50th Streets
(212) 245-5973
Subway: B,D,F,M to 47th-50th Streets-Rockefeller Center;
4,6 to 51st Street
stores.lego.com
Monday–Saturday 10am–8pm; Sunday 11am–7pm

Although it's located in exceptionally busy Rockefeller Center, the Lego store is manageable, clean, orderly, and organized, and reflects the quality and design aesthetic of the brand. Throughout the store charming scenes of New York City constructed from Legos are displayed behind glass windows on a child's-eye-view level (the Brooklyn Bridge, the Circle Line boat, a subway platform, and more). Undoubtedly, the centerpiece of the store is the painstakingly detailed and utterly astonishing model of Rockefeller Center, constructed with tens of thousands of Legos. The complete line of Lego sets are for sale here—far beyond the assortment you'd find in a typical toy store. There's a Pick a Brick wall of dozens of sizes and colors (fill a large container for $14.99 or a small one for $7.99), a kiosk with components to build your own mini figure (3 for $9.99), as well as affordable souvenirs (key chains, and a Statue of Liberty Lego set for $5.49). Last but not least, the staff is friendly, energetic, and knowledgeable.

The NBA Store

590 Fifth Avenue, between West 47th and 48th Streets
(212) 515-6221
Subway: B,D,F to 47th-50th Streets-Rockefeller Center;
E to 5th Avenue-53rd Street
www.nba.com/nycstore
Monday–Thursday 10am–9pm; Friday–Saturday 10am–10pm;
Sunday 10am–8pm

As the only official NBA store in the U.S.—the other two are in Beijing—the NBA store is a not-to-be-missed stop for any true hoops fan. While the new location isn't as interactive as the much larger original store, it's still a browser's paradise. With a full array of both current and hard-to-find throwback merchandise (jerseys, hats, shorts, shirts, pants, pajamas, shot glasses, pencils, note-books, baby bottles and much more), there's something for the NBA enthusiast of any age.

The ground floor offers items currently "trending" and there's a somewhat limited sneaker department in the back. Upstairs is where the real fun begins; you'll immediately be struck by the floor's bursts of color and pulsating hip-hop beats that make it feel more like a playoff party than a shopping experience. While the store isn't exactly inexpensive, the merch is not overpriced; splurge on an authentic jersey of your favorite current or former player, or track down the various sale racks for an impressive array of affordable treasures.

Central Park

Central Park

From 59th Street to 110th Street and Fifth Avenue to Central Park West
(212) 310-6600
www.centralparknyc.org

Bike rental (see NYC by bicycle, page 27)

Self-guided tours: www.centralparknyc.org/visit/tours

Free app: www.centralparknyc.org/digital.html

Audio guides: Look for the green signs throughout the park with a phone number to call to access an audio guide explaining a nearby feature of the park.

Current children's activities in the park (dance, music, puppets, stories, free for 3–8 with adult): centralparknyc.org/sandbox

Throughout the summer, the Central Park Film Festival screens many movies perfect for kids; bring a picnic and view such classics as *Raiders of the Lost Ark*, *West Side Story*, or *Hook*. (Sheep Meadow; rain or shine; gates open at 6:30pm; a guest DJ spins until the film starts at 8pm; free.)

Within the park are food options (see restaurants map). To pick up a picnic or snack before you enter the park, swing by the Plaza Food Hall (page 376).

Beyond the obvious family-friendly wide-open spaces and play-grounds, Central Park is a treasure trove of child-friendly activities. The itinerary below takes you through the south part of the park, where features of interest to families are in the closest proximity (for northern Central Park, see page 238). First go to the website www.centralparknyc.org/maps/downloadable-maps and print out the General Map, the Map of Restaurants and Restrooms, and the Map of Playgrounds.

To start at the zoo, enter the park at 59th Street and Fifth Avenue, and be sure you take the pedestrian walkway closest to and parallel to Fifth Avenue, and not the sidewalk closest to the roadway on the left. If it's near the half hour, don't miss the striking of the Delacorte Clock, when its hippo, monkey, and other animals dance and play seasonal tunes ("April Showers," "Deck the Halls") on their musical instruments.

The Central Park Zoo is everything that most zoos aren't: compact and easy to navigate. Even those who find zoos depressing respond to the sweet "storybook come alive" nature of this zoo. California sea lions take center stage in the central pool; these rascals perform daily at their mealtimes (11:30am, 2pm, and 4pm). Windows below water level provide great viewing for kids. Next, venture into the penguin house to see those dapper creatures swim, dive, and frolic. Outside, move on to the floating and swimming polar bears and, beyond, on the outer path, look for the snow monkeys, snow leopards, and other animals.

Next, enter the indoor tropical zone where the leafcutter ants toil and exotic birds fly overhead in the warm, humid, closed building that recreates a rainforest environment. You'll see snakes, reptiles, and more. Staffers are happy to answer questions, provide information, and engage children.

Outside again, walk north, beyond the Delacorte Clock to the Tisch

Children's Zoo, which offers little children a chance to observe and pet animals including ducks, goats, sheep, alpacas, and pot-bellied pigs. Some of the animals may be fed by hand; coin-operated machines dispense feed. Paths and climbing areas make this a sweet play space for the smallest kids.

(Central Park Zoo: Summer Monday–Friday 10am–5pm; weekends and holidays 10am–5:30pm; Winter 10am–4:30pm. Last ticket sold 30 minutes prior to closing. Main zoo and Tisch zoo: adults $12, 3–12 $7; Total Experience [main zoo, Tisch zoo, 4-D theater] adults $18, 3–12 $13; 4-D theater 3 and up $7)

Leaving the Children's Zoo, continue north along the path, go right at fork, and take a sharp right to the Billy Johnson Playground. It's ideal for toddlers as well as older children: there's a bridge, a sandbox, a mini-amphitheater, and baby swings. The main attraction is a granite slide set into a hill; local kids bring pieces of cardboard to sit on to accelerate the ride down.

Exiting the playground, return to the fork in the path, look left, and try to spot the bronze statue of Balto. He's the Siberian husky sled dog who, in 1925, took medicine to combat an outbreak of diphtheria in Nome, Alaska, that doctors feared would spread among the city's children.

On the right, at the fork of the path, the huge rock topped by a gazebo provides a fun climb. Throughout the park you'll see many examples of exposed Manhattan schist, the ancient bedrock and foundation on which Manhattan is built.

Continue north, passing the large and well-equipped 72nd Street Playground. This is a good place for one parent to stay with the kids

while the other visits the Frick Collection across Fifth Avenue at 1 East 70th Street, considered by many the most exquisite museum in New York City.

On to the Conservatory Water, popularly called the model boat pond. At the boathouse, you can rent a radio-controlled boat (April–October, $11 for 30 minutes; Monday–Thursday 11am–6pm; Friday 11am–8pm; Saturday 1pm–8pm; Sunday 10am–7pm). A staffer makes the rounds along the pond to help children sail their vessels. There's a **restroom** at the boathouse, an ATM machine, and a small **cafe** with cereal, bagels, hot dogs, and alcoholic beverages. (Overheard one Saturday morning at 9:30am: a young mother with a wailing newborn and demanding toddler eyeing the bar and asking her husband, "Is it too early for a cocktail?")

North of the model boat pond is the beloved Alice in Wonderland statue that kids love to climb; it's an iconic photo op, too. On the western side of the pond is a statue of Hans Christian Andersen where story times are held on Saturdays at 11am, June–September.

Head west, and deeper into the park, crossing the road to find the Loeb Boathouse. Outside, a casual **cafe** serves veggie burgers, salads, and sandwiches. Inside, the upscale **Lakeside Restaurant** has expansive views of the lake, and is a lovely setting for a meal with older well-behaved children. Reservations are accepted for all meals except brunch. (Lunch Monday–Friday noon-4pm; brunch Saturday, Sunday 9:30am–4pm; dinner, April–November only, Monday–Friday 5:30pm–9:30pm; Saturday–Sunday 6pm–9:30pm.)

Weather permitting, you can rent rowboats at the nearby shack, and go out on the picturesque lake (April–November, 10am–6pm, $15

for the first hour; $3 each additional 15 minutes; $20 returnable cash deposit required; no credit cards; maximum 4 people per boat). An hour might seem like time enough, but the lake is larger than it appears, and you'll want to take your time viewing Bethesda Fountain and other picturesque park scenes from the water.

At this point you may want to exit the park at Fifth Avenue and 72nd Street. Or, back on land, walk to Bethesda Fountain (see * page 345) where you can loop back along the west side, to end up near where you started on Central Park South.

If you want to explore further, continue north through the Ramble, 38 acres of rustic woodland that seems a million miles away from

the rest of the park. The paths are unmarked, and can be confusing, but keep heading north and you'll find Belvedere Castle, where the official New York City weather is recorded, including temperatures and snowfall. Inside, climb up the steep and narrow stairs for views of the park and city beyond. Young birdwatchers can borrow (no charge) backpacks with binoculars; pocket guides with which to identify birds, trees, wildflowers, and wildlife; colored pencils; and a bird journal to keep.

Near the castle and the 79th Street entrance to Central Park, the Swedish Cottage holds hour-long marionette shows. The puppets are engaging but the recorded audio isn't. (18 months–12, $7; 13 and up, $10; check performance times at www.cityparksfoundation.org/arts/swedish-cottage-marionette-theatre)

Now, retrace your steps south and westward to Bethesda Terrace.

* At Bethesda Terrace, you'll find a grand fountain, views of the lake, a tunnel leading to steps (with restrooms on either side), and wedding couples posing for photos. Walk up the steps to the Mall, with its fun and energetic street performers who always draw a crowd.

From the Mall, you'll see the Dairy, a visitor center and gift shop with an affordable selection of fun and educational nature-related items. Beyond is the Chess and Checkers House where boards and playing pieces may be borrowed to play on the stone tables. On Saturday mornings in warmer weather, a long horseshoe-shaped table is set up on the terrace to accommodate young chess players. Although the tranquility of the park can sometimes be interrupted

by performers, crowds, and other activities, under this pergola, you feel as if you've entered a quiet room within the park. Children and adults are deep in concentration while a grand master chess instructor plays the entire group simultaneously. He moves from player to player, watches each kid make a move, makes a counter move, offers a comment on strategy, and moves on to the next player's board. (April–October, Tuesday–Sunday 10am–5pm; November–March, Wednesday–Sunday 10am–5pm; free lessons on some Saturdays; 25 players can be accommodated, first come first served)

Continue to mid-park, at 64th Street, where the 57-horse carousel provides rides for 250,000 visitors a year (daily 10am–6pm, April–October, weather permitting; November–March, call ahead, (212) 439-6900 ext. 12; $3 per ride, cash only).

In the winter, Wollman Rink offers a beautiful ice skating experience, especially at night, surrounded by the skyscrapers; the scene is iconic and the setting magical. In the summer, the rink is closed and the smallish Victorian Gardens amusement park set up. Outside, grab an organic chicken breast, grilled organic chicken sausage, or a foot-long hot dog with homemade sauerkraut at the **Wollman Grill**.

As you exit the park, Heckscher Playground to the west is the largest playground in Central Park. Contiguous to it are spectacular rocks that New York kids have been climbing for centuries.

PLAY

EAT

SHOP

Upper East Side

PLAY

Ancient Playground

Fifth Avenue, at East 85th Street
(212) 310-6600
Subway: 4,5,6 to 86th Street
Daily 8am–dusk

After a visit to the Metropolitan Museum, kids may need a little
outdoor time just to let off some steam. Central Park might work—
it's right in the museum's backyard—but younger kids might
prefer a more structured play area. If so, head to the lovely Ancient
Playground. In a nod to the Museum's Egyptian holdings, swings
and elevated walkways are built upon pyramid-like bases. Other features include monkey bars, tire swings, a circular sandbox with two
short slides emerging from an obelisk in its center, and a pair each
of swings for babies and bigger kids.

Cooper-Hewitt Design Museum

2 East 91st Street, between Fifth and Madison Avenues
(212) 849-8400
Subway: 4,5,6 to 86th Street
www.cooperhewitt.org
Free
Closed for renovation until 2014; check website for updated details

Good design can include just about everything, and The Cooper-
Hewitt collection reflects that. The museum's holdings include
Bloomingdale's shopping bags, travel posters, furniture, textiles, tea

sets, Swatch watches, lace, and buttons. This is a place that will appeal to older kids—there have been exhibitions on the fashion label Rodarte, the Tata Nano mini-car, and Van Cleef & Arpels. You can get a good sense of what's in the collection by logging on to the website's Object of the Day feature (under the Explore Design tab), in which curators choose and explain favorite pieces. The museum holds drop-in toddler programs and workshops on everything from book making to tie-dying to designing a Muppet. The Cooper-Hewitt also has one of the best museum shops in the city filled—natch—with beautifully designed practical and cool things for toddlers, teens, and parents, from watches and jewelry to toys and art kits.

Four Seasons Children's Day

The Four Seasons Restaurant

99 East 52nd Street, between Park and Lexington Avenues

(212) 754–9494

Subway: 6 to 51st Street

www.fourseasonsrestaurant.com

Once a year, in August, children dine free at this iconic restaurant, with its stunning modernist setting that includes a pool, glimmering Philip Johnson "curtains," a Picasso tapestry—and incomparable food. No lowering the culinary standards, either. The restaurant treats this event like the rite of passage it is; children order off the a la carte menu. For many adults, dining here is the quintessential New York experience; taking your child to a first meal here is a milestone for both. As would be expected, reservations are required if you hope to have a spot, and must be made well in advance (only two children, ages 5–14, per adult). Check the website for current dates.

The Jewish Museum
1109 Fifth Avenue, at East 92nd Street
(212) 423-3200
Subway: 6 to 96th Street; 4,5,6 to 86th Street
www.thejewishmuseum.org
Saturday–Tuesday 11am–5:45pm; Wednesday closed;
Thursday 11am–8pm; Friday–11am–4:00pm
Adults $15; students $7.50; under 18 free; Saturdays free;
Thursdays 5pm–8pm pay what you wish
Strollers may not be able to be accommodated in the special exhibition galleries although umbrella strollers are welcome in the rest of the museum. A limited number of strollers are available for loan from the coatroom.

Adults who were intrigued by archaeology in their youth will be as excited as their children to explore the Jewish Museum's kids exhibition, *Archaeology Zone: Discovering Treasures from Playgrounds to Palaces.* In it, children are able to do what archaeologists do: piece

together objects, weigh and examine them, figure out how they were made and their uses, and interpret symbols, as well as see original artifacts from the museum's collection. Before you visit, view the video on the museum's website, "What Happened to King Hezekiah's Jar?" about the discovery of this artifact, which is displayed at the entrance to *Archaeology Zone*. At certain times, children can enter the sand-filled portion of the room that simulates an archaeological dig and search and sift for buried objects (call for hours).

Sundays at the museum are filled with family activities, including drop-in art workshops for ages 3 and up, gallery tours, story time, and *Archaeology Zone* (all free with museum admission). Concerts and theater performances are held throughout the year (check website for current schedule).

The museum often has temporary exhibitions that engage children, including shows devoted to the creators of Curious George, the art of Ezra Jack Keats (*The Snowy Day*), and the art and magic of Houdini. Even if the current show isn't child-centered, the museum has designed a five-stop walking tour for children, *Animals in Art*, that will lead them from object to object through the galleries (it can be found online). Family activity guides relating to current exhibitions are available at the front desk, free with admission. A self-guided audio tour, *Culture and Continuity: The Jewish Journey*, featuring an introduction to the museum plus short discussions of 21 pieces of art, is available at the fourth floor lobby (Sunday, Monday, Tuesday, Thursday & Friday; for ages 6 and up with an adult; free).

Lox at Cafe Weissman serves certified kosher food, including salmon flown in from Scotland, bagels, challah French toast, herring (cured in-house), potato latkes, grandma's tuna sandwich, pastries and more; (212) 423-3200. A museum ticket is not required to dine at Lox. Closed Saturday.

The museum's shop may be one of the best places to pick up a quintessentially NYC souvenir: a wooden bagel yoyo ($10); a rainbow Star of David Slinky ($2.50); a purse in the shape of a hot dog ($6.50); and for parents who have been hauling all their kids' stuff around the city, a Schlep Tote ($25). Closed Saturday.

Madeline Tea at the Carlyle Hotel

35 East 76th Street, between Madison and Park Avenues
(212) 744–1600
Subway: 6 to 77th Street
www.rosewoodhotels.com/en/carlyle
Saturdays in November and December at 10am and 12:45pm
Check website for updated schedule and prices; reservations required

Annually, on Saturdays in November, the posh Hotel Carlyle holds Madeline Teas for children in its elegant Bemelmans Bar, the walls of which were painted with scenes of Central Park by Ludwig Bemelmans, author and illustrator of the Madeline books. The buffet overflows with kid-friendly food (the early seating has breakfast items such as brioche French toast, croissants, muffins, scrambled eggs, cereal, yogurt parfaits, and more; the afternoon tea includes tea sandwiches, macaroni and cheese, crudités and fruit salad cups, iced shrimp, cupcakes and cookies). Madeline dolls and books round out the decor.

Museum of the City of New York

1220 Fifth Avenue, between East 103rd and 104th Streets
(212) 534-1672
Subway: 6 to 103rd Street; 2,3 to Central Park North-110th Street
www.mcny.org
Daily 10am to 6pm
Suggested admission: adults $10; students $6; families $20
(max. 2 adults); 12 and under free

The Stettheimer dollhouse is the attraction for children at the MCNY; it's sweet, but the reason it's well known is that the miniature paintings on the wall are by distinguished early 20th-century artists, including Marcel Duchamp and Gaston Lachaise. Is that of interest to most kids? Maybe not. The 20-minute *Timescapes* film, while fascinating, will appeal only to older children interested in the history of New York City. If an adult in your group wants to see one of the museum's changing exhibitions, the airy second-floor cafe overlooking Central Park can provide a spot for the kids to sit down and have a snack. Or, check ahead and find out what free family programs, such as a Father's Day scavenger hunt through the museum or a walking tour of the murals of East Harlem, are scheduled.

Roosevelt Island Tramway

Manhattan station at Queensboro Bridge, East 60th Street and
Second Avenue

(212) 832-4543

Subway: 4,5,6 to 59th Street; F to Lexington Avenue-63rd Street;
N,Q,R to Lexington Avenue-59th Street

rioc.ny.gov/tramtransportation.htm

Sunday–Thursday 6am–2am; Friday–Saturday 6am–3:30pm
(departs at 15-minute intervals)

This is a little gem within New York's mass transit system. Secured
to a cable 250 feet above the East River at its highest point, this
glass-walled commuter tram offers breathtaking views of the

Midtown Manhattan skyline and the Ed Koch Queensboro Bridge as it makes its three-minute crossing from Manhattan to Roosevelt Island. One-way passage costs the same as a subway fare payable via a MTA Metrocard. Passengers must disembark at Roosevelt Island but may re-board upon paying another fare. The tram departs from each side of the river every fifteen minutes, and continuously during rush hours.

Solomon R. Guggenheim Museum
1071 Fifth Avenue, at East 89th Street
(212) 423-3587
Subway: 4,5,6 to 86th Street
www.guggenheim.org/new-york
Sunday–Wednesday, Friday 10am–5:45pm; Thursday closed; Saturday 10am–7:45pm
Adults $22; students $18; under 12 free; Saturday 5:45pm–close pay what you wish

There was a time when the main attraction the Guggenheim for kids was the trip down the spiraling gallery at the center of this Frank Lloyd Wright building, and if you could interest them in the art, so much the better. It's still one of the coolest experiences around. Now the museum's abundant kids programming provides yet another way to introduce kids to art, and to keep them interested. Try to plan your visit to coincide with one of those programs (www.guggenheim.org/new-york/education/families-kids-teens). You'll find tours and art workshops for families, kids, tweens, and teens. The Guggenheim's Tips page (www.guggenheim.org/new-york/education/families-kids-teens/tips) offers guidance on how to prepare for and enjoy a visit. When you arrive, don't forget to pick up an activity guide, with a journal and pencil, to use as you walk the exhibitions. The gift shop inventory changes, but plenty of items are designed for kids such as waterproof bibs, smocks with exuberant Keith Haring prints, silver backpacks with the smiling Guggenheim Kids logo ($18), and floaty pens ($8).

The Asia Society

725 Park Avenue, between East 70th and 71st Streets
(212) 288-6400
Subway: 6 to 68th Street-Hunter College
www.asiasociety.org
Tuesday–Sunday 11am–6pm; closed Monday

If you have a special interest in Asian and Asian-American art, by all means visit this sublime and serene museum. Special features for kids are on the website (kids.asiasociety.org) and include stories, games, crafts, and language instructions (Learn Hindi with students from India, count to twelve in Chinese). If you're in the neighborhood, though, the **Garden Court Cafe**, in a sky-lit lobby, serves well-priced and highly regarded food in a casual setting (lunch Tuesday–Sunday 11am–5pm; limited menu 3:30pm–4:30pm; closed Monday). The clientele includes Park Avenue ladies-who-lunch as well as young neighborhood parents with strollers and older kids who like the dumplings and other Asian-inspired food.

The Metropolitan Museum of Art

1000 Fifth Avenue, at East 82nd Street

(212) 535–7710

Subway: 4,5,6 to 86th Street

www.metmuseum.org

Sunday–Thursday 10am–5:30pm; Friday, Saturday 10am–9pm

Recommended admission: adults $25; students $12; under 12 free.

To avoid waiting in lines, advance tickets may be purchased online; they are valid for up to one year after the date of purchase.

Fee includes same day admission to the Main Building and The Cloisters museum and gardens (see page 485). Guided tours, available in 10 languages, are free with admission.

One-hour audio guides, appropriate for ages 6–12, are available at the Audio Guide desk in the Great Hall ($7; under 12 $5).

On Saturday and Sunday, family greeters stationed in the Great Hall are available to answer questions and give family tips; look for their red aprons.

Other information of particular interest to families:

All bags and backpacks must be checked, so to avoid lines, don't bring them into the museum.

Strollers (except oversized and jogging strollers) are permitted in most galleries.

Most restrooms have changing stations.

The Met is America's Louvre: vast, magnificent, and—even without children in tow—overwhelming. The key to a successful visit is to focus on your family's interests, realistically assess your stamina, and map out a plan before you arrive.

"The floor space of the Museum is as large as thirty football fields," according to *Inside the Museum, A Children's Guide to the Metropolitan Museum of Art*—and it may feel even larger if you try to cover too much territory. Distances aside, time is another consideration. With young children, spending an hour in the museum seems to be a reasonable goal. Older children will be able to handle a longer visit. Prioritize what you want to see, start with the art that is most important to you, and work your way down the list, gauging their energy as you go.

Before you go

Even minimal advance planning will repay your efforts a hundred-fold. The Met's website is invaluable for this. If you do nothing else, go to the website and under the Learn tab, click on For Kids, take a look at the Family Map, and get a general idea of the route you want to take through the museum. It's much easier than deciphering the map once you've arrived in the always busy and sometimes very loud and crowded Great Hall.

Prepping your children at home sets the stage for a memorable visit. Show your children images of artworks on the Met's website. Seeing the photos of the art, and then, at the museum, the actual work, will be a revelation. A photo can't begin to convey the shimmering light of a Tiffany stained glass window, the beautiful reality of Degas's Little Dancer sculpture, or the scale of "Washington Crossing the Delaware" (let the fact that the painting is more than 12 feet high and 21 feet long be a surprise). The goal is to have a visit filled with "aha!" moments.

Online, look at the Met's archive of Family Guides and find those that most interest your kids (on the Met's home page, on the pull-down menu under Learn, click on For Kids, then scroll down under Family Map and Guides). Some of the Family Guides have maps and point out objects to look for as families walk through the galleries—you'll want to take them with you to the museum; others, such as *Mysterious Mummies,* provide background information that can be used to interest your children before the visit. The Family Guides are available in PDF form to print out. Some, but not all, are available at the Great Hall Information Desk, so if there's one you're particularly interested in using at the museum, print it out and bring it with you.

Another fun way to see the museum: if your child has read *From the Mixed-Up Files of Mrs. Basil E. Frankweiler* by E. L. Konigsburg, be sure to show them The "Mixed-Up Files" guide on the website. The Met has designed a walk through the galleries, pointing out the actual objects, or similar ones, mentioned by Claudia and Jamie in the book. There's even a suggested project for kids, and those who complete it and either send it to the museum or drop it off at the front desk are promised a "museum goodie."

Remember: No matter which way you approach the museum you'll feel as if you haven't even begun to scratch the surface. *Inside the Museum* offers this consolation: "There are more than two million objects in the Museum's collection. If you spent a minute looking at each one, you would have to come to the Museum every day for more than thirteen years to see them all." Keep that in mind, and know that even if you pause in front of only a handful of artworks, you'll see many more unplanned delights en route from one to another. Even a detour to the nearest restroom can take you across continents and millennia, and show you marvels you never could have imagined.

When you arrive

At the Great Hall Information Desk, take time to pick up these free materials:

- a Museum Map, which has galleries identified by number, essential when trying to find a certain artwork;

- a Family Map, which is less detailed and has galleries identified by department only (Greek and Roman Art). Being simpler, it's an "at a glance" way to find restrooms, changing facilities, water fountains, and dining options.

- the Family Guides, some available in Spanish, which are self-guided mini-tours of the collections for children by subject. A caveat: one of these, a walking tour of the Top Ten kids' favorite artworks, encompasses the entire museum, and can be too long and cover too much territory for all but the most intrepid families.

- Today's Events list, which usually includes at least two activities for families which are usually free with admission.

- a Family Activities brochure, a complete calendar of events and activities for children, including Saturday Sketching (ages 11–18) in the Museum's galleries, with guidance from an artist-instructor, materials provided; Story Time in the Nolen Library Children's Reading Room (ages 18 months to 3 years); an Art Trek (ages 5–12); Start with Art at the Met (ages 3–7), which includes drawing and story time. Programs change, but they are free and only a few require advance registration. Check the website for the current schedule.

Note: Sometimes objects are moved and galleries are closed for renovation or to prepare for an exhibition; ask a guard and have a Plan B. Museum guards, stationed throughout the museum, are unfailingly knowledgeable and cordial.

It's cringing to reduce the Met's treasures to a handful, but if you want to see the "greatest hits" without walking miles, here is a manageable plan. Start at the Temple of Dendur and Egyptian galleries, then, depending on your interests, walk through or stop at Arms and Armor on the way to the American Wing, which is on both the first and second floors. If you're still good to go, continue on across the building to 19th- and early 20th-century European Paintings and Sculpture (where you'll find the Impressionists). Or, if you have a child interested in mythology, after the American Wing, walk to the

Greek and Roman galleries on the first floor. The Chinese Garden in the Asian Art Gallery is a tranquil alternative to any of these stops. Or, at any point, take the elevator to see what's on exhibit on the roof; it's refreshing and the view is incomparable.

If parents want to see more of the museum but the children have reached their limit, adults can also take turns attending the Children's Story Hour or one of the Family Activities. A wonderful refuge in the Met is the Children's Reading Library in the Nolen Library. It's a good place to go when a young child needs a break. It's open to all museum visitors daily from 10am to 5pm, and has a collection of art books for children, as well as computers with art-

related games and stories. If your little ones are ready for a breath of fresh air, the Ancient Playground in Central Park is adjacent to the museum (page 350).

The Met makes a point of saying that children are welcome in all the **dining venues**, and they are, but the self-service cafeteria on the ground floor is the most child-friendly venue of all, with booster seats and high chairs and a pleasant and slightly chaotic atmosphere—lots of people, lots of food stations. Adults can choose among the sushi, pasta, main courses, pastries, antipasti, and grill stations. At the grill, a Taxi Cab meal for children under 12 offers a choice of a grilled cheese, a hot dog, whole wheat penne with marinara sauce, or chicken tenders, each with fruit, chips or fries, and juice or milk ($6.25). The cafeteria also has soft-serve yogurt and wine. Older children may enjoy lunch or afternoon tea at the Petrie Court Café, with its views of Central Park, or the American Wing Café, which serves breakfast and light fare adjacent to the grand sky-lit Charles Engelhard Court.

At the rear of the vast book and gift shop on the first floor is a curated selection of items for children, including lots of things for budding archaeologists, much with Egyptian and Medieval themes. The video, *Don't Eat the Pictures*, features the Sesame Street characters visiting the Met.

The Whitney Museum of American Art
945 Madison Avenue, between 74th and 75th Streets
(212) 570-3600
Subway: 6 to 72nd Street
www.whitney.org
Wednesday, Thursday, Saturday, Sunday 11am–6pm; Friday 1–9 pm
Adults $20; 19–25 $16; 18 and under free
Note: The Whitney is scheduled to relocate in 2015;
the new address will be Washington Street at Gansevoort Street in
the West Village.

This is the museum where on every wall kids will discover an
American artist whose work they'll forever recognize and remember:

Edward Hopper, Georgia O'Keeffe, Jacob Lawrence, Frank Stella, and more. The most obvious attraction for kids is undisputedly (Alexander) Calder's Circus. The artist used found materials, including corks, wire, and buttons, bottle caps, scraps of cloth, wood, and more, to create this work of great charm and whimsy. In the Whitney's location on Madison Avenue, only a few elements of the Circus have been on display recently, with a black-and-white film of Calder manipulating the Circus played on a small screen set into the wall—at 45 minutes, too long for children to watch while standing. As of this writing, plans for the installation of the Circus in the new Whitney weren't finalized.

If you want to see the galleries, but are reluctant to take a very small child along, Whitney Wees provides a family program that seems luxurious by any standards, especially to New Yorkers used to navigating around crowds while pushing strollers through galleries. The program's one-hour tours for parents and children up to 18 months are held when the museum is closed to the public and are conducted by PhD candidates in art history; strollers are not only allowed, but the website reassures parents "crying babies are welcome" ($35 per adult; registration required). Other programs for older children include drawing workshops and tours for ages 4–5, 6–10, and 8–12 (registration recommended, drop-ins welcome if space is available, $10 per family fee includes admission to the museum before public hours). Check the website for current programs and schedules. You don't have to wait for your visit to the Whitney to start making art: the kids page on the museum website is filled with fun activities appropriate for young artists ages 8–12. (whitney.org/ForKids)

Hungry? If you've wanted to sample restaurateur Danny Meyer's excellent food—but a meal at the Union Square Cafe is not in the plans—the restaurant **Untitled** is the place to eat well, and affordably, in a casual setting. Michelin has given it a "Bib Gourmande" for excellence on a budget. The setting in the lower lobby, under the soaring windows, is bustling, lively, and kid-friendly. The kids menu offers pancakes, grilled cheese, or a hamburger, $6–$12 (Wednesday and Thursday 11am–6pm; Friday 11am–9pm; Saturday and Sunday for brunch, 10am–6pm).

EAT

Candle Cafe

1307 Third Avenue, between East 74th and 75th Streets
(212) 472-0970
Subway: 6 to 77th Street
www.candlecafe.com
Monday–Saturday 11:30am–10:30pm; Sunday 11:30am–9:30pm

You don't have to be a vegan to enjoy—really enjoy—the organic, vegan, farm-to-table food served here. The modest prices, not easy to find on the Upper East Side, only heighten the appreciation. For adults, there's kale salad, an Aztec salad (bi-color quinoa, black beans, red onion, and corn topped with spiced pumpkin seeds and barbeque grilled tempeh, served over mixed field greens with toasted cumin vinaigrette, $17), and a Paradise Casserole (layers of sweet potato, black beans, and millet over steamed greens with country gravy, $16). Even unadventurous young eaters will like the spring rolls, manicotti ($14), quesadilla, spinach ravioli, guacamole and chips, and the affordable $4–$5 side dishes, including mac and cheese and corn on the cob. Beverages include juices and smoothies, wine by the glass and bottle, and organic ales.

Additional Location: Candle Cafe West 2427 Broadway (Upper West Side)

El Café in El Museo del Barrio

1230 Fifth Avenue, between East 104th and 105th Streets
(212) 831-7272
Subway: 6 to 103rd Street
www.elmuseo.org/en/el-cafe
Tuesday–Friday 11am–3:30pm (full menu); Saturday noon–3:30pm
(limited menu); closed Sunday and Monday

Only a handful of objects from the permanent collection are on display at El Museo, but if you find yourself in the neighborhood, and
it's mealtime, you may want to check out the museum's El Café. The
menu changes every other week, and features delicious, reasonably
priced dishes from Latin American and Caribbean countries—the
cultures represented in the museum's holdings. The room is
flooded with light, and the graffiti mural on the wall is super cool.

Forty Carrots at Bloomingdale's

1000 Third Avenue, between East 59th and 60th Streets, seventh floor
(212) 705-3085
N,Q,R to Lexington Avenue-59th Street; 4,5,6 to 59th Street;
F to Lexington Avenue-63rd Street
www1.bloomingdales.com
Daily 10am until one hour before store closing

Frozen yogurt had its New York City debut in 1975 at the much-loved
Forty Carrots, a colorful and sleek child-friendly setting. The frozen
yogurt (small $5, large $7) has a devoted following, aficionados cit-
ing its perfect balance of sweetness and tang. The rest of the menu
is healthy, too, with soup, fruit cups, salmon, and veggie burgers
and, for calorie-counting parents, lots of salads and a no-mayo

tuna salad sandwich served on organic bread. The kids menu offers grilled cheese, tuna salad on a pretzel roll, pizza, or spaghetti with a fountain soda or milk and a dessert-size frozen yogurt ($9). There's a good smoothie selection, too, and fresh fruit and vegetable juices.

Lexington Candy Shop

1226 Lexington Avenue, at East 83rd Street
(212) 288-0057
Subway: 4,5,6 to 86th Street
www.lexingtoncandyshop.net
Monday–Saturday 7am–7pm; Sunday 8am–6pm

On a recent afternoon, three diners here were eating: a grilled cheese sandwich, a scoop of chocolate ice cream in a metal dish, and a hamburger with a fried egg on top. That pretty much sums up the classic American food served at this old-fashioned soda fountain and luncheonette that has survived unchanged since 1925, owned and operated continuously by three generations. Go here for a malted, a root beer float, or a tuna melt. Sit on a stool at the counter and watch the celebrated milkshakes being made, or tuck into a booth. Breakfast is served anytime: squeezed-to-order orange juice,

eggs any way, pancakes. The magazine *Travel and Leisure Family* calls the Candy Shop "The perfect destination for a family breakfast."

Nectar
1090 Madison Avenue, between East 81st and 82nd Streets
(212) 772-0916
Subway: 6 to 77th Street
Daily 7am–10pm

If you're near Museum Mile, hungry and thirsty, but don't want to eat in a museum or at a posh Upper East Side restaurant, this traditional coffee shop/diner, a block from the Metropolitan Museum of Art, will come to the rescue. Even when busy, as it often is, service is fast and friendly. The space is small, but it's casual enough to accommodate kids. You can have poached eggs or pancakes ($9.95) at breakfast, a cup of chicken noodle soup or a BLT at lunch.

Pastrami Queen
1125 Lexington Avenue, between East 78th and 79th Streets
(212) 734-1500
Subway: 6 to 77th Street
www.pastramiqueen.com
Daily 10am–10pm

If the long lines at Katz's on the Lower East Side are too much for your family to handle, you can have a similar experience, on a much smaller scale, at this tiny, friendly kosher deli. The menu is classic: overstuffed sandwiches (pastrami, corned beef, brisket, tongue, "by themselves a hearty meal," $14.95), royal-size combo sandwiches ("for the large appetite," $18.95), triple-deckers ("you won't believe

you ate the whole thing," $21.95), platters, open sandwiches, and—
for the faint of heart—salads and omelets. There's a kiddie menu for
children under 10 (hamburger, hot dog, mini salami or bologna
sandwich served with fries, $9.95). The "colossal" side orders
include knishes, kasha varishkes, potato pancakes, and pickles.

Plaza Food Hall

in the Plaza Hotel
1 West 59th Street, at Fifth Avenue
(212) 986-9260
Subway: N,Q,R to 5th Avenue-59th Street; F to 57th Street; 4,5,6 to 59th Street; E,M to 5th Avenue-53rd Street
www.theplazany.com/dining/foodhall
Monday–Saturday 8am–9:30pm; Sunday 11am–6pm
Hours vary by purveyor

Yes, there's food in Central Park, but with a few exceptions, it's hot dogs and pretzels from carts. For an array of choices, to take out or eat there, visit the upscale Plaza Food Hall, which includes The Todd English Food Hall.

Accessed by escalators located on the 58th Street and the Central Park South sides of the hotel, the Plaza Food Hall has outposts of many popular local gourmet retailers specializing in pastries, baked goods, tea, coffee, subs, lobster rolls, and more.

On the pricier side, but with many choices, the adjacent Todd English Food Hall has a number of different food stations, including salads, panini, seafood, sushi, pizza, and pasta. Prices range from $14 for a plain flatbread pizza or soba noodles with mushrooms, to $18 for a burger and $24 for linguini and clams.

Serendipity 3

225 East 60th Street, between Second and Third Avenues
(212) 838-3531
Subway: N,Q,R to Lexington Avenue-59th Street; 4,5,6 to 59th Street;
F to Lexington Avenue-63rd Street
www.serendipity3.com
Sunday–Thursday 11:30am–midnight; Friday–Saturday 11:30am–1am

Serendipity an iconic tourist destination and the frozen hot chocolate is a cherished childhood memory for many New Yorkers, but be
prepared for a long wait if you only want dessert. Reservations are
taken for meals only; make them well in advance. The shabby chic
Victorian decor is a glimpse of a sweeter, simpler time, and once
you've done Serendipity, you can always say you've been there. The
restaurant doesn't have room for strollers.

SHOP

Armani Junior

1223 Madison Avenue, at East 88th Street

(212) 828-6920

Subway: 4,5,6 to 86th Street

www.armani.com/us/armanijunior

Monday–Saturday 10am–6pm; Sunday noon–5pm

The clothing here is beautifully designed, all along the Armani aesthetic—elegant yet preppy, very Milan-meets-the Hamptons. The refined and cohesive palette means most of the pieces are interchangeable, so everything works together. You may not want to allocate your resources for an Armani T-shirt or pair of cargo pants, but perhaps for a special outfit for a grandparent's 80th birthday party? An anniversary celebration? A family portrait? There are occasions that merit the splurge.

Barbour

1047 Madison Avenue, at East 80th Street

(212) 570-2600

Subway: 6 to 77th Street

www.barbour.com

Monday–Saturday 10am–8pm; Sunday 11am–7pm

Originally designed for hunters and equestrians, this classic British outerwear is now popular street wear. This branch carries the children's line where you'll find several versions of the classic waxed canvas jacket, with corduroy collar and tartan lining and preppy quilted jackets for both boys and girls, in classic navy, dark olive, black, or brown. Grab some Wellies, and your child will be ready for a canter across the countryside at Balmoral, or jumping through puddles on Fifth Avenue.

Bonne Nuit

1193 Madison Avenue, at East 81st Street
(212) 472-7300
Subway: 4,5,6 to 86th Street
Monday–Friday 9am–7pm; Saturday 10am–7pm; Sunday noon–5pm

This boutique offers an unusual combination: European children's wear and fine lingerie for women. At the front of the shop are racks and racks of elaborately smocked dresses for girls in pastels, ginghams, and seersucker with coordinating garments for little sisters and brothers. A glass case is filled with tiny crocheted baby shoes and a hanging rack displays an assortment of navy and white *mariniere* striped garments. All the basics for kids are stocked, too (birth to size 10/12 for boys, 12/14 for girls), from socks to rain jackets. At the rear of the shop are women's pajamas, gowns, and robes, some available in mother-daughter sizes. This is a traditional shop that somehow manages not to be fusty: perhaps it's the fact that every inch of the shop is jammed, from floor to ceiling, and that the staff is cheerful, welcoming, and helpful.

Dylan's Candy Bar
1011 Third Avenue, at East 60th Street
(646) 735-0078
Subway: 4,5,6,N,Q,R to 59th Street;
F to Lexington Avenue-63rd Street
www.dylanscandybar.com
Monday–Thursday 10am–10pm; Friday, Saturday 10am–11pm;
Sunday 10am–9pm
Café: Monday–Thursday 10am–10pm; Friday, Saturday 10am–11pm;
Sunday 10am–9pm

Long into adulthood, New York kids who've grown up with Dylan's still love to pop in it's a rockin' place, with a great playlist on the sound system, and Candyland-come-to-life decor. There's always something new at this sweet tooth's dream-come-true: white fudge-dipped Bugles, chocolate-covered fortune cookies, bars in unique flavors (Angel Food Cake, red velvet cake, banana cream pie, $3 each or 4 for $10). Who can resist a little sprinkle-covered pink cup-cake tin, filled with cupcake-shaped mints ($4)? You'll find kosher and sugar-free options, too. Out-of-towners can find some fun NYC-themed souvenirs.

On the lower level, you'll find fudge and more merchandise. On the second floor, in the café, you'll find savory and dessert pizzas, sun-daes, frozen hot cocoas, various peanut butter sandwiches, and desserts to share. There's an ice cream counter with neon blue mint chip and birthday cake among the flavors.

Adults: it's not all about the kids. Dylan's Candy Bar has a small cocktail bar, too, in the café, with stools that look like peppermint drops. Will some brave soul please check out the Pop-Arita (a

margarita with Pop Rocks) and the Sour Patch Margarita (with Sour Patch Kids), and report back?

E.A.T. Gifts

1062 Madison Avenue, between East 80th and 81st Streets
(212) 861-2544
Subway: 4,5,6 to 86th Street
www.elizabar.com
Monday–Saturday 10am–6pm; Sunday noon–5pm

This is where tony Upper East Siders find imaginative stocking stuffers, charming party favors, and fanciful gifts for adults as well as children. The boutique is a treasure trove of wind-up toys, Pez dispensers, glittery phone chargers, sparkly jewelry and barrettes, gourmet candy, games, toys, books, totes, and stationery items. There are all sorts of luxuries large and small, including—appropriately for this little shop where every inch is crammed with delights—a little porcelain dish with a Mae West quote: "Too much of a good thing can be wonderful."

Eloise Shop at the Plaza Hotel

1 West 58th Street, between Fifth and Sixth Avenues
(212) 546-5460
Subway: N,Q,R to 5th Avenue-59th Street; F to 57th Street
www.theplazany.com/shops/eloise-at-the-plaza
Monday–Saturday 10am–8pm; Sunday 11am–6pm

It's all Eloise all the time at this shop and event space devoted to the Plaza's most famous fictional resident. Eloise devotees can purchase an iconic Eloise outfit (black pleated skirt with suspenders and a white blouse) and Eloise-esque garments (tutus, princess dresses, smocked dresses with teapot motifs). Pink glittery T-shirts are decorated with an image of Eloise and a quote: "My absolutely favorite color is pink pink pink" ($28). You'll find cotton candy bubblebath and shampoo, jewelry, candy, hooded terry robes, notepads, playing cards, "Do not disturb" door hangers. The Eloise movie loops in an adjoining room, where kids can watch while perched on pink glitter ottomans. Check the shop's online calendar for events: There's a Rawther Fancy Tea on Fridays ($100 for one "Eloise Fan" and Mostly Companion, $75 per additional fan); fashion, cooking, and magic events, mostly starting at about $40, though there are free Every Child A Reader story times (check Eloise-at-The-Plaza on Facebook).

FAO Schwarz

767 Fifth Avenue, between East 58th and 59th Streets
(212) 644-9400
Subway: N,Q,R to 5th Avenue-59th Street; F to 57th Street;
4,5,6 to 59th Street
www.fao.com
Sunday–Thursday 10am–8pm; Friday, Saturday 10am-9pm

New York has the long-cherished FAO Schwarz. It's a store where you can find just about anything, and it's an experience as much as a shopping destination.

A real-life Toy Soldier greets visitors at the door of this enormous store; in fact, the first thing you may notice is how big everything is, including plush animals (Ride-on Bambi, $199.99; Seated Snow Leopard, $899.99; Ride-on Elephant, $1,349.99), The Big Piano, and the oversized signs pointing in the direction of Action Figures, Dolls, Games, Lego, Vehicles. The people traffic along the center aisle can feel like Grand Central Terminal at 5:30pm on a weekday, but plenty of staff members assist shoppers. The majority of items on the first floor are within the area designated FAO Schweetz. Perhaps you're looking for a ten-inch-tall five-pound gummy bear ($39.99) or a 1.5-pound box of Mike & Ike ($6.99)? You're at the right place. Many candies are sold in bulk ($15.96/pound).

Miss Piggy fans: pass through the candy section and you'll arrive at the Muppet Whatnot Workshop, where you can purchase a custom outfitted Muppet puppet with your choice of the Muppet's body, eyes, nose, hair, and outfit ($99, 30 minutes to produce).

Apparel, infant toys, and equipment are on the lower level. The second floor showcases the heart of the store's inventory. Several themed sections occupy their own areas; some change depending on trends *du jour*. The items offered on this floor make FAO Schwarz such a special place: the Astro Gallery of Gems, Ravensburger puzzles, Science and Education, Vehicles and Remote Control, Plants and Weather, Candy Chemistry, Mega Blocks, Lionel Trains. Oh, and that Big Piano. You can purchase a small Big Piano (70" long) for $79.99, or splurge on one like the floor model: it's 22' 8" long and goes for $250,000. Have any been sold? "Two!" says a sales clerk.

Glaser's Bake Shop

1670 First Avenue, between East 87th and 88th Streets
(212) 289-2562
Subway: 4,5,6 to 86th Street
www.glasersbakeshop.com
Tuesday–Friday 7am–7pm; Saturday 8am–7pm; Sunday 8am–3pm; closed Monday

Though all of the sweets at this classic Upper East Side bakery will delight, this is the place to try an iconic New York cookie. The "black and white" is the city's spin on a classic old-fashioned drop cake, its consistency more cake-like than cookie-like. The top is iced half and half with vanilla and chocolate. Its fame extended beyond the boroughs after Episode 77 of "Seinfeld," when Jerry told Elaine, "I love the black and white! Two races of flavor living side-by-side in harmony. It's a wonderful thing isn't it? . . . If people would just look to the cookie, all our problems would be solved!" It's a treat available all around the city, but Glaser's, since 1902, makes what is arguably the best in town.

Lemonade

1038 Lexington Avenue, between East 74th and 75th Streets
(212) 585-4371
Subway: 6 to 77th Street
Monday–Saturday 10:30am–6pm

The owner of this sweet little children's shop grew up in the neighborhood, so the clothing here naturally reflects the Upper East Side aesthetic, a refined yet lighthearted look that moves easily from private school weekdays to Hamptons weekends. The little girls' clothing doesn't feature pink as often as it does countryside florals; there's sparkle, but "mild sparkle," the owner says. Where there's smocking, it's not on an Alice-in-Wonderland-type frock, but on a little Indian cotton shift by the London brand ilovegorgeous. Instead of a tutu, there's a wisp of a sundress inspired by a tutu from one of the shop's favored lines, A Girl and a Mouse. There are different price points, and different looks. Customers love the wide selection of pajamas, including one with a Madeline print.

Magic Windows
1186 Madison Avenue, at East 87th Street
(212) 289-0028
Subway: 4,5,6 to 68th Street
www.magicwindowskids.com
Monday–Friday 10am–6pm; Saturday 11am–5pm; Sunday closed

This immaculate store, with its high ceilings, pale aqua walls,
creamy traditional woodwork, and shimmering pink Murano glass
chandelier, evokes the Upper East Side carriage trade whose needs
and desires it deftly fulfills. No neon here, except for the bathing
suits in lively prints. The layette shelves are filled with gentle pink,
blue, and white cotton garments; a glass-fronted wardrobe protects

exquisite christening gowns. This is a shop filled with pristine white pique dresses, blouses with Peter Pan collars, kilts, cable knit cardigans, grosgrain bows, and headbands. The boys clothing, too, is traditional and refined: white tennis sweaters, Bermuda shorts, and, for special occasions, ring bearer outfits, tuxedos, and suits. Many items can be monogrammed, including white linen crib pillows, diaper covers, and baby blankets. Alongside clothing, you'll find children's tea sets, European Corolle dolls, and a book on teen manners and etiquette.

H.L. Purdy Opticians

1195 Lexington Avenue, between East 81st and 82nd Streets
(212) 737-0122
Subway: 4,5,6 to 86th Street
www.hlpurdy.com
Monday–Friday 9:30am–6:30pm; Saturday 10am–5pm;
Sunday closed

The Upper East Side branch of this long-established traditional eyeglass store has a boutique dedicated to children's eyewear, with a wide selection of fashionable frames from around the world. Italian brands are known for fun colors (lavender, red, transparent); Denmark's Lindberg brand for delicate wireframes in aqua, violet, pink. The shop also carries full ranges of Juicy Couture, Ray Ban, Ralph Lauren, and Adidas brands, as well as sports and non-prescription optical-quality glasses for kids. The ultimate eyeglass fashion statement: Purdy's own line of plastic frames for kids can be made to order in any combination of color and shape.

Tiny Doll House

314 East 78th Street, between Second and Third Avenues

(212) 744-3719

Subway: 6 to 77th Street

www.tinydollhouseny.com

Hours vary, call ahead

Even if your child doesn't have a dollhouse, a visit here may be an unforgettable experience, for both girls and boys; the world reduced to a Lilliputian scale is mesmerizing. But if you're furnishing a tiny cottage or castle—any dollhouse, modest or magnificent—you'll be able to find something here. Anything. You can also find the house itself (a Colonial, a brick brownstone, a Tudor cottage, $500–$1000). And while the scope of the offerings is impressive, the quality is absolutely staggering. Diminutive etched glass hurricane lamps, a Majolica asparagus dish, coromandel screens, a Knole sofa, a pair of gilded pier mirrors, a lacquered étagère, objects seemingly as ornate and delicate as those housed over on Museum Mile.

They are displayed behind glass in exquisitely designed themed dioramas—a library, a patisserie, a holiday room, a nursery—about two dozen in all. The miniatures are sourced from around the world, many, like a beautiful little leather-upholstered wooden armchair ($295), signed by the artist who made them. Despite its elegance, the shop has many objects that children can afford.

Vilebrequin

1007 Madison Avenue, at East 78th Street
(212) 650-0353
Subway: 6 to 77th Street
us.vilebrequin.com
Monday–Saturday 10am–6pm; Sunday 11am–5pm

Saint Tropez, circa 1971: sun, sand, Brigitte Bardot. Vilebrequin's iconic French swimming trunks—designed then and there—were originally made out of spinnaker canvas and were a striking alternative to the swim briefs popular at the time. Inspired by surfers' shorts, then as now, the classic men's trunks come in a wide range of colorful prints (turtles, shells, fruit, flowers), as well as solids, and now also come in boys sizes that fit ages 6 months to 12 years ($135–150). Tailored, not baggy, they now are made of quick-drying

100% polyamide, and are still the ultimate in chic. The boutique also carries classic linen shirts, piqué polos, and other beach essentials.

Additional location 436 West Broadway (Soho)

Yummy Mummy

1201 Lexington Avenue, between East 81st and 82nd Streets
(212) 879-8669; toll free (855) 879-8669
Subway: 4,5,6 to 86th Street
www.yummymummystore.com
Monday, Tuesday, Thursday, Friday 10am–6pm;
Wednesday 10am–8pm; Saturday 11am–6pm

This is an invaluable resource if you're a nursing mother and you find yourself in New York City needing any breastfeeding-related products. The boutique has a wide selection of nursing bras (some from Elle Macpherson's line), swimwear, and maternity and post-partum apparel; body pillows, lumbar support pillows; oils and salves for pre- and post-partum care; books and DVDs; and bottle-feeding basics and accessories. Yummy Mummy also has a well-established program to rent hospital-grade breast pumps. In addition to all the material goods you may need, the shop offers a support system for nursing mothers—classes, a website filled with information, resources, and referrals to counselors and educators.

Zitomer

969 Madison Avenue, between East 75th and 76th Streets

(212) 737-5560

Subway: 6 to 77th Street

www.zitomer.com

Monday–Friday 9am–8pm; Saturday 9am–7pm; Sunday 10am–6pm

Zitomer is a drugstore and a pharmacy where many residents of exclusive zip code 10021 have their prescriptions filled. And, in a neighborhood where chain drugstores are a hike away, it's handy to know about a place to find bandaids and sunscreen. But Zitomer has far more than the basics. The first floor is an Ali Baba's cave, a mega boutique of luxury makeup brands, cosmetics, travel accessories, hundreds of headbands, and all the accoutrements of the luxe life; and fun browsing. Upstairs, though, is what families will want to know about—toys (balls, Playmobil sets, craft kits, Star Wars figures), stuffed animals, games, clothing, and baby equipment.

Kids Shoes

Camper

635 Madison Ave, between East 59th and 60th Streets
(212) 339-0078
Subway: N,Q,R to 5th Avenue-59th Street; 4,5,6 to 59th Street
www.camper.com
Monday–Saturday 10am–8pm; Sunday 11am–6pm

Campers is a family-owned Spanish company with a history dating back to the late nineteenth century. The shoes are cute and quirky, and might be just the thing for your cute and quirky little child. The Twins collection—two shoes that are a pair, but not identical—are whimsical and witty. You'll find red Mary Janes with cupcake decoration, one topped with a cherry, the other with a chocolate drop; white Mary Janes ($70), one with a kitten's face, one with a puppy's, and more. The styles, including sneakers, are known for their comfort as well. Sizes will fit infants through big kids (U.S. size 6).

Additional locations: 522 Fifth Avenue (Midtown),
125 Prince Street (Soho), 270 Lafayette Street (Little Italy/Nolita)

Geox

575 Madison Avenue, at East 57th Street
(212) 355-3029
Subway: 4,5,6 to 59th Street; N,Q,R to Lexington Avenue-59th Street; F to Lexington Avenue-63rd Street
www.geox.com
Monday–Saturday 10am–8pm; Sunday 11am–7pm

This Italian shoe brand ("the shoe that breathes") is the second-best selling brand of sports shoes in Europe, and is distinguished by its design and technology. The perforated outer sole features a waterproof membrane that lets feet breathe, but prevents water from penetrating (science lesson: the membrane's micro-pores are larger than water vapor molecules but smaller than water droplets). Breathable, non-slip, flexible, anti-bacterial, and waterproof or water-resistant, they're ideal for kids. The full line is carried in this U.S. flagship store.

Athletic shoes for boys include styles with soccer ball motifs, a style in neon lime and yellow, a white high-top with zipper closure, and a more subdued suede boating shoe. The girls' line includes athletic shoes, casual Mary Janes, studded denim high-top sandals, and a silver mesh ballet flat with a shoelace on the toe and neon lime trim. The kids shoes run from $60 to $80. Geox carries Italian sizes 26 through 37/38 (U.S. sizes 9 through 5½), and fit toddlers through about age 8. There's a smattering of kids apparel in the store, as well as the full range of men's and women's shoes and apparel.

Additional locations: 731 Lexington Avenue (Upper East Side), 862 Broadway (Union Square to Madison Square)

Jack Rogers

1198 Madison Avenue, between East 87th and 88th Streets
(212) 259-0588
Subway: 4,5,6 to 86th Street
www.jackrogersusa.com
Monday–Thursday 10am–7pm; Friday, Saturday 10am–6pm;
Sunday noon–5pm

The iconic Jack Rogers Palm Beach Navajo sandals made famous by Jackie O are now available in little girl sizes here at the flagship boutique. Think matching mother and daughter sandals in classic combinations (gold/gold, turquoise/silver, fuscia/white, and more), as well as college and sorority colors (Carolina blue, matte silver, royal and pink, orange and navy, and more). The ultimate indulgence: sandals are now also available in the full range of colors, monogrammed in white with white whip stitching. They're available in little girl size 9 through girl size 4 (classic $79, monogrammed $98; women's classic $110, monogrammed $168). Wide and narrow sizes are also available.

Little Eric

1118 Madison Avenue, between East 83rd and 84th Streets
(212) 717-1513
Subway: 4,5,6 to 86th Street
No website
Monday–Saturday 10am–6pm; Sunday noon–6pm

Mary Janes, ballet flats, boating shoes, sandals, moccasins, sneakers, loafers—almost every style of shoe for both everyday and for "good"—in a variety of materials from gold satin to Liberty of London prints to calf and suede, offer both children and their adults a wide array of choices at this welcoming boutique. Little Eric manufactures its own shoes; Made in Italy means the shoes are beautifully constructed of quality materials, and the fact that it's family owned means the customer service is top notch. The congenial owner himself will probably wait on you. The stack of packages by the door are addressed to destinations around the world—apparently, once you shop at Little Eric, you want to be a repeat customer no matter where you live. Custom shoes can be ready in four weeks, at no extra charge. The toys and the 25-cent (complimentary) mechanical horse ride are the icing on the cake.

Tod's

650 Madison Avenue, at East 60th Street
(212) 644-5945
Subway: N,Q,R to 5th Avenue; 4,5,6 to 59th Street
www.tods.com
Monday–Saturday 10am–7pm; Sunday noon–6pm

If your *bambini* demand nothing but the best, this Italian luxury leather goods brand has a tiny selection of classic suede loafers for small children at its swank and sleek store. The mini-version of the brand's iconic hand-stitched pebble-soled driving moccasins will fit infants through 3 years ($140).

Also see Harry's Shoes, page 434

PLAY

EAT

SHOP

Upper West Side

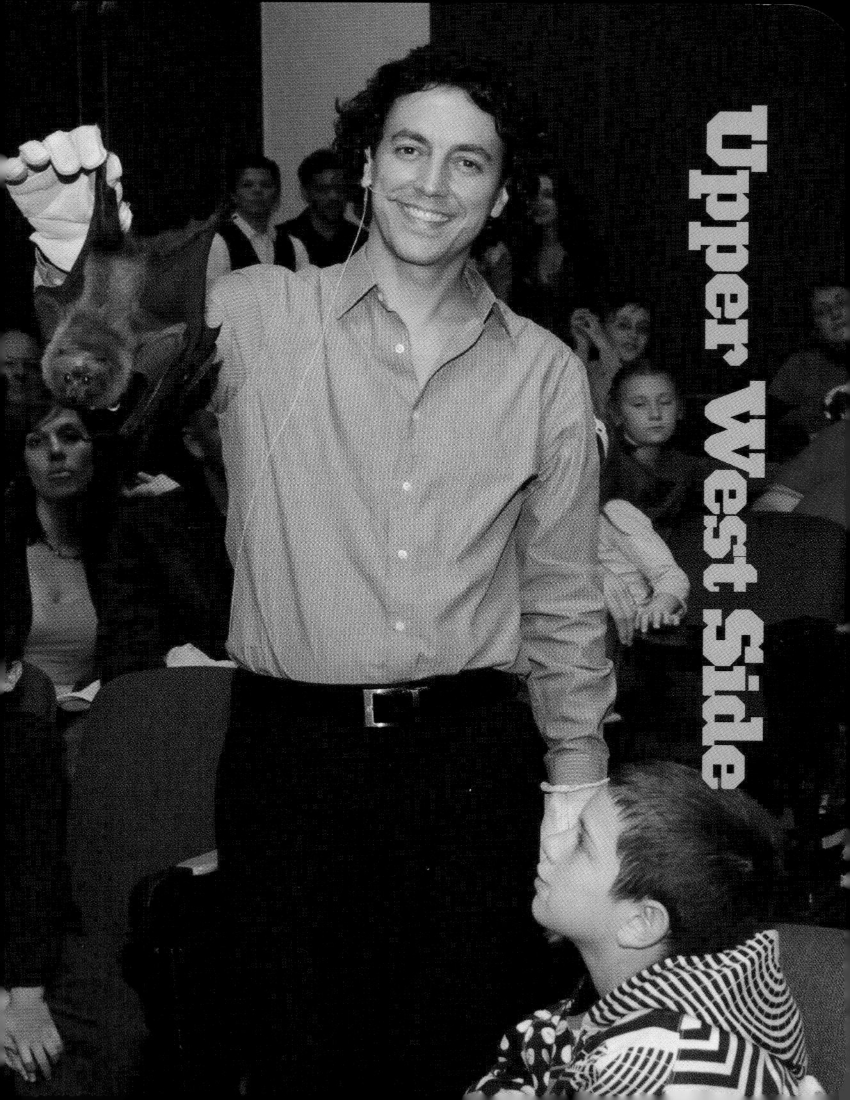

PLAY

Diana Ross Playground
Inside Central Park at West 81st Street and Central Park West
Subway: B,C to 81st Street-Museum of Natural History

With a fun central climbing structure that includes bridges, fire poles, slides, and ladders, this shaded playground is a great place to visit before or after museum visits on the Upper West Side.

ABS Atrium and Museum of Biblical Art
1865 Broadway, at West 61st Street
Atrium (212) 408-1200; Museum (212) 408-1200
Subway: 1,A,B,C,D to 59th Street-Columbus Circle
www.americanbible.org
Atrium: Monday–Friday 8am–6pm;
Museum: Monday–Friday 10am–6pm
Free

With floor-to-ceiling windows that face bustling Broadway, this modern, sunlit public space provides a rare place for passersby to sit down on comfortable chairs, use the free Wi-Fi, and maybe order a bite to eat at the small café counter at the rear. Billing itself "Columbus Circle's Rest Stop," the Atrium is indeed a calm and welcoming haven, as befitting a space in the headquarters of the American Bible Society. ("Recharge your body, your soul, and even your phone," says the brochure, and a staff member says that the staff is there to answer questions but not to proselytize.) A huge screen offers an interactive Biblical experience, where interested visitors can click on Timeline, Atlas, or other topics, and call up virtual reconstructions of sites in the Holy Land, maps, verses, and other visuals that bring the Bible to life. It's impressive.

Upstairs, the two small galleries that comprise the Museum of Biblical Art have rotating art exhibitions inspired by both Jewish and Christian traditions. Each show offers a free guide for adults and one for children. Whether the subjects are of obvious interest to children or not, there's sure to be a piece or two that will capture their attention; one show displayed the vast canvas, *Good Samaritan*, by Jared Small, a realistic depiction of the Bible story, perfect for children.

American Ballet Theater

Check website for seasonal locations
(212) 477-3030
www.abt.org/education
Tickets are available at the Metropolitan Opera House box office, online, or by phone (212) 362-6000

The one-hour ABTKids Performance, held annually, is an introduction to dance narrated by a member of the ABT's artistic staff. Designed for ages 4–12, the event features child-friendly highlights from the company's repertoire ($25 per person). The ABT also offers pre-performance workshops held before Saturday matinees to prep children 12 and under for what they'll be seeing; ABT teaching artists guide them through a ballet warm-up and a short piece of choreography ($20; tickets to the accompanying performance are required).

American Museum of Natural History and Rose Center for Earth and Space

Central Park West at 79th Street

(212) 769-5100

Subway: B,C to 81st Street-Museum of Natural History; 1 to 79th Street, 1,2,3 to 72nd Street

www.amnh.org

Daily 10am–5:45pm

Suggested admission, which includes both the museum and the Rose Center: adults $22; students with ID $17; 2–12 $12.50

There is an additional charge for special exhibitions and events (IMAX, *Dark Universe* in the Hayden Planetarium, The Butterfly Conservancy, etc.); in order to add one or more of those, you must pay the suggested admission to the museum. Various price and package options are available at the museum and online. Online tickets include a service charge.

The ticket lines are often long; it's usually quicker to buy tickets from the automated kiosks in the lobby, but tickets purchased at the kiosks are charged the suggested admission price. Tickets are also sold at the West 81st Street entrance, where lines are usually shorter. However, if you choose to follow the suggested tour we've mapped out below, keep in mind that it is oriented from the main Central Park West entrance.

More families visit the American Museum of Natural History than any other museum in New York. Galleries are often filled with hundreds of grade school students; upon exiting, it's not unusual to see dozens of yellow buses parked outside. To avoid the biggest crowds, visit on a school day after 2pm when the schoolchildren will have

departed. But even if you can only visit on a rainy and terribly crowded Saturday, do. This museum is unforgettable; ask generations of New Yorkers who love it above all others.

Before you go

As with any vast museum, even minimal advance planning will repay your efforts a hundredfold. On the website and under the Plan Your Visit tab, click on Interactive Floor Plan and get a general idea of the route you want to take through the museum. It's much easier than deciphering the map once you've arrived.

If you want to plan your own tour through the museum, or choose among tours created by the AMNH, download free iPhone/iPod

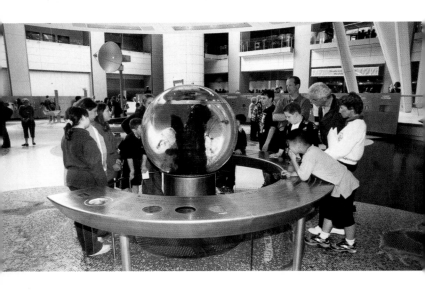

apps at www.amnh.org/apps. Or, borrow a pre-loaded device at the museum. The tours created by the AMNH include the guaranteed-to-please Dino Tour (estimated time, 2 hours), Highlights Tour (3 hours), and the Night at the Museum Tour (2 hours). These same tours are available online (click Plan Your Visit on the home page).

There's nothing wrong with wandering through the museum without a plan, but if you do want to see the "greatest hits," we've mapped out a suggested route that includes the dinosaurs, Indians, birds, mammals, the Hall of Diversity, ocean life, and, if you're still standing, the Rose Center for Earth and Space. If the directions seem convoluted, that's because they are: the museum itself is confusing and maze-like, but these directions include enough detail to keep you from getting lost or disoriented.

Once you've arrived

The main entrance opens into the Theodore Roosevelt Memorial Hall. Two large dinosaur skeletons greet you, including the five-stories-high Barosaurus skeleton, "the tallest free-standing dinosaur model in the world."

A map is essential. Pick one up in the lobby the minute you arrive. Note: to avoid confusion be aware that the main entrance on Central Park West is considered the second floor of the museum, not the first.

If you have a very young child who may not be up for a long visit, we suggest going directly to the Millstein Hall of Ocean Life where there's plenty to engage a toddler. It's magical: the huge model of a blue whale hovers above, underwater scenes flicker on the ceiling, a video plays on the lower level, and a play area in the center of the lower level allows small children to romp. The Hall of North American Mammals is manageable and fun, too, and the AMNH app includes a scavenger hunt to spot hidden details in the legendary dioramas. The Discovery Room (also described below) is another spot for young children who are tired of walking through the galleries and need some down time or unstructured activities.

If you want to see the "greatest hits," begin your exploration on the top floor, where the dinosaurs are exhibited. Before starting, visit the Wallach Orientation Center and view the 10-minute film, *The Evolution of Vertebrates in Nature*, narrated by Meryl Streep. To get to the Wallach Orientation Center: After showing your ticket, walk to the left, to the left again, and through the Hall of Asian Mammals. Continue on, keeping to the right, through Asian Peoples (you'll pass wonderful models of trade cities, a reconstructed Korean scholar's studio, model ships, a golden Buddha, and more).

Emerging from Asian Peoples, you come to an elevator on your left. Take it up to the fourth floor and enter the Wallach Orientation Center where the film is shown. The film plays continuously with two-minute breaks between showings. It explains evolution of vertebrates and, therefore, the logic and progression of exhibits on this floor—it makes the museum make sense. The seating is casual (kids climb and move around the benches) and even if the content is above their age level, even the youngest viewers are engaged by the visuals. **Restrooms** with changing tables are adjacent.

After viewing the film, enter the Hall of Vertebrate Origins. Don't miss stupendemys, a giant turtle. Continue through the gift shop and to the right, walk through the Saurischian Dinosaurs. Continue through and down the hall to the right, and then the left, to arrive at Ornithischian Dinosaurs. Your kids may like to find the protoceratops protecting their nest of eggs. Continue on to Mammals and their Extinct Relatives; if you need to sit down, take a break on one of the benches in the bright corner overlooking Central Park.

Finish up at the Milstein Hall of Advanced Mammals. In the second room, look for the seven murals near the ceiling, and don't miss the mammoth or the models of the North American miniature camels, stenomylus. Nearby is the **Café on 4**, with stroller parking outside, counter service with snacks, fruit, and beverages, and a small seating area.

This brings you back to the Orientation Center. Take the steps or elevator down to the third floor. From the steps, turn right to enter Primates (**bathrooms** are on the right). Walk through Primates and

continue straight to the Eastern Woodlands and Plains Indians, where children love to look at the small models of teepees, long houses, and dwellings of different tribes. Behind those galleries is the Margaret Mead Hall of Pacific Peoples.

If there's a birdwatcher among you, instead of entering the Indians halls, you may want to emerge from Primates, turn right, and visit the Leonard Sanford Hall of North American Birds. Don't miss the mural of the flamingo colony and the dioramas of nocturnal animals that are presented in near darkness. From there, follow the path through the small and rather neglected-looking hallway where New York mammals and birds are displayed to the Akeley Hall of African

Mammals. This gallery overlooks a downstairs gallery, also of African Mammals, the centerpiece of which is a herd of elephants. Through African Mammals, exit and turn right. If you want to go to Reptiles, do it now by continuing past the stairs. When you reach the impressive child's-eye-level American Crocodile and American Alligator, you'll know you've arrived.

Or, head down to the second floor, and make a loop through the lower level of African Mammals, emerging where you entered.

From here, you may continue on to the Hall of Biodiversity and Milstein Hall of Ocean Life on the first floor. Go down the flight of stairs at the right of the entrance to African Mammals (you'll go past the entrance to the museum shop). At the bottom of the stairs, pass the lower-level museum shop entrance, make a left and a quick right to the Hall of Biodiversity. From the giant jellyfish overhead to displays of thousands of insects and other organisms, the Hall of Biodiversity could entertain children, and adults, for an entire day—or lifetime.

From there, continue to the Milstein Hall of Ocean Life, a favorite spot in the museum for the youngest children. Another great destination for small children is the Jill and Lewis Bernard Family Hall of North American Mammals, next to the Hall of Ocean life (separated by the museum shop). Look for the immense Alaska brown bears.

At this point, many families are ready to rest and regroup. Others may want to explore the Spitzer Hall of Human Origins where hands-on science activities are held every weekend (free, no reservations necessary).

Beyond Human Origins includes meteorites, minerals, and gems in darkened galleries, the illuminated artifacts seeming nothing short of magical and mysterious.

In the middle of the Rose Center for Earth and Space is a huge sphere, divided into two halves. The top half is called the Hayden Planetarium, where the movie *Dark Universe* is screened. After ascending via elevator, visitors wait in a large darkened room before entering the theater (attendants will store strollers). The lower half of the sphere is the Hayden Big Bang Theater, where visitors can watch the short video presentation, *Big Bang*, about the beginnings of the universe (free).

There are exhibits throughout the sphere that explore the history of the universe and the concept of cosmic scale.

The Cullman Hall of the Universe further explores stars, galaxies, planets, and the universe. Don't miss the space scales built into the floor of the area. Each is calibrated to calculate weight based on the gravitational differences of various celestial bodies. Visitors can find out how much they would weigh on those bodies, as well the sun and Mars.

In addition to the galleries, and worth an extended visit in itself, The Discovery Room offers hands-on activities for children ages 5–12. It resembles a fun-filled classroom with tons of things to do, play with, examine, and explore. Upstairs, older kids can handle a live Madagascar hissing cockroach, an African walking stick, an albino leopard gecko, and more (not the Chilean rosehair tarantula, however, although the staff member will be happy to have you watch as he pulls silk out of its spinneret). Monday afternoons, the snake is fed (rats) and on Wednesday afternoons, the bearded dragon is given his weekly bath. There's a microscope, a seismograph that registers earthquakes worldwide, and more; enthusiastic staffers make this hidden gem in the museum a real delight.

The AMNH has a lively roster of family activities featuring live animals, performances, and workshops, led by naturalists and biologists. Events for children include bird watching in Central Park and a Live Bat Encounter ($12). Visit www.amnh.org for tickets and information or call (212) 769-5315. Adventures in Science Workshops are free and are designed for children Pre-K through grade two (each child must be accompanied by one adult). Topics include whales, stars, robots, and frogs. Visit amnh.org/ais or call (212) 769-5708.

The impressive—huge!—gift shop and its satellites are stocked with thousands of books and toys.

The **food court** is located on the ground floor. For **other eating options** near the museum, see pages 426, 428, 429.

Outside, on the northern side, the museum's Arthur Ross Terrace provides a breath of fresh air and a place for kids to stretch their legs. The garden's imaginative design appeals to both adults and children. Tiny sapphire mirrors reflect the sky above; twinkling fiber optic lights in the shape of the constellation Orion provide a light show at night; water jets bubble up intermittently.

Children's Museum of Manhattan

212 West 83rd Street, between Broadway and Amsterdam Avenue
(212) 721-1223
Subway: 1 to 86th Street;
B,C to 81st Street-Museum of Natural History
www.cmom.org
Sunday, Tuesday–Friday 10am–5pm; Saturday 10 am–7pm;
closed Monday
Adults and children $11; under 12 months free; first Friday of every
month 5pm–8pm free

Occupying four floors and a backyard of a building on a residential
Upper West Side block, the Children's Museum of Manhattan hosts
indoor activities for young children. The first floor theme is the
human body and how it works, and the gallery includes an oversized
toilet called Royal Flush, that, with a high definition monitor in
the "bowl," shows guests what "a perfect poo" should look like
(no kidding).

Once kids have explored the first floor, head upstairs for more activities suited for a variety of ages. The second floor's Adventures with
Dora & Diego is geared toward ages 3–4. The third floor's PlayWorks
for Early Learning is filled with toddlers climbing cushiony geometric
objects such as spheres, cubes, and triangles. Themed play areas
include a fire engine, a bus, and the Little Apple Deli.

The fourth floor has a basic crafts room decorated with work by artist Red Grooms and is manned by a teaching artist who oversees a
project of the day; available one afternoon were cardboard boxes,
strips of streamer paper and cardboard, markers, tape, and straws

to make double-decker cutouts of New York based on the work of the artist.

In the backyard, water games show kids how water currents work and include "fishing" with toy rods and magnetic fish.

Columbia Astronomy Public Outreach

Pupin Physics Laboratory, Columbia University (Enter the main gate of the Columbia University campus at Broadway and 116th Street. Look for the tall building in the northwest corner of the campus, with a green dome on top. Upon reaching Pupin, follow the posted signs to the event room.)
Subway: 1 to 116th Street
outreach.astro.columbia.edu
Friday evenings; check website for dates and times. Note: Observing depends on clear skies (check the website on the day of the event for observing status), but the lecture, Q&A, slideshows, sometimes films, and observatory tours occur regardless.
Free

If you and your kids would like to stargaze with astronomers, make your way to the Physics and Astronomy Department on a Friday evening. There, at the Rutherfurd Observatory, astronomers hold a weekly stargazing event with the opportunity to look through a variety of high-powered telescopes positioned on the roof. (Bring warm clothes: it's often windy or cold.) The rooftop portion takes place after a 30-minute lecture, but attendance at the lecture isn't required and the public is free to come and go during the 90-minute stargazing session. Lectures are at "a public level" and have been on such topics as comets, the Milky Way, the sounds of the stars, and the

Voyager. A sentence on the website explains why there is no charge for these events: "As scientists and researchers who receive the bulk of our funding from public sources (NASA, NSF, etc.), we feel it is our duty to give back to the public through free educational events."

Museum of Arts and Design

2 Columbus Circle, at Broadway and Central Park South
(212) 956-3535
Subway: A,B,C,D,1 to 59th Street-Columbus Circle; F to 57th Street; N,R,Q to 57th Street
www.madmuseum.org
Tuesday, Wednesday, Saturday, Sunday 10am–6pm; Thursday, Friday 10am–9pm; closed Monday
Adults $16; students $12; 18 and under free; Thursday 6pm–9pm pay what you wish

Although most of the exhibits here (floors 2–5) won't be of obvious interest to children—shows focus on subjects such as wood and contemporary glass—the Open Studio program can be lots of fun for both kids and parents. On the sixth floor, artists work on their projects and talk to visitors about the process. You may see an artist create a sculpture, silkscreen, piece of jewelry, crochet, puppet, or ceramics; there's been a pipe cleaner sculptor in seasons past (Tuesday–Sunday 10am–1:30pm and 2:30pm–5pm; Thursday, Friday 6pm–8:30pm; free with admission).

Moms: if a shopping trip to Barneys isn't in the cards, one could do worse than to take home a piece of jewelry from the museum shop at MAD. To the right of the entrance (no admission required to browse the store), the centerpiece of the boutique is a large oval showcase that holds beautifully deisgned, chic, and high-end jewelry, for a perfect souvenir of fashion-forward New York City.

New York City Ballet

David H. Koch Theater at Lincoln Center
Between West 62nd and 65th Streets and Columbus and Amsterdam Avenues
(212) 496-0600
Subway: 1 to 66th Street-Lincoln Center
nycballet.com

Kids can get up close and personal with members of the corps de ballet in a variety of events at the New York City Ballet. Children's workshops held before matinees explore the music and themes of the upcoming performance. During the 45-minute event, NYCB teaching artists lead children through a warm-up, movements, and a performance (ages 5–8, $12 per person, no prior dance training needed). In Motion Workshops, for children ages 9–12, follow a similar format.

Several other programs introduce children to the world of classical ballet: Saturday Family Programs feature members of the company, who might describe a day in their lives or show children how a choreographer works. The presentations are one hour long and are appropriate for families with children 5 and older ($20 per person). Friday evening Dancer Chats, appropriate for all ages, are free but reservations must be made prior to 4pm on the day of the event.

New-York Historical Society DiMenna Children's History Museum

170 Central Park West, at West 77th Street
(212) 873-3400
Subway: B,C to 81st Street-Museum of Natural History;
1 to 79th Street, 1,2,3 to 72nd Street
www.nyhistory.org
Tuesday–Thursday, Saturday 10am–6pm; Friday 10am–8pm;
Sunday 11am–5pm; closed Monday
Adults $18; 5–13 $6; 4 and under free; Friday 6pm–8pm pay what you wish

Time travel is a powerful concept, and the curators and designers at the New-York Historical Society have done their best to transport young visitors through 300 years of New York and American history by showing it through the eyes of children of the past. As you enter the museum, pick up the scavenger hunt pamphlet, "Can You Spot It?" Then, make your way downstairs to the DiMenna Children's History Museum.

A long banquette greets families as they arrive if they need to rest for a few moments. After entering the galleries, kids can wander through and find what interests them. There are interactive features: touchscreens, artifact-filled drawers to open and shut, earphones, and maps with sliding magnifying glasses. Orphans, newsboys, baseball players from New York's past... you'll meet them all here.

Other family activities are scheduled through the week, and attendance at these events is included with admission, so if they interest you, plan your visit to coincide with them. There's a family film series (*Ghostbusters*, *West Side Story*), complete with popcorn; a

Little New Yorkers program (a song, a story, and a related craft project for ages 3–5); a story time for ages 4–7; and a cross-stitch circle (the museum's loom is available at the same time so kids can also try their hand at this historic craft). One-off programs are worth exploring on the website's calendar of family programs; your young ones might be interested in a July 4th Independence Day Scavenger Hunt, the History of Ice Cream, a game with a Civil War historian, or a one-man show during which an entire circus emerges from his suitcase.

The expansive gift shop has quality toys and souvenirs: a colonial soldier costume, T-shirts with inspirational quotes, old-fashioned games (marble, jacks, pick-up sticks, yo-yos), and a plush Liberty the Dog, the endearing mascot of the museum ($14.95).

Museum Overnights for Families

In E. L. Konigsburg's 1967 classic, *From the Mixed-Up Files of Mrs. Basil E. Frankweiler*, two children run away to the Metropolitan Museum of Art and end up spending the night. Until several years ago, museums hadn't been so keen on the idea of stowaways, and while you and your family won't be able to spend the night in the Met, other options abound in New York City. Each institution below offers different activities. Slots tend to fill up well in advance (sometimes more than a year), so plan ahead and book your spots. Most programs include a meal and snack, free admission to the museum, and a goody bag. These overnights are the stuff of dreams—and those dreams are sure to be inspired by all the wild, ancient, and beautiful things that surround your children as they sleep.

For most of these overnights, cots are provided, but each participant needs a sleeping bag (Eastern Mountain Sports Upper West Side location rents sleeping bags, (212) 873-4001), a pillow, flashlight, camera, toothbrush and toothpaste, and warm comfortable clothing to sleep in. Check individual websites for specifics.

A Night at the Museum

American Museum of Natural History
Central Park West, between West 77th and 81st Streets
(212) 769-5100
Subway: B,C to 81st Street-Museum of Natural History
www.amnh.org/plan-your-visit/amnh-sleepovers
$145 per person (one adult chaperone minimum per three children)
6pm–9am; check website for dates

This program, for ages 6–13, started in 2008, was modeled after the movie *A Night at the Museum,* and has been wildly successful ever since. Go on a fossil fact-finding mission, with the lights dimmed and a flashlight in hand. Watch a show at the planetarium or see the IMAX feature. Sleep beneath the famous blue whale. An evening snack and light breakfast, as well as museum admission the next day, are included.

Knightwatch Medieval

The Cathedral Church of St. John the Divine
1047 Amsterdam Avenue, at West 112th Street
(212) 316-5819
Subway: 1 to Cathedral Parkway-110th Street
www.stjohndivine.org/families/nightwatch
$135 per person (one adult chaperone per 1–3 children)

Helena Kubicka de Bragança/Courtesy the Cathedral of St. John the Divine

The world's largest Gothic Cathedral is candle-lit, and a noble title and coat of arms await your group. Actors guide children through a scavenger hunt and a minstrels' serenade, and a storyteller tells a bedtime story before participants go to sleep in the nave (ages 6–12).

Operation Slumber

Intrepid Sea, Air, & Space Museum
Pier 86, Twelfth Avenue and West 46th Street
(212) 245-0072
Subway: A,C,E to 42nd Street-Port Authority;
1,2,3,7,N,R to Times Square-42nd Street
www.intrepidmuseum.org
$120 per person (one adult chaperone per child)
This overnight for ages 6–17 (ideal for 8–12) features a flashlight scavenger hunt, a special visit to the flight deck, the Hangar Deck (with the hands-on Exploreum, and space pinball), a ride on the Cosmic Coaster, and access to the Space Shuttle Enterprise.

Live Music Performances for Families

The musical "crown jewels" of New York City work hard at attract-
ing new generations of audiences by mounting enchanting and
educational performances for children, from tots through teens.
No visit to New York would be complete without taking children
to one of these world-class events, designed with them in mind,
usually held in an impressive setting.

Each organization has several performances throughout the year,
in the fall through spring; check online for current schedules.
Although tickets are initially sold by subscription, by August or by
Labor Day individual tickets are put on sale.

Jazz at Lincoln Center

Rose Theater, in the Time Warner Center
Broadway, at West 60th Street
(212) 258-9999
Subway: A,C,B,D,1 to 59th Street-Columbus Circle
jalc.org
Tickets start at $12. Tickets are available at Centercharge (212)
721-6500, or at the box office (Monday–Saturday 10am–6pm;
Sunday noon–6pm). Individual tickets are available starting in
mid-August.

The joint is jumpin' and the kids are, too, at JALC's two Jazz for
Young People Concerts each year. Concerts are one hour long—
the time flies!—and are best suited for children ages 6 and
younger. Recent events have been Jazz Meets Gospel and a Dave
Brubeck Festival. A family-friendly matinee, featuring the Jazz at
Lincoln Center Orchestra with Wynton Marsalis, is held each
December.

New York Philharmonic

Avery Fisher Hall at Lincoln Center
1941 Broadway, between West 65th and 66th Streets
(212) 875-5656
Subway: 1 to 66th Street-Lincoln Center
nyphil.org
$12–$39; single tickets are available starting in August online,
at the box office, by phone at (212) 875-5900, or by mail

The Young People's Concerts, held in the fall through spring, help
children ages 3–6 explore classical music by bringing them up
close to a major orchestra. The concerts were started in 1922,
and brought to worldwide attention in the 1960s when Leonard
Bernstein conducted them on live TV. Before each concert, the
Kidzone Live! portion of the program, included in the ticket price,
introduces children to the musicians, lets kids try some instruments, and allows them to ask about the music they're about
to hear (12:45pm–1:45pm, on all tiers of Avery Fisher Hall). The
concert portion is half an hour long; there is no intermission.

Symphony Space

2537 Broadway, at West 95th Street
(212) 864-5400
Subway: 1 to 96th Street
www.symphonyspace.org
Saturday, October–April
$13–$25; single tickets are on sale by August 1 for the
following season

Symphony Space's Just Kidding series has one of the most ambi-
tious schedules of all the organizations that program for children,

with weekly concerts October through April. Symphony Space is a multi-disciplinary performing arts center, so the events might focus on dance, music, puppetry, magic, or performance art. The types of musical concerts give you an idea of the scope: bluegrass, funk/soul/gospel, and "kindie rock." "Beats, Rhymes & Breaking," which introduces kids to breakdancing, focuses on the "strength, grace and agility" required for that dance form. "DiNO-Light" is a glow-in-the-dark event that utilizes electroluminescent wire to bring dinosaurs to life. Guest artists come from both the U.S. and around the world.

The Chamber Music Society of New York

Alice Tully Hall at Lincoln Center
1941 Broadway, between West 65th and 66th Streets
Subway: 1 to 66th Street-Lincoln Center
www.chambermusicsociety.org/seasontickets/concerts_for_kids_and_families
$10–$30; individual tickets are available after August 1 at the box office at Alice Tully Hall; (212) 875-5788 or online

The Meet the Music! series usually schedules one concert in the fall and two in the spring, and is aimed at children 6–11. The performances are fun and funny. One program, "Red Dogs and Pink Skies," explored the similarities between music and painting; in "Leave it to Ludwig," Beethoven "himself" appeared on stage "to help a young pianist play his music as he meant it to be played." Each event is approximately one hour long with no intermission.

The Little Orchestra Society

(212) 971-9500

www.littleorchestra.org

Tickets start at $17. Single tickets may be purchased starting August 1 by calling the New York City Center (212) 581-1212 or at the City Center box office starting September 3.

For almost 70 years, The Little Orchestra Society has staged live classical music for young audiences: the Happy Concerts for ages 6–12, held at Avery Fisher Hall, Lincoln Center, and at the New York City Center; and the Lolli-Pops for ages 3–5, held at the Kaye Playhouse at Hunter College. Performances, held in November and again in the spring, may draw from the LOS's classic repertoire (*Hansel and Gretel*, *Peter and the Wolf*, *Carnival of the Animals*, Bach, Beethoven, and Brahms) or be a modern work (*The Composer Is Dead*, written by Daniel Handler aka Lemony Snicket). In December, the LOC performs Music Under the Big Top at the Big Apple Circus.

EAT

Absolute Bagels

2788 Broadway, between West 107th and 108th Streets
(212) 932-2052
Subway: 1 to Cathedral Parkway-110th Street
www.absolutebagels.com
Daily 6am–9pm

If it's a "good" bagel you seek, you can find one just about anywhere that makes them fresh daily; if it's an exceptional one, try Absolute. At this no-frills bagelry, they're neither too big nor too small, they're not too sweet, they're perfectly chewy, and because the place is often busy, it's likely you'll be able to taste them hot from the oven. You can get bagels unadorned ($1 each), with cream cheese (a slew of options, $1.95–$3.55), with smoked fish ($7.50–$8.45), and made into sandwiches ($4–$5). There are a few tables.

Fred's

476 Amsterdam Avenue, at 83rd Street
(212) 579-3076
Subway: B,C to 86th Street
fredsnyc.com
Sunday–Thursday 5pm–11pm; Friday, Saturday 5pm–midnight; Saturday, Sunday brunch 10am–3:30pm; Saturday, Sunday twilight menu 3:30pm–5:30pm

It's not open for lunch, but Fred's has a "twilight" seating on week-ends, from 3:30pm–5pm that might be perfect for an early family dinner. The walls of this laid-back hangout are lined with photos of neighborhood dogs; the restaurant itself is named after one of them, a female black Lab, who was adopted from Guiding Eyes for the Blind. The owner's statement, "Fred epitomizes everything that this establishment stands for: loyalty, reliability, an ingrained need to please, and a playful spirit," explains the sweet and friendly vibe. The kids menu includes all the faves: penne, grilled cheese, mac and cheese, chicken fingers, or sandwich ($5.95–$8.95). There's plenty here that pleases all ages: burgers, fried calamari, pork chops, and standout Mom's meatloaf ($16.95). The outdoor terrace provides front row viewing of the Upper West Side during good weather. Lighter fare includes a vegetarian wrap and a Healthy Choice fajita.

Island Burgers & Shakes

422 Amsterdam Avenue, between 80th and 81st Streets
(212) 877-7934
Subway: 1,2 to 79th Street;
B,C to 81st Street-Museum of Natural History
www.islandburgersandshakes.com
Sunday–Thursday noon–10pm; Friday, Saturday noon–10:30pm

The original Hell's Kitchen location was founded by two friends who realized there wasn't a place in that neighborhood to get a char-broiled burger as opposed to a griddle-style patty found in many NYC coffee shops. Now, both locations, with sit-down service, serve more than 64 options of burgers and grilled chicken sandwiches, called churrascos. From the mild to hot, they include the Bangkok (with Thai Chili, curry, and peanut sauce), the Mike's Pool Hall (with jack cheese and sautéed onions on dark rye), and the Crescent City (blackened, bayou mayo, onion, sourdough). There are milkshakes, small and main-course salads, appetizers (chili, grilled asparagus), and baked potatoes; beer is served.

Additional location: 766 Ninth Avenue (Midtown)

Landmarc
Time Warner Center
10 Columbus Circle, between Central Park West and Broadway, Third floor
(212) 823-6123
Subway: 1,A,B,C,D to 59th Street-Columbus Circle;
N,Q,R to 57th Street-7th Avenue
www.landmarc-restaurant.com
Daily 7am–2am

Impressive views, glamorous dining room, and crowd-pleasing New American cuisine make this a festive place to have dinner and watch the sun set over Central Park. There's lots of seating (and stroller parking), and a staff that is used to a large bustling dining room with lots of families. Landmarc's large kids menu offers the usual (grilled cheese sandwich, PB&J, pasta, burger, mac and cheese, $6–$10) and slightly more sophisticated children's meals as well (whole-wheat quesadilla with chicken, cheese, and vegetable, or sliced skirt steak served with steamed broccoli and cheesy brown rice, both served with sliced apples and bananas, $12). For adults, the starters, especially, shine: warm goat cheese profiteroles ($12); smoked mozzarella & ricotta fritters ($13); roasted marrow bones with onion marmalade and grilled country bread ($16). Adult entrées include a daily pasta special ($15–$20); main-course salads (around $20); and more expensive fish, beef, or pork entrées. The wine list is distinguished by its quality and low markup, and a large selection of half bottles.

Additional location: 179 West Broadway (Tribeca)

Luke's Lobster
426 Amsterdam Avenue, between 80th and 81st Streets
(212) 877-8800
Subway: 1 to 79th Street;
B,C to 81st Street-Museum of Natural History
www.lukeslobster.com
Sunday–Thursday 11am–10pm; Friday, Saturday 11am–11pm

This sweet little spot seems to have blown in on a nor'easter. Committed to sustainable fishing, Luke's uses no middleman or distributor to supply the lobsters. You know where they come from—straight from the docks in Maine—and a portion of the profits goes to the Maine Lobstermen's Community Alliance. The Lobster Roll ($15; with beer, chips, and a pickle, $20), the Taste of Maine (half of a lobster, half of a crab, and half of a shrimp roll, $20), and New England Clam Chowder ($8) are all delicious; the Lobster Bisque is a show stopper. Buns are buttered and toasted in true New England style.

Additional locations: 93 East 7th Street (East Village), 242 East 81st Street (Upper East Side), 26 South William Street (South Street Seaport and Lower Manhattan), 1 West 59th Street in the Plaza Food Hall (376).

Oaxaca Taqueria

424 Amsterdam Avenue, between 80th and 81st Streets
(212) 580-4888
Subway: 1,2 to 79th Street;
B,C to 81st Street-Museum of Natural History
www.oaxacatacos.com
Monday–Thursday, Sunday 11am–midnight;
Friday, Saturday 11am–1 am

There's no waiting for servers here; customers place orders at the counter. The Korean-influenced taco (the especiale), is one standout, and it's hard to find a better deal than the lunch specials (two tacos or enchiladas with rice and beans, half a torta or a quesadilla with a salad or soup, for under $7). Try the elote, an ear of corn grilled with cotija cheese and chili powder; if your kids want it without the chili powder, it can be made that way. Pick up a Corona on the way; you can BYOB, making this the perfect spot for an inexpensive early supper or to unwind after visiting the American Museum of Natural History. There are a handful of small tables and some counter stools.

Additional locations: 48 Greenwich Avenue (West Village), 125 East 7th Street (East Village)

Pain Quotidien

50 West 72nd Street, and Central Park West
(212) 712-9700
Subway: 1,2,3 to 72nd Street; B,C to 72nd Street
www.lepainquotidien.us
Monday–Friday 7:30am–7:30pm; Saturday, Sunday 8am–7:30pm

This is a child-friendly option where you really can't go wrong. The beautiful and delicious baked goods and the well-prepared meals are never disappointing. Nothing about these restaurants feels like a "chain." The food is simple yet sophisticated, organic when possible, and the setting is warm yet Euro-chic. A communal table stretches down the center of each location, with smaller individual tables at the perimeter of the room. There's always a child, or four, eating a bite of this or a spoonful of that. The menu includes classic sandwiches (grilled chicken, smoked salmon, roast turkey and avocado), salads, quiche, cheeses, soups, and wine and beer.

There are 30 locations in Manhattan; for addresses, see www.lepainquotidien.us/#/en_US/locations/new_york

Peacefood Cafe

460 Amsterdam Avenue, at West 82nd Street
(212) 362-2266
Subway: 1 to 79th Street;
B,C to 81st Street-Museum of Natural History
www.peacefoodcafe.com
Daily 10am–10pm

For a healthy meal just a few blocks from the AMNH, lots of young neighborhood families are big fans of the vegan Peacefood Cafe. Kids favorites include brown rice with cashew cheese ($6) and baked soy nuggets ($7). You'll find a Mediterranean panini ($11.95), a creamy and flavorful broccoli soup ($5.95), fruit smoothies, fresh juices, and any number of homemade desserts, which are not only non-dairy and eggless, but made without refined sugar.

Additional location: 41 East 11th Street (Washington Square & the West Village)

Sugar and Plumm

377 Amsterdam Avenue, at West 78th Street
(212) 787-8778
Subway: 1 to 79th Street;
B,C to 81st Street-Museum of Natural History
www.sugarandplumm.com
Monday–Thursday 9am–10pm; Friday 9am–11:30pm;
Saturday 8:30am–11:30pm; Sunday 8:30am–10pm

Child-friendly is an understatement at this "purveyor of yumm." It's not a free-for-all, but one young diner was seen exiting the restaurant on his scooter, while three others ran from their table to the ice cream counter to the gift shop and back—several times. They didn't seem disruptive or ill-behaved, just completely at home at this large, congenial restaurant. The premise: parents can dine on good food (house-smoked free-range wings [$14], crispy-skin salmon with lemon hollandaise [$24], and more); and not worry that the kids are disturbing the peace. The lighthearted and cool design adds to the vibe: door handles at the entrance that look like two giant lollipops; a large mosaic of candies and an ice cream sundae; pendant lights that look like bonbons. There's a kids menu, for ages 12 and under, for breakfast (ranging from a yogurt parfait to the Little Lumberjack) and dinner (sliders, mac and cheese, etc.). Desserts are big: Earthquake in a Fishbowl ($17), banana splits, milkshakes, and sundaes. Next to the ice cream counter, crepes are made—kids can watch.

Additional location: 257 Bleecker Street (Washington Square & the West Village)

SHOP

Bank Street Bookstore
610 West 112th Street, at Broadway
(212) 678-1654
Subway: 1 to 116th Street-Columbia University
www.bankstreetbooks.com
Monday–Friday 8am–8pm; Saturday, Sunday 10am–8pm

This children's bookstore is affiliated with the Bank Street College of Education, and the discerning selection of books reflects the expertise of the institution. The store is on a corner, with lots of windows, and occupies two stories. In practical terms this means lots of space, and thus a greater selection than one normally sees in a children's bookshop. To get an idea of the range of the store's offerings, go to the website, where books are organized into almost 100 categories (chapter book series, scary, historical fiction picture books, human body, new sibling, time travel, etc.). Another feature on the website of value to parents is the list of the winners of the annual children's book awards given by the affiliated Children's Book Committee, founded 75 years ago to guide librarians, educators, and parents to the best books for children published each year. Try to schedule your visit to coincide with one of the frequent story hours or book signings (check the website for upcoming events). The selection of toys in the shop, many under $12, are of the same top quality as the book selection.

Harry's Shoes for Kids
2315 Broadway (84th Street)
(212) 874-2034
Subway: 1 to 86th Street
www.harrys-shoes.com
Tuesday, Wednesday, Friday, Saturday 10am–6:45pm;
Monday, Thursday 10am–7:45pm; Sunday 11am–6pm

In a world of big-box retailers, it's comforting to know a Harry's Shoes still exists—a store with trained personnel who know how to properly measure a child's foot, recommend a style that will fit well, and find options for children with hard-to-fit feet. Here, customers are offered old-fashioned service.

Harry's is the offspring of the parent store half a block away, which has been serving the Upper West Side since the 1930s. Like the main store, the inventory is extensive. There are small-fry versions of big people's fashion brands: Kors by Michael Kors, Steve Madden, Stuart Weitzman, Polo, Kenneth Cole Reaction, and Florsheim. For sport, choose among a wide range of athletic shoe brands, including Sperry, Geox, Hush Puppies, Campers, Birkenstock, Converse All Stars, Keen, and Skechers. For the girly girls, there are shoes encrusted with beads and sequins, butterflies and flowers. You'll also find well-made and beautifully designed shoes from Japan, Italy, and France…and the classic American brand Stride Rite.

PLAY

EAT

SHOP

PLAY

The Cathedral of St. John the Divine

See Museum Overnights, page 416

Central Park

110th Street, between Fifth and Lenox Avenues

(212) 860-1370

Subway: 6 to 110th Street; 2,3 to Central Park North-110th Street

centralparknyc.org

Daily 10am–5pm

In the northeast corner of Central Park at the tranquil lake called the Harlem Meer, park rangers run a fish-and-release program. Fishing poles can be borrowed at the nearby Charles A. Dana Discovery Center (picture ID required); instructions and bait are provided (Monday–Saturday 10am–3pm; Sunday 10am–1pm; ages 5–15). If you're in town on Halloween, don't miss the annual Pumpkin Sail, a flotilla of candlelit jack-o'-lanterns launched on the Meer. Next to the Meer is the beautiful Bernard Family Playground.

Hamilton Grange National Memorial

St. Nicholas Park

414 West 141st Street, between Convent and St. Nicholas Avenues

(646) 548-2310

Subway: 1 to 137th Street; A,B,C,D to West 145th Street

www.nps.gov/hagr/index.htm

Wednesday–Sunday 9am–5pm; ranger-guided tour 10am, 11am, 1pm, 2pm, and 4pm. Historically furnished floor may be seen only accompanied by a ranger.

Free

Overlooked in part because of its off-the-beaten-path location, Hamilton Grange, home of Founding Father Alexander Hamilton, is nonetheless a gem. Historic houses can leave kids unimpressed, but if parents have an interest in visiting, there's an interesting video that will keep the kids occupied while you admire the restored rooms. The home, built in 1802, has been relocated twice, and the video documents the move and restoration. A film about Hamilton, who grew up as an orphan on the island of Nevis in the Caribbean, and who ultimately became Secretary of the Treasury and George Washington's "right-hand man," is shown continuously in a space adjoining an informative exhibit. Three trading cards about the Grange are given to kids who visit since this is a National Park Service site related to civil rights and the Civil War.

Historic Tour of the Apollo Theater

253 West 125th Street, between Frederick Douglass and Adam Clayton Powell Boulevards
(212) 531-5337
Subway: 2,3 to 125th Street; A,B,C,D to 125th Street
www.apollotheater.org
Tour times vary; reservations are required (by telephone only)
$14–$18 per person, depending on day of the week and size of group

Director Billy Mitchell's tour of the Apollo Theater celebrates the theater and its rich history, Harlem as a neighborhood, American entertainment, and the African-American experience. Mitchell provides an aura of intimacy and authenticity often missing from tours of famous places. He started running errands at the theater in 1965 at age 15. James Brown paid for his education.

At one point in the tour, tour goers are invited to perform on stage during a Mock Amateur Night Show. "No boos, please," Mitchell reminds the audience. The warm introduction of each "performer" and the applause each receives after his/her act makes even the shyest performer comfortable.

The tour finishes with a visit backstage to the dressing rooms, where Mitchell entices visitors to imagine the old stars "sitting in these very chairs" getting ready for their shows. "Imagine, here you are, right where Billie Holiday sat practicing before her show. 'Good morning heartache / Here we go again,' she would have sung. And Louie Armstrong warming up with 'I see skies of blue.' And of course, James Brown with, '1-2-3 HIT IT.' "

Jazzmobile
Summerfest: various locations throughout the city
Great Jazz on the Great Hill: Central Park from West 103rd to
107th Streets
www.jazzmobile.org

Jazzmobile's Summerfest concerts are free performances held in neighborhoods throughout the city and at large venues such as Grant's Tomb and Marcus Garvey Park. Each year, Great Jazz on the Great Hill transforms the northwest corner of Central Park into a huge jazz festival and dance floor. Jazzmobile suggests: "Bring a blanket or lawn chairs and a cooler for a true 'New York City moment.'" Check the website for dates, times, and details.

Jeffrey's Hook Lighthouse (the Little Red Lighthouse)

Fort Washington Park
178th Street and the Hudson River
For a schedule of tours, call 311 and ask for the Urban Park Rangers.
Subway: A to 181st Street
Walk west to Plaza Lafayette. Cross the footbridge and take a left down the path under the overpass. Cross over the railroad tracks and follow the path to the left (south). The lighthouse is almost directly under the George Washington Bridge.
www.nycgovparks.org/parks/fortwashingtonpark/monuments/810
June–October, second Saturday of the month: 1pm–4pm
Free

The subject of the beloved children's book, *The Little Red Lighthouse and the Great Gray Bridge*, Manhattan's only remaining lighthouse is tucked under the George Washington Bridge, dates from 1880, and was a beacon for ships as they navigated the channel between New Jersey and New York. Slated for demolition after it was overshadowed in 1951 by the newly constructed bridge, it was saved through a nationwide campaign by the loyal young readers of the classic story (see page 21).

If you don't make it to the lighthouse itself, you can see it from the Totally Kid Carousel (page 448).

Morris-Jumel Mansion and Row Houses

65 Jumel Terrace, between West 160th and West 162nd Streets
(212) 923-8008
Subway: C to 163rd Street-Amsterdam Avenue; 1 to 157th Street
www.morrisjumel.org
Wednesday–Sunday 10am–4pm
Adults $5 (Saturday and Sunday before noon $2); students $4;
under 12 free

This is the oldest house in Manhattan, but its fame also rests on
the fact that it was Washington's headquarters for a month in 1776,
and later the site of a legendary dinner he held as President (among
those in attendance were Vice President John Adams and Secretary

of State Thomas Jefferson). When the home's second owner, Stephen Jumel, passed away, his widowed wife married the former Vice President, Aaron Burr. The museum provides a four-page Scavenger Hunt for children that, if completed, will earn them a prize. Questions in the Scavenger Hunt are along the lines of, "How many windows are there in George Washington's Office/Room?"

Museum for African Art

Fifth Avenue at 110th Street
Subway: 2,3 to Central Park North-110th Street; 6 to 110th Street
www.africanart.org

When this guide went to press, the Museum for African Art had not yet moved into its new home on "Museum Mile." Check the website for updates.

Schomburg Center for Research in Black Culture

515 Malcolm X Boulevard
(212) 491-2200
Subway: 2,3 to 135th Street
www.nypl.org/locations/schomburg
Monday, Friday, Saturday 10am–6pm;
Tuesday–Thursday 10am–8pm; closed Sunday

This branch of the New York Public Library is a research library with a focus exclusively on African culture. The Langston Hughes Lobby features *Rivers* (Houston Conwill), a memorial to the author and to Arturo A. Schomburg. The cosmogram at the center of the floor incorporates song lines, text, literary symbols, and the final words of Hughes's famous poem, "The Negro Speaks of Rivers." Underneath are the interred cremated remains of the poet.

Check the Schomburg's website: many of the events held at the center may be fun to attend with children, in particular the Carnegie Hall Neighborhood Concerts and Films. One of the films screened here, *Little Ballers*, profiled four eleven-year-old boys and their coach in their pursuit of an AAU National Championship in basketball. Both the concert and the movie programs are free, but registration is required.

Another reason to visit the Schomburg with children may be the small library shop that has jewelry, dolls, and other gifts, but that offers a most impressive inventory of children's books on African and African-American subjects.

Sylvia's Gospel Brunch

Sylvia's Restaurant
328 Malcolm X Boulevard/Lenox Avenue, between West 126th and 127th Streets
(212) 996-0660
Subway: 2,3 to 125th Street; A,B,C,D to 125th Street; 4,5,6 to 125th Street
sylviasrestaurant.com
Gospel Brunch musical performance from 12:30pm–4pm
Restaurant hours: Monday–Saturday 8am–10:30pm; Sunday 11am–8pm

It may be filled with tourists, many of whom have arrived via that bus you see parked out front, but there's nothing inauthentic about the gospel brunch at Sylvia's. When married duo Ruth and Clay Simpson take the stage, the place comes to life and everyone comes together. Clay plays the keyboard and sometimes sings. Ruth, the star of the

show, moves seamlessly between the three dining rooms, greeting people at every table, asking them where they're from, welcoming them ("Spain is in the house, let's give it up for Spain"), and posing for photos, all of it occurring during the uplifting chorus of "Let It Shine." So much fun!

The live music lasts for three and a half hours and tables turn over along the way, but the best strategy for getting in without having to wait is to arrive around noon. The food is solid soul food brunch fare, with eggs, waffles, sausages and bacon, fried chicken, rib steak, cornmeal-dusted fried catfish, and a number of sides, including collard greens, macaroni and cheese, and candied yams. (Most brunch items are $12.95–$16.95 and include a mimosa, Bloody Mary, soft drink, coffee, or tea.)

Of course, you can go to Sylvia's any day of the week—its location near 125th Street makes it a convenient place for a meal in Harlem—but Sundays are best because the neighborhood really comes to life then. Be sure, if it's a Sunday, to stroll down 128th Street between Malcolm X Boulevard and Fifth Avenue, where the music and preaching from at least three churches spill out into the street.

Totally Kid Carousel

Harlem Riverbank State Park
Riverside Drive and 145th Street
Subway: 1 to 137th Street-City College
June–October; hours vary
$1

Unlike other merry-go-rounds, the animals on this one were designed by an artist, based not on his own designs, but on children's drawings. It's a trek to the western shore of the island of Manhattan, but in addition to the ride, you'll be rewarded with sweeping views of the Hudson River, the George Washington Bridge, and the Little Red Lighthouse (page 443).

Statues of Famous African-Americans

Four impressive statues commemorating renowned African-Americans stand within several blocks of each other in Harlem. A walking tour linking them can provide a chance to recount to children the contributions, achievements, and legacies of these significant figures.

Adam Clayton Powell Jr. (Branly Cadet)

163 West 125th Street at Adam Clayton Powell Jr. Boulevard
In front of the state office building named for him, this statue

depicts the civil rights leader striding up an incline (the statue is called "Higher Ground"). Before being elected to Congress to represent Harlem, Adam Clayton Powell Jr. organized the community to protest against unfair employment and housing practices and went on to become a national figure involved in important civil rights legislation.

Frederick Douglass (statue, Gabriel Koren; memorial, Algernon Miller)
110th Street and Frederick Douglass Boulevard
The great abolitionist writer, orator, statesman, and intellectual is honored here. Throughout his life, he campaigned for full rights not only for African-Americans, but for women, Native Americans, and immigrants. The circular memorial represents a wheel—many fugitive slaves escaped via wagon—and the paving designs depict quilt patterns. (Some claim that quilts were used to communicate secret messages and as coded maps to assist travelers on the Underground Railroad.)

Duke Ellington (Robert Graham)
Duke Ellington Circle, 110th Street at Fifth Avenue
Legendary jazz composer and musician Duke Ellington stands next to a concert grand, supported by the Muses, 25 feet above street level here at the northeast corner of Central Park.

Harriet Tubman
Harriet Tubman Triangle, St. Nicholas Avenue at West 122nd Street and Frederick Douglass Boulevard
Harriet Tubman is best known for conducting hundreds of slaves to freedom on the Underground Railroad. Perhaps less well

known is her work as a scout, spy, and nurse for the Union Army during the Civil War, for equal rights for African-Americans and women, and for caring for the disadvantaged of all races.

"Swing Low: Harriet Tubman Memorial" (Alison Saar)—with lots for children to discover—depicts Tubman tearing out the roots of slavery. Have your children look at Tubman's skirt and find the faces, based on West African passport masks, symbolizing the people she conducted to freedom. Look, too, for shackles, a key, the sole of a shoe with holes, and other references to her work. Along the base of the statue are panels depicting episodes in her life interspersed with squares depicting patchwork quilt patterns. When the statue was erected, a controversy ensued because it was facing south, not north.

EAT

Amy Ruth's

113 West 116th Street, between Malcolm X Boulevard/Lenox Avenue
and Adam Clayton Powell Boulevard
(212) 280-8779
Subway: B,C to 116th Street; 2,3 to 116th Street; 6 to to 116th Street
www.amyruthsharlem.com
Monday 11:30am–11pm; Tuesday–Thursday 8:30am–11pm; Friday
8:30am–5:30am; Saturday 7:30am–5:30am; Sunday 7:30am–11pm

Though its exact roots are debatable, one account of the chicken
and waffle combination places its genesis at a late-night jazz club
in Harlem. At the close of a late performance, so the story goes, the
hungry musicians couldn't decide between breakfast and supper
food, so they combined the two.

This cheery Harlem restaurant has devoted much of its menu to
that theme of waffles, and expanded the protein options to include
steak, fish, and shrimp. The basic "Al Sharpton" combo is a light
and fluffy waffle topped with a pristinely crisp and juicy piece of
bone-in fried chicken ($11.45–$12.45); unforgettable. The rest of the
menu options are deftly prepared Southern classics: fried, smoth-
ered, baked, or barbecued chicken ($13.95), fried or smothered pork
chops ($14.95), fried whiting ($13.95), various traditional sides, and
delicious desserts, including creamy banana pudding, sweet potato
pie, and peach cobbler.

Dinosaur Bar-B-Que

700 West 125th Street, at Twelfth Avenue
(212) 694-1777
Subway: 1 to 125th Street
www.dinosaurbarbque.com
Monday–Thursday 11:30am–11pm; Friday, Saturday 11:30am–1am;
Sunday noon–10pm

The heavenly aroma and roadhouse vibe will win you over before
you sit down, but once you start eating, you'll be even more
delighted. Choose among platters and sandwiches; pork, beef,
chicken, ribs, catfish; salads and plenty of sides, each better than
the last. Everything's stellar, but standouts have to be the Harlem
Potato Salad, the BBQ Beans with Pork, and the fresh-cut fries.

Prices are reasonable: sandwiches with one side $10–$12, second side $1.50; half-rack of ribs with cornbread and two sides $17.95. The kids menu, at $5.95, includes an entrée (BBQ sliders or chicken, macaroni and cheese, and others) plus two sides. Dessert, in particular the peanut butter pie (thick peanut butter on an Oreo crust with chocolate on top), is off the charts.

Additional location: 604 Union Street (Brooklyn)

Harlem Shake

100 West 124th Street at Lenox Avenue
(212) 222-8300
Subway: 2,3 to 125th Street
harlemshakenyc.com
Sunday–Thursday 11am–11pm; Friday, Saturday 11am–2am

The Formica counters, chrome stools, catsup and mustard squeeze bottles on the tables may be retro, but the food is up-to-date at the large and lively Harlem Shake. In addition to burgers, "griddled smashed-style for crisp browning," there's a ubiquitous kale salad. The shakes, including a red velvet milkshake, are made with Blue Marble ice cream and organic milk. Burgers include the Pigskin Classic, topped with fried pork rinds; a Jerk Fry Burger, topped with jerk fries and jerk mayo; and the Hot Mess, with pickled cherry pepper-bacon relish, American cheese, and smoky chipotle mayo (all $8.50). You'll find grilled cheese sandwiches, melts, and fried chicken sandwiches, too. Vegans and vegetarians can request that fries be cooked in vegetable oil.

Harlem Tavern

2153 Frederick Douglass Boulevard, at West 116th Street
(212) 866-4500
Subway: B,C to 116th Street; 2,3 to 116th Street
www.harlemtavern.com
Monday–Friday noon–2am; Saturday, Sunday 11am–2am

A friend who lives in Harlem describes the Tavern as, "definitely a great place for families, always an incredibly lively and fun crowd, super friendly. The food is affordable and tasty." That about covers the bases. The menu is big and varied, with kid favorites such as burgers, catfish bites, grilled chicken skewers, wings (all about $10) and entrées that appeal to adults: cedar-planked salmon, bourbon-braised beef short ribs, or Cajun mahi-mahi (all about $20). Cocktails and wine are served, but beer is the star here, with foreign and domestic lagers, ales, stout, porters, seasonal beers, ciders, and even a couple of gluten-free options. There's a sprawling dining room and in fair weather lots of outdoor seating under umbrellas at communal tables.

Harlem's Original Floridita

2276 Twelfth Avenue, near West 125th Street
(212) 662-0090
Subway: 1 to 125th Street
harlemsfloridita.com
Sunday–Wednesday 8am–11:30pm; Thursday–Saturday 8am–1:30am

This old-school Cuban restaurant has been serving delicious food with true barrio flavor at low prices since 1969. For breakfast, opt for traditional fare like eggs, pancakes, or French toast with or without bacon, ham, or sausage ($2.95–$7.95), or head into Latin flavors with one of the best items here, mangu (mashed boiled plantains drizzled with olive oil, topped with pickled red onions, served with fried queso blanco and your choice of breakfast items such as eggs and bacon). For lunch and dinner, opt for a Cuban sandwich (roast pork, ham, Swiss cheese, pickles, and mustard cooked in a sandwich press, $5.50) or mofongo (fried plantains, mashed with garlic, served with chicken, pork, or cheese, and a chicken or beef gravy, $8.95).

The kid's menu offers chicken fingers, grilled cheese, and rice and beans ($2.50–$4.50).

Make My Cake

121 St. Nicholas Avenue, at 116th Street
(212) 932-0833
Subway: B,C to 116th Street; 2,3 to 116th Street
www.makemycake.com
Monday–Thursday 8am–8pm; Friday 8am–9pm;
Saturday 9am–9pm; Sunday 9am–7pm

You'll find international tourists sampling Harlem specialties (red velvet cupcakes, sweet potato cheesecake, key lime pie) and giggling high school girls grabbing an after-school treat at this popular bakery and pretty café. Another house specialty is the German chocolate cake featured on Bobby Flay's Food Network show, "Throwdown!"

Margie's Red Rose Diner

275 West 144th Street, between Adam Clayton Powell and
Frederick Douglass Boulevards
212-491-SOUL (7685)
Subway: A,B,C,D to 145th Street; 3 to 145th Street
www.facebook.com/pages/Margies-Red-Rose-
Diner/112044248848712
Wednesday, Thursday 10am–8pm; Friday, Saturday 10am–9pm;
Sunday 10am–6pm; closed Monday and Tuesday, check Facebook
page for updates to hours

A warm welcome is extended to every guest at this small and
immaculate restaurant. Margie's daughter Coco and Coco's
husband Michael now run the restaurant, and they have not only
continued its tradition of serving delicious down-home soul food,
but have added some Coco originals, such as a cool and soothing
lemonade pie.

You may have to wait a little longer than at other places for your
meal because Coco prepares everything herself, one item at a time,
to maintain quality and freshness. The wait is well worth it. The
fried fish is superb—arguably the best in Harlem—and the sage
sausage, slow-cooked turkey legs, and other soul food classics
demonstrate the truth of the restaurant's motto, painted on the wall:
"Happiness is homemade."

Patisserie des Ambassades and Cafe

2200 Frederick Douglass Boulevard (Eighth Avenue), between
118th and 119th Streets
(212) 666-0078
Subway: B,C to 116th Street; 2,3 to 116th Street
patisseriedesambassades.com
Monday–Sunday 7am–3am

This is an easy place to stop in for a simple croissant and café au lait or for a full meal. The vibe here is laid-back and local. The cooks are mainly from Senegal, and the menu has international flavors that range from Africa to the Caribbean, with maybe a touchdown in France: kabobs and curries, croque Monsieurs and Madames, lamb shanks, plantains, and more. Prices are reasonable (dinner entrées well below $15), portions generous, and the service relaxed.

Patsy's Pizzeria

2287 First Avenue, between East 117th and 118th Streets
(212) 534-9783
Subway: 6 to 116th Street
www.thepatsyspizza.com
Monday–Thursday 11am–11pm; Friday, Saturday 11am–midnight;
Sunday 11:30am–10 pm

East Harlem was once known as Italian Harlem when it was home to the city's largest population of Italian immigrants. The Italians may have left the neighborhood but Patsy's hasn't, and here, you can taste why this style of pizza—thin and chewy with a lightly-charred bottom, a sweet and simple tomato sauce, and just the right amount of cheese—has evolved into New York's favorite. Be

sure to take the kids next door to the pizzeria section of the restaurant, where they can marvel at how efficiently the pizza men prepare new pies and how quickly those pies cook in the super-hot oven in about one minute. If all you want is a quick pie and you don't mind standing, you can grab a pie there (plain cheese, $11). The full Italian menu in the main restaurant will satisfy anyone who doesn't want pizza: soups, salads, pastas, heros, and Italian entrées that range from $11–$17. There's plenty of seating and many original details, such as a vintage tile floor.

Red Rooster Harlem

310 Lenox Avenue, between West 125th and 126th Streets

(212) 792-9001

Subway: 2,3 to 125th Street; A,B,C,D to 125th Street;
4,5,6 to 125th Street

www.redroosterharlem.com

Monday–Friday 11:30am–3pm, 5:30pm–10:30pm (11:30pm on
Friday); Saturday 10am–3pm, 5pm–11:30pm; Sunday 10am–3pm,
5pm–10pm

Everyone—from customers to hostesses, servers, and celebrity
chef/owner Marcus Samuelsson himself—seems delighted to be at
Red Rooster. The restaurant, named in honor of a legendary Harlem
speakeasy, is congenial, appealing, and buzzy, from the horseshoe
bar up front to the dining room and open kitchen in the back. The
menu might be called Melting Pot Modern, a mix of soul food (fried
green tomatoes and yard bird) with Scandinavian touches that hark
back to Samuelsson's childhood (Swedish meatballs, gravlax) with
international accents such as coconut rice and curry peas. Entrées
range from $20 to $30. The "Yes, chef" cocktail (mint-infused
vodka, berbere spice, pineapple and lemon) gets raves.

On Sunday, a gospel buffet brunch is served downstairs in Ginny's
Supper Club, from 11am to 3:30pm, with performances at 10:30am
and 12:30pm by Vy Higgensen's Gospel for Teens choir ($39.95 per
person, $19.98 for children under 12, reservations recommended).

If you only want a snack, pop in and check out the Nook, a "pocket"
within Red Rooster serving the pastry chef's Whoopie pies and red
velvet cake and sandwiches from the main menu, including the
Chickety Split (fried chicken thigh with chili mayo and bread and

butter pickles on a biscuit), the Shrimp Shorty (Gulf shrimp on brioche,), and a Swedish-style hoagie piled with meatballs. A Red Rooster T-shirt may be the coolest NYC souvenir ever.

Settepani

196 Lenox Avenue/Malcolm X Boulevard at 120th Street

(917) 492-4806

Subway: 2,3 to 116th Street

settepani.com

Daily 9:30am–11pm

This chic and casual Italian eatery, run by a husband-and-wife team (he's Italian, she was born in Ethiopia and lived in Kenya) is clearly at home in the 'hood, and happy to be there—there's a real feeling of community here. The fresh seasonal cuisine is appealing, too, and the outdoor seating provides a great place to perch and watch a vibrant Harlem street scene. The menu includes paninis, salads, pastas (around $15), and entrées that range from sophisticated (octopus stew over couscous or marinated rabbit with beans, $22–$24) to simple (cavatelli pasta au gratin with tomato, mozzarella, and basil, $15), so there is something for everyone.

SHOP

Grandma's Place

84 West 120th Street between Malcolm X Boulevard and
Fifth Avenue

(212) 360-6776

Subway: 2,3 to 116th Street; B,C to 116th Street

Tuesday–Thursday 11am–8pm; Friday, Saturday 10:30am–8:30pm;
Sunday 10:30am–6:30pm

This small family-run store has a carefully chosen inventory of toys
of the highest quality, many wooden, from car seat ABCs to doll-
houses, play farms, and arts and crafts kits. The books, many with
multicultural themes, reflect the insight of the buyer, Grandma
herself, who has degrees in education and children's literature. Baby
dolls, Raggedy Anns, ballerinas, Barbies, all with skins in a variety
of hues, are another treasure in this beautiful and beautifully cared-
for shop.

Studio Museum of Harlem

144 West 125th Street, between Adam Clayton Powell Jr. Boulevard
and Malcolm X Boulevard/Lenox Avenue
(212) 864-4500
Subway: 2,3 to 125th Street; A,B,C,D to 125th Street
Thursday, Friday noon–9pm; Saturday 10am–6pm;
Sunday noon–6pm
www.studiomuseum.org
Suggested donation: adults $7; students $3; under 12 free;
Sunday free

The changing exhibitions here may or may not be of interest to children (check website for current shows), but if you're on bustling 125th
Street with kids you may want to peek into the bright and spacious gift
shop that has an inventory that includes handcrafted jewelry.

Also see the bookshop at **Schomburg Center for Research in Black
Culture** (page 445).

Brooklyn

If you haven't been there during the past 15 years or so, you'll find that a lot has changed in Brooklyn. The hundreds of individual communities scattered throughout its 71 square miles, many clinging to their historic roots, others changing to accommodate fresh arrivals, make Brooklyn interesting and fun for children and adults alike. Below are three fun and family-friendly excursions worth taking.

For large-scale grandeur, nothing beats a walk over the Brooklyn Bridge. Begun in 1867 and completed in 1883, the Brooklyn Bridge, America's first steel wire suspension bridge, boasts enormous gothic pylons and commanding views of lower Manhattan and New York Harbor.

The walkway, which straddles the bridge's center above the auto traffic, is rather narrow for the crowds it handles, but it does widen in two areas. These spots provide opportunities to consider the views and the history of the bridge itself.

Allocate at least 45 minutes for a one-way walk across the bridge. From Manhattan, a round trip to and from Brooklyn, walking one way and taking the subway the other way, will take at least 90 minutes, depending on the crowds, how often you stop along the way, and where in Manhattan you return to. For those who need to rest, benches line the path for the entire span.

To begin in Manhattan, cross the street from City Hall Park (4,5,6 to Brooklyn Bridge; J to Chambers Street; N,R to City Hall; 2,3 to Park Place) and follow signs to the bridge's pedestrian walkway.

To begin in Brooklyn, take the A,C to High Street, cut through the park at Cadman Plaza, walk north onto Cadman Plaza East (the eastern border of the park), and follow signs onto the bridge (you'll go up a set of stairs).

For activities, shopping, and food on the Manhattan side, see the downtown sections of this book. To explore the Brooklyn side of the bridge for a bit, here are some favorite places:

New York's revitalized waterfront is at its best in Brooklyn Bridge Park, which encompasses a series of connected piers and manicured grassy areas north and south of the bridge, and includes playgrounds and children's activities, restaurants and kiosk food vendors, a beautiful glass-encased carousel on the water, and a number of recreation areas. Some details are below, but for more information including maps and descriptions that will reflect new construction (much of the park is open but some sections are still in development), visit www.brooklynbridgepark.org.

To the north of the Brooklyn Bridge is the neighborhood DUMBO, which stands for "Down Under the Manhattan Bridge Overpass." This waterfront area includes a large grassy lawn, with perfect views of the Brooklyn and Manhattan Bridges and the lower Manhattan skyline, and the nautically-themed "Main Street Playground." The highlight of this section, however, is the award-winning Jane's Carousel, a meticulously restored 1922 carousel with spectacular views. It has 48 horses and two chariots and, most important, an absolutely gorgeous setting. Tickets are $2 per ride (or 12 tickets for $20); for hours of operation and more details, visit janescarousel.com.

To the south of the Bridge is Pier 1, which offers 9.5 acres with idyllic East River and Manhattan views. It begins at Fulton Ferry Landing, which was, in 1642, the site of the first ferry service between Manhattan and Brooklyn and the inspiration for Walt Whitman's famous poem, "Crossing Brooklyn Ferry" (its lyrics are woven, along with Brooklyn Bridge imagery, onto the rails along the dock's edges). No matter what day of the week, you'll likely see a number of brides and grooms posing for pre-wedding photos against the beautiful backdrop.

Pier 1 includes two sprawling hillside lawns, a children's playground, and tree-lined pathways, one of which flanks the water's edge, all of them excellent spots for relaxing, tossing a Frisbee, or eating a pizza picked up from nearby Grimaldi's or Juliana's (see below). Eventually, Pier 1's many amenities will also include a 200-room hotel.

At the southern end of Pier 1, you'll encounter Squibb Bridge, a zig-zagging and bouncing wooden "trail bridge" that connects Brooklyn Bridge Park with the neighborhood of Brooklyn Heights (and its famous Promenade).

To the south from Pier 1, Brooklyn Bridge Park continues along the waterfront with playing fields, bicycle and pedestrian paths, and plenty of grassy and paved areas for impromptu play or picnics. The Picnic Peninsula is an area located between Piers 3 and 5 offering plenty of space and tables for enjoying a picnic with a view, as well as two playgrounds.

Finally, at the southern end of Brooklyn Bridge Park is Pier 6, a play area that offers separate sections with swings, an enormous sandbox with shady seating along the perimeter, slides (including one built out from a "treehouse"), and water (streams, valves, steps, wading pool). The free ferry to Governors Island departs from Pier 6 (see p. 482).

There are a number of **food concessions** within the Brooklyn Bridge Park, with many bunched up near Pier 1. For an up-to-date list of food options, go to www.brooklynbridgepark.org/visit/concessions-restaurants.

For an interactive map of Brooklyn Bridge Park and its many offerings, go to www.brooklynbridgepark.org/interactive-map.

For the classic view-packed stroll in elegant Brooklyn Heights, the historic neighborhood that abuts the Brooklyn Bridge, walk south along any of the streets parallel to the river (Columbia Heights, Willow Street, Hicks Street, or Henry Street) to Remsen Street, and go to the right. Remsen Street deadends at Columbia Heights. From there, follow the path toward the Promenade. There are two city playgrounds near the corner of Columbia Heights and Middagh Street: Harry Chapin Playground, on the eastern side of Columbia Heights, and Squibb Park, on the western (water) side. The nearest subway stations are the 2,3 at Clark Street, the R at Court Street, and the 2,3,4,5 at Borough Hall. You can also access this area via the Squibb Bridge from Pier 1.

Your child needn't be a train fanatic to go gaga at the New York Transit Museum, where the sheer number of hands-on displays will interest kids of all ages and bring out the inner child in many grown-

ups: parking meters with coin slots and turning dials (long gone from NYC streets), turnstiles, and more. Even the entrance is fun: it looks like a subway station—because it was one (now decommissioned). The real draws are the old subway train cars and streetcars that visitors can enter. They're perfectly preserved, right down to the 1950s-era leather seats and the vintage advertisements.

You can easily navigate this museum on your own by first exploring the historic displays upstairs (the permanent exhibit "Steel, Stone, and Backbone" presents the history of the subway system) and a number of interactive exhibits, including a full-size cutout "fishbowl" bus to pretend-drive and -ride. Then head downstairs to the Court

Street Station, built in 1936 but long since decommissioned, where train cars from many different eras are yours to enter and explore.

If you visit on a weekend, consider the free, guided tour for children 5 and older. It's an informative way to experience the museum, and later on you can explore on your own. Guided tours vary in content, but generally last an hour and include visits to several vintage cars and some history of public transportation in New York.

In addition to tours, the museum also offers free programs for children on weekends and destination rides on old trains during certain dates in the summer. Among recent "nostalgia rides" was a two-hour ride to Coney Island aboard cars from the 1930s (advance tickets required, adults $50, children $25).

Wrap up your visit with a stop at the Transit Museum store. In addition to Metropolitan Transit Authority branded souvenirs (T-shirts, shower curtains, and train sets), the store also sells some vintage items, including old subway tokens and conductor's badges. For higher-priced real artifacts such as line signs and seats, visit www.mta.info/nyct/materiel/collectsales.

(New York Transit Museum, Boerum Place and Schermerhorn Street, Brooklyn Heights; (718) 694-1600; Tuesday–Friday 10am–4pm; Saturday, Sunday 11am– 5pm; closed Monday; adults $7, ages 2–17 $5; see www.mta.info/mta/museum for updated programming details)

Located almost directly underneath the bridge, **Grimaldi's** has long been one of NYC's most popular pizza stops. Its coal oven pies, pristine mozzarella, and simple tomato sauce make a truly delicious pizza. **Juliana's**, a half-block away, is run by the original owner of Grimaldi's, and now serves pizza that is every bit as good as Grimaldi's, but without the long lines. Both are in the shadow of the Brooklyn Bridge, in Brooklyn Heights. (Grimaldi's, 1 Front Street, (718) 858-4300, large regular pizza is $14; Juliana's, 19 Old Fulton Street, (718) 596-6700, large regular pizza $19)

The several blocks of Henry Street between Middagh and Montague Streets offer several restaurant options, all of which are kid-friendly. **Noodle Pudding** is a favorite spot with locals that remains under the tourist radar, in part due to its strange name. It offers Manhattan-quality Italian food at Brooklyn prices (gnocchi with butter and sage or tomatoes, $12.50; rigatoni with roasted eggplant, tomatoes, and fresh ricotta, $14). (38 Henry Street, (718) 625-3737, dinner only, from 5:30pm)

Siggy's is a favorite casual spot serving organic and homemade food at gentle prices. The flank steak sandwich, at $11, is amazing and big enough to share; the burger selection includes beef, turkey, veggie, and wild salmon ($10). Other sandwiches, salads, soups, and juices are also reasonably priced (76 Henry Street, (718) 237-3199, closed Monday). Siggy's has a second location in Manhattan (292 Elizabeth Street, (212) 226-5775, closed Sunday).

If your family prefers a totally informal meal in the park, pick up sandwiches, baked goods, and sweets from **Cranberry's** (48 Henry Street, (718) 624-3500).

For small-batch ice cream with a view, the **Brooklyn Ice Cream Factory** at Fulton Ferry Landing can't be beat. There's often a line, but it moves fast. Stroll along the pier or into the adjacent Pier 1 Park, or if you're visiting between Memorial and Labor Days, you can sit under a tent by the water. Prices start at $3 for a single scoop.

If you've walked to Pier 6 and don't mind proceeding another 10–15 minutes further, make your way to **Brooklyn Farmacy & Soda Fountain**, at the corner of Henry and Sackett Streets (follow bike/walking path from Pier 6 two blocks along Atlantic Avenue to Henry Street, go right and walk eight blocks to Sackett Street). Everything in this impeccably recreated retro soda fountain/sweet shop is done with style and is locally sourced. Try a single scoop ($3.75), an "extra-thick" shake ($7), or a sundae ($9–$-12), an old- fashioned New York egg cream, or an ice cream float. There's a menu with offerings beyond ice cream. See brooklynfarmacy.blogspot.com.

Whether or not your visit coincides with summer, Coney Island is a place that merits an entire day. Whatever this New York City beach may be lacking in terms of pristine water and clean sand, it surely makes up for with fun. Besides the beach and boardwalk, several cultural, culinary, and amusement attractions also intrigue and thrill kids and adults alike.

Ride the D,F,N,Q train to the Coney Island-Stillwell Avenue Station. The exit at the front of the train is one block from the boardwalk. From Bryant Park, the ride on the F or the N train clocks in at just over one hour.

You can visit the beach during the crowded summer months or during its relatively tranquil offseason. Along the side streets leading to the beach are shops that sell umbrellas, sunblock, beach chairs, towels, souvenirs, and anything else your family might need.

You can also head to either or both of Coney Island's two large amusement areas, or to the Cyclone, a vintage 1927 wooden roller coaster, one of only four on the U.S. National Register of Historic Places. (Surf Avenue near West 10th Street)

On the boardwalk near West 12th Street is Deno's Wonder Wheel Amusement Park, the older of the two amusement areas. It features rides for young children: fire engines, flying elephants, boats—things that go in circles. Tickets are $3 each. Bumper cars, the 150-foot Wonder Wheel, and a couple of other rides are geared toward older kids and adults. (Wonder Wheel and bumper car tickets are $7. Discounts are available for quantity purchases and via coupons on the park's website, www.wonderwheel.com.)

Coney Island's newer amusement area, Luna Park, opened in 2010, classifies its rides according to "thrill" levels, and admits passengers, not by age, but by height. Zamperla, the Italian company that owns Luna Park, considers it a showcase for its state-of-the-art amusement rides. Among the milder rides suitable for young children are the Circus Coaster (36" height minimum, a great first roller coaster for kids 5 and older) and Wild River (42" height minimum to ride alone or 36" with a "capable" companion, a flume-like ride featuring free fall with many splashes).

Older kids and adults will enjoy The Tickler, a roller coaster with spinning teacups for cars, and the Cyclone roller coaster, with a

fantastic initial drop that carries with it significant G-force and great ocean views.

At Luna Park, instead of tickets, guests must buy a card, from which amounts are deducted per ride. A four-hour wristband for $29 is also available, but it does not include the Cyclone and certain other (mostly "Extreme") rides. Cyclone tickets are also sold separately at the ride ($9 each).

Luna Park's main entrance is at 1000 Surf Avenue; secondary entrance at the boardwalk near West 10th Street.

A five-minute walk along the boardwalk from Luna Park is the wonderful New York Aquarium (602 Surf Avenue, at West 8th Street). It features walruses, sea otters, a sea lion performance (included with the $9.95 admission), sharks, penguins, and a schedule of changing exhibitions.

Plenty of food options line the boardwalk in Coney Island; we especially recommend Nathan's for hot dogs and, for pizza, Totonno's, a few blocks away from the boardwalk.

The historic hot dog stand, **Nathan's Famous** (1310 Surf Avenue at Stillwell Avenue), is good for a quick snack or a meal. As you step up to the counter to order hot dogs for the gang, admire the old-fashioned food shop interior. There's also a Nathan's on the boardwalk a block away where the lines are usually longer. For those who hanker for seafood, not hot dogs, Nathan's also has clams on the half shell, fried clams, and even frog's legs. On the Fourth of July Nathan's holds a famous hot dog eating contest.

Totonno Pizzeria Napolitano alone is worth a trip to Coney Island from Manhattan (1524 Neptune Avenue, between West 14th and West 15th Streets—a 5–10 minute walk from the Stillwell Avenue station). This is the pizza first served in 1924 by Anthony "Totonno" Pero, the grandfather of the current owners. White pizza at Totonno's, unlike the New York standard, has no ricotta. Instead, mozzarella, olive oil, fresh minced garlic, and a grated aged cheese, conspire to make a truly tantalizing pizza. If you're ordering only one pie, it can be made half white and half red. No slices. A large plain pie is $19.50; toppings are $2.50 each.

Paul's Daughter (on the boardwalk, at West 10th Street) is low-cost quick stop for clams on the half shell and an ice-cold glass of beer.

About ten minutes' walk past the Aquarium is Brighton Beach, a neighborhood that may share a boardwalk with Coney Island but in reality is a completely different place. Primarily home to people from the former Soviet Union, Brighton Beach is a little slice of Eastern Europe right here in Brooklyn. Its cultural uniqueness becomes apparent two blocks north of the boardwalk along Brighton Beach Avenue, an under-the-elevated-train street lined on both sides with mainly Russian retailers. Check out **Gold Label Gourmet Food** (281-285 Brighton Beach Avenue, between Brighton 2nd and Brighton 3rd Streets), a shop specializing in appetizers and treats from the Baltic region. Try the puffy fried pierogi filled with potato ($1.50 each) and the Ukrainian pear soda. The pierogi and other homemade pastries, both savory and sweet, are available through a window facing the sidewalk in front of the store. For another Odessa-by-the-sea experience, stop in for lunch at **Cafe Restaurant Volna** (3145 Brighton 4th Street, at the boardwalk), which has outside seating. Food options range from herring to salads ($9–$15) and soups (cold or hot, red or green borscht, and others) to dumplings. The B,Q train to Manhattan leaves from the Brighton Beach station at Brighton Beach Avenue and Brighton 6th Street.

Governors Island

Governors Island is open every Saturday, Sunday, and Holiday Monday (Memorial Day and Labor Day) from Memorial Day weekend until the last weekend of September.

Free ferries depart from the Battery Maritime Building (corner of South and Whitehall Streets) in Manhattan, and from Pier 6 / Brooklyn Bridge Park (at the western end of Atlantic Avenue) in Manhattan. Ferry schedules can be found at www.govisland.com/html/visit/directions.shtml.

www.govisland.com

The East River Ferry Service also stops at Governors Island. One-way tickets are $4 per person. Details are at same webpage as above www.govisland.com/html/visit/directions.shtml).

A map of Governors Island can be found here: www.govisland.com/downloads/pdf/map.pdf.

Calendar of events is posted here: www.govisland.com/html/visit/calendar.shtml.

The State of New York purchased Governors Island from the federal government in 2003 for $1 and the 172-acre island, formerly a military base, was opened to the public for the first time.

Every weekend day throughout the summer, the island, chock-a-block with family-friendly activities and great views, may be explored on foot or by bike. Bring your own bike, or rent bicycles or quadcycles from Bike and Roll, located at the southwest corner of the Parade Ground. However you choose to get around, be sure to explore not only along the interior paths that pass Colonels Row but also the path that traces the island's perimeter.

Two former military installations still located on the island are Castle Williams, a circular fortification located at the northwest tip of the island, and Fort Jay, a star-shaped fortress located just inland from the Manhattan ferry dock. Fort Jay, with its dry moat and original cannons in position to defend the city, is a place where rambunctious youngsters can let their imaginations run wild. Castle Williams is open to visitors only via the National Park Service's free 30-minute guided tour, on the half hour from 10:30am–4:30pm.

Governors Island also plays host to several annual and special exhibits that justify full-day visits. Children gravitate toward the very homemade-looking (but plenty sturdy) tree house, located in the parade grounds, and the equally homemade-looking mini-golf course, both produced by Figment, a non-profit arts organization. Also check out the Saturday ARTery classes for all ages, and the Children's Museum of the Arts weekend programs (both free). Special installations vary each year; in 2013, vintage French carousels were exhibited.

Three blocks inland from Yankee Pier (East River Ferry / Brooklyn Ferry) there are a number of **food options**. The longest line may be at the Veronica's Kitchen food truck, where Caribbean foods such as jerk chicken, fried fish, and chicken roti are served with two sides ($7, $9). Other food vendors include Little Eva's beer garden, Hibachi Heaven, Perfect Picnic, Pyramid Coffee, and a Mr. Softee ice cream truck.

Governors Island can get crowded, but by arriving early in the day (and leaving before the last ferry), you can minimize the impact of crowds. A new multi-featured park is scheduled to open on 30 acres of the island in 2014; it will include a grove of 50 red hammocks, a maze of gardens, ball fields, and children's play areas.

Restrooms are located throughout the island.

Fort Tyron Park

The Cloisters

99 Margaret Corbin Drive, in Fort Tryon Park
(212) 923-3700; questions about Family Workshops (212) 650-2280
Subway: A to 190th Street, then walk north along Margaret Corbin
Drive, or transfer to the M4 bus and ride north one stop.
www.metmuseum.org/visit/visit-the-cloisters
Admission (recommended): adults $25; students $12;
children under 12 free.
Hours: March–October 10am–5:15pm;
November–February 10am–4:45pm

A visit to The Cloisters is a welcome reprieve from the intensity of
Manhattan. Anyone with an interest in medieval gardens, medieval
art and architecture, or unicorns—or with a half-day of time on their
hands—should go there. The seven famous unicorn tapestries
aren't the museum's only draw for families. The medieval collection
contains thousands of works displayed in the building itself and its
three cloistered gardens.

The Garden Tour (free with admission, May–October, daily 1pm–
2pm) may be a bit lengthy and detailed for children, but visitors are
welcome to peel off at any point. (Your kids may not want to, especially if they are fans of *Harry Potter*: here's a chance to see what a
mandrake looks like.)

The Cloisters offers Family Workshops that vary by topic and according
to the instructor. At the Medieval Merchant Adventurers program,
families explored the museum in search of art on the topic, then did

a craft project (ages 4–12, free with admission, some Saturdays and Sundays, 1pm–2 pm, check online calendar).

For a more structured visit, families can opt for an Art Hunt; ask for the free guide at the admissions desk. Or, rent a Family Audio Guide geared toward children ages 5–7 ($5).

One weekend in June each year, The Cloisters hosts a Family Festival, a day of exhibition-related activities organized to help children enjoy the collection.

Among other things, the gift shop sells unicorn-themed items, including books, coloring books, tote bags, and magnets, as well as books on medieval themes, such as *The Knight and the Dragon* and *How to Find Flower Fairies.*

Queens

Museum of the Moving Image

36-01 35th Avenue, between 36th and 37th Streets
(718) 777-6888
Subway: M,R to Steinway Street; N,Q to 36th Avenue
www.movingimage.us
Wednesday, Thursday 10:30am–5pm; Friday 10:30am–8pm;
Saturday, Sunday 11:30am–7pm; closed Monday and Tuesday

The Museum of the Moving Image features an engaging collection of exhibits that celebrate the technology and history of film and television. Much of the museum comprises interactive experiences appealing to both children and adults.

The museum's core exhibition, "Behind the Screen," on floors 2 and 3, presents a range of artifacts (early cameras and projectors, costumes from famous films, items from classics like *Star Wars* and *Star Trek*, vintage video arcade games).

Interactive stations include ones about sound effects (choose a movie clip, listen to how a sound effect was created, then hear the result), stop-motion animation (use provided 2D objects to record up to 100 frames to save as a ten-second animation file that you can e-mail to yourself), and voiceovers (your voice is dubbed over those of characters in famous films, including Dorothy in *The Wizard of Oz* and Dewey Finn in *School of Rock*). Another enables the creation of a flipbook that stars the visitor (five seconds of recorded video become 40 separate stills that are then printed, bound, and available for purchase in the museum store, $10).

Classic movie serials such as *Superman* and *Flash Gordon* are screened daily in Tut's Fever, a Red Grooms- and Lysiane Luong-designed theater that pays homage to movie palaces of the 1920s and '30s. Theaters on the ground floor screen motion pictures including silent films with live accompanying music, new releases with the filmmakers present for Q&A, and movies geared toward children. For the schedule, see the Calendar section of the website. Admission to films is often included with museum admission.

On some Saturdays during the year, from noon to 5pm, the museum features a drop-in media-making studio for kids and their parents. With the guidance of museum educators, children can work on a number of film- and programming-related projects such as the creation of hand-drawn flipbooks and basic video games.

While very young children will find much at the museum engaging, the exhibits are designed especially for those 8 and up.

Stadium Tours

Barclays Center

Home of the Brooklyn Nets and (as of 2014) the New York Islanders

620 Atlantic Avenue, Brooklyn

(718) 933-3000

Subway: 2,3,4,5,B,D,N,Q,R to Atlantic Avenue-Barclays Center;
C to Lafayette Avenue; G to Fulton Street

www.barclayscenter.com/events-tickets/vip-tours

Twice daily, on select days, 10am and 1pm

Adults $24; 12 and under $12

Citi Field

Home of the New York Mets

123-01 Roosevelt Avenue, Flushing, Queens

(718) 507-TIXX

Subway: 7 to Mets-Willets Points (Note: the 7 train can be erratic
and service is often suspended; express service is not available on
weekday afternoons or on weekends, and the local train is slow,
crowded, and makes 19 stops from Times Square. Instead, take the
Long Island Railroad from Penn Station, a comfortable two-stop,
18-minute ride to Mets-Willets Point. This is also the best way to get
to the U.S. Open. On-peak $9.50 each way; off-peak $7 each way
[station, not on-board, rates].)

newyork.mets.mlb.com/nym/ballpark/tours/index.jsp

Mets Hall of Fame & Museum is open during home games; free
admission with a ticket to the game. Access on non-game days is
only available with the tour. Check website for updated schedules.

Adults $13; 12 and under $9

MetLife Stadium

Home of the New York Giants and the New York Jets

1 MetLife Stadium Drive, East Rutherford, NJ

(201) 559-1515

There is no subway line to MetLife Stadium, but New Jersey Transit provides rail transportation. From 34th Street-Penn Station, purchase a round-trip ticket to Meadowlands Sports Complex Station. Take the NJ Transit train to Secaucus Junction, and follow signs to transfer to the Sports Complex.

www.metlifestadium.com/your-stadium-tours.php

Saturdays at 10am and 1pm (times may change because of special events; check website for the current schedule).

Tickets available exclusively through Ticketmaster:

www.ticketmaster.com, (877) 469-9849

Adults $20; 5–12 $14.75

Madison Square Garden

Home of the New York Knicks, the New York Rangers, and the New York Liberty

Pennsylvania Plaza, between West 31st and West 33rd Streets

(212) 465-5800

Subway: 1,2,3 to 34th Street-Penn Station;

B,D,F,M to 34th Street-Herald Square

www.thegarden.com/tours

Tickets are available exclusively through Ticketmaster. Tour times change frequently; check www.ticketmaster.com for current schedule.

Adults $34.45; 12 and under $22.95

Yankee Stadium

Home of the New York Yankees

1 East 161st Street, Bronx

Tickets may be purchased 10 days in advance of the tour date via Ticketmaster (877) 469-9849 and the website yankees.mlb.com/nyy/ballpark/stadium_tours.jsp.

Tickets also may be purchased at any Yankees Clubhouse Shop in New York City and at Yankee Stadium; check website for details. Online tickets purchased from the Yankees website: adults $20; 14 and under $20; 3 and under free. Tickets purchased through other outlets vary in price.

Staten Island

Staten Island Ferry
Whitehall Terminal
4 South Street, at Battery Park
311
Subway: 1 to South Ferry; R to Whitehall Street; 4,5 to Bowling Green
www.nyc.gov/html/dot/html/ferrybus/staten-island-ferry.shtml
Daily, 24 hours. Departures every 15 minutes during rush hour and
every half hour at night and on weekends; see website for detailed
schedule including holiday changes.
Free

There is no better value when it comes to riding a boat in
New York than the Staten Island Ferry. This five-mile, 25-minute
ride offers views of the Statue of Liberty, Ellis Island, the Lower
Manhattan skyline, and New York Harbor. The boat features indoor
and outdoor seating on multiple levels and a snack bar. You must
disembark at Staten Island's St. George Terminal, but you can
return to Manhattan immediately by re-boarding the same boat.
If you wish to briefly explore Staten Island, there are a few good
restaurants within a short walk of the ferry terminal.

Exit the ferry terminal, go left to Bay Street (cross at the crosswalk)
and continue to 76 Bay Street, where you'll find **Pier 76**, owned by
the same family that owns Rubirosa (page 132). It feels more like a
sports bar restaurant than an old school pizza joint, but you will find
excellent pizza with an ultra-thin crust, a coating of juicy, naturally
sweet tomato sauce, and dots of mozzarella. The fried calamari is
also noteworthy.

Two other dining options near the ferry terminal are **The Gavel Grill** (9 Hyatt Street), that serves a good grilled cheese sandwich and cheeseburger deluxe, among its typical luncheonette offerings, and **Enoteca Maria** (27 Hyatt Street), an Italian restaurant that features a rotating roster of Italian grandmothers who make foods from their personal repertoires. **Enoteca Maria** opens at 3 pm, so plan for a late lunch or early dinner and be sure to reserve ahead.

ABOUT THE AUTHORS

Angela Hederman is an editor of travel guides and cookbooks at The Little Bookroom. She and her husband have lived in Greenwich Village for more than 30 years, are the parents of five grown children, and have four young grandchildren.

Michael Berman is a photographer and writer specializing in food, restaurants, and travel. His blog is pizzacentric.com. He lives with his wife and young daughter in Brooklyn.